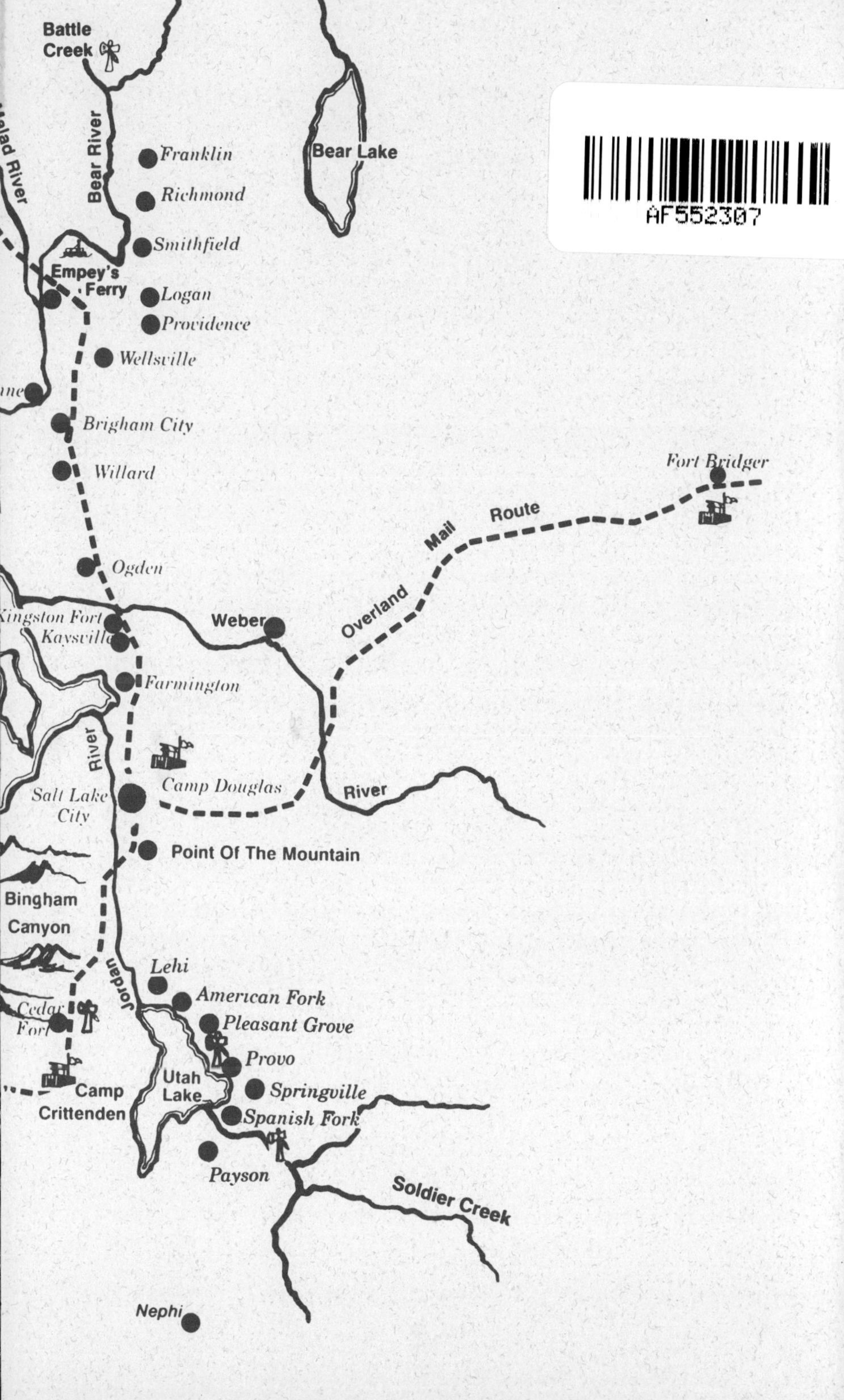
Battle Creek
Bear River
Bear Lake
Franklin
Richmond
Smithfield
Empey's Ferry
Logan
Providence
Wellsville
Brigham City
Willard
Fort Bridger
Overland Mail Route
Ogden
Weber
Farmington
River
Camp Douglas
Salt Lake City
River
Point Of The Mountain
Bingham Canyon
Jordan
Lehi
American Fork
Cedar Fort
Pleasant Grove
Provo
Utah Lake
Camp Crittenden
Springville
Spanish Fork
Payson
Soldier Creek
Nephi

GREAT WEST AND INDIAN SERIES, VOLUME FIFTY-TWO

Brigham and the Brigadier:

General Patrick Connor and His California Volunteers in Utah and Along the Overland Trail

Brigham and the Brigadier:

General Patrick Connor and His California Volunteers in Utah and Along the Overland Trail

by

JAMES F. VARLEY

WESTERNLORE PRESS . . . 1989 . . . TUCSON, ARIZONA

Library of Congress Catalog Number 89-051214
ISBN 0-87026-069-3

PRINTED IN THE UNITED STATES OF AMERICA BY WESTERNLORE PRESS

To Peggy,
for her loving support and advice.

Table of Contents

Introduction

In the backwash of America's great Civil War, events were occurring in the Intermountain West and along its lines of communication that would be of great importance both to the region's settlement and its future conformation.

During that war, California raised almost 16,000 volunteer soldiers, more than the entire United States Army at the war's commencement. The state would ultimately furnish two full regiments of cavalry, eight of infantry, one battalion of native California cavalry and one battalion of "mountaineer" infantry. In addition, several companies of California volunteers would serve in the East as part of the Massachusetts and Washington Territory contingents. Nevada sent into the field six cavalry companies and four of infantry, totaling some eleven hundred troops. These Californians and Nevadans, who volunteered in the West, remained on duty there for the duration, assigned the sometimes mundane, sometimes terrifying task of manning lonely outposts erected for the control of Indians.

This work concerns certain of those Nevada and California volunteer soldiers, many of them former miners, who were charged with protecting the overland mail, telegraph and emigrant routes while most of the nation's army was engaged in a death struggle in the East. Unfortunately, the events involving these soldiers generally have been overshadowed by that larger conflict. Even today, their significant impact on Indian relations and policy, the Mormon religion and Utah statehood, and the socioeconomic development of the West remains little known because of scant attention from historians.

Central to these happenings, along with his nemesis Brigham Young, was Patrick Edward Connor, the fiery Irish-born leader of the volunteer troops. Connor, a fascinating study, was an entirely self-made man — a sort of Horatio Alger with a brogue and a large dash of Diamond Jim Brady. His life before, during and after the Civil War displayed remarkable variety and excitement. Personally courageous, aggressive, and innovative in his vision, Connor could be viewed as the archetypal nineteenth century man who wrested this nation from adversaries and tamed its wilderness, while striving to make his fortune.

Patrick Connor seems to have always been on the leading edge of America's "Manifest Destiny" — at first in starting to move Indians westward; then in the conflict with Mexico; in the Gold Rush and awakening of California; and finally in the pacification and development of America's Great Basin and plains states. He was in San Francisco during its earliest brawling, booming days. He jumped from one newly opened area to another, helping make new towns grow and founding towns of his own; he was the first to open vastly wealthy new areas to mining; he tried to provide transportation and roads where previously none had existed, always motivated by a fierce desire to go where others had not. His business dealings and expansive schemes were representative of all that was good and bad in that age.

Connor acted as a patriot of the finest order, laying his life on the line for his adopted country, without hesitation, time after time. At the outset of the Civil War, at age forty-one, even though he had accumulated a considerable fortune and lived comfortably as a respected citizen of Stockton, California, he chose to answer the call to Union arms. Most of his Western contemporaries and many prominent men of the era held him in high esteem. Yet some recent authors have portrayed him as little better than a murderer, or as a bombastic and overconfident Irishman who was motivated solely by a hunger for glory. In writing this history I hoped to discover for myself which assessment was closer to the truth.

This is not a biography of Patrick Connor in the conventional sense, although the work contains most available facts of interest concerning his life. I have, rather, tried to use his story as the glue to stick together the tale I really hope to tell — that of the fascinating events surrounding the man during the building of the nation in the second half of the last century. By using as much of the original language and description as possible, I also hope the story will give the reader a feel for the temper of the times and what it was like to have lived in that era of open emotions. The simpler approach to both life and death, and the greater degree of refinement and nuance in speech, manners and the written word are so alien to us today that they might have occurred a thousand years ago, instead of a mere one hundred or so.

In addition to the fact that General Connor and his volunteers have never received adequate recognition for their accomplishments, previous historians have largely avoided certain aspects of the story that should be told. These include such matters as the intense antagonism between the soldiers and Mormons, some of the less heroic events in Patrick Connor's life, and the brutal repression of the Morrisite sect by Mormon-controlled governmental authority.

On a more personal plane, this rough-and-tumble history fascinates me because I grew up near the scene, and my great-grandparents were recent immigrants in Salt Lake City when the events herein took place. I have often pondered the extent of their participation in the conflicts, and wondered about their outlook toward the "Gentiles" in blue who had come amongst them from the mines of California and Nevada.

I owe a large debt of gratitude to the many who have helped in the research of the story of the volunteers. Special thanks are due to Mrs. George Goodlett for providing me with Kate Connor's reminiscences; to Donald DeVere, Curator of the Fort Douglas Museum, for the photographs of old Camp Douglas; and to Mary Joerger of the College of Southern Idaho for her tireless help in obtaining books and films from other libraries.

James F. Varley

Twin Falls, Idaho
1989

Major-General Patrick Edward Connor, ca. 1866.
(Courtesy Utah State Historical Society)

The Call to Arms 1

"Men of the North and West,
Wake in your might.
Prepare, as the rebels have done,
For the fight!"

— from "Men of the North and West,"
Richard Henry Stoddard[1]

I

In the uncertain first days of the Civil War following the Union disaster at First Manassas, the United States Government sent forth an urgent request to the various states for volunteer troops. Only a few weeks earlier, on July 4, 1861, President Lincoln had called on Congress for four hundred thousand men with whom to prosecute the war. Initially, California was asked to supply an infantry regiment and five companies of cavalry but, soon afterward, a second call increased the levy on the state to a total of four infantry regiments and two of cavalry.

Within a few days, in late August, Governor Downey offered command of one of the new California infantry regiments to Patrick Edward Connor, a fellow Irishman and prominent citizen of Stockton. Connor promptly accepted the commission and was duly sworn in as a colonel of California Volunteers. One Stockton newspaper noted that it was a well-merited tribute to a gallant officer who had seen hard service. While the editor confessed that he was opposed to the war and Lincoln's administration, he had respect for brave men. This fellow Connor was said to be a strict disciplinarian, but was experienced, and would use his men well if they did their duty.[2]

When Patrick Connor was offered command of the Third California Volunteer Regiment of Infantry, he and a partner had just been awarded a contract to continue work on the state capitol in Sacramento after the original contractor was unable to fulfill his obligations. The new colonel, whose income from all his enterprises at the time of war's outbreak was said to be the considerable sum of over $8,000 per year, was released from his contract when he accepted his commission.

The road to such respectability and prominence for Connor had been neither easy nor dull. And certainly his circumstances in that first year of the war were a far cry from his beginnings. He had come into life as an "O'Connor" — as Irish as Paddy's pig — born on Saint Patrick's Day, in the year 1820. His first years were spent in County Kerry, Ireland, near the Lakes of Killarney but, when he was about sixteen, O'Connor immigrated with his parents to New York City.

As a poorly-educated member of a despised Irish-American minority, young "Paddy" O'Connor may well have felt his best path to success could be in military service, where a man would be judged more on skill and bravery than on his former nationality or religion. In answer to a call for soldiers during the Florida War, in November 1839 he enlisted in the First U.S. Dragoons as a private soldier of Captain James Allen's Company I. The nineteen-year-old Irish lad was described at enlistment as being of slight build, 5 feet, 6½ inches in height, with blue eyes, brown hair and a fair complexion.[3] Not noted in the records was a rather large pair of ears.

The First Dragoons was a top-notch regiment with a great deal of pride and hauteur. It was the first unit formed in an attempt to find a more effective means of fighting the Indians, and its commander, Colonel Stephen W. Kearny, had worked his men hard to improve the regiment ever since its inception just a few years prior to O'Connor's enlistment. These dragoons trained as infantrymen, used infantry organizational designations, and their horses served merely as a quick means of locomotion.

While its companion regiment, the Second Dragoons, was chasing Seminoles in Florida, the First did its duty on the plains. Allen's company served in the vicinity of Fort Leavenworth until moving to Fort Atkinson, Iowa Territory, in August 1842. Not long after this, the unit went to serve at Fort Sanford, the Sac and Fox agency, where it remained until the post was abandoned on May 17, 1843. Next, Allen and his men were called upon to build the second Fort Des Moines at the confluence of the Des Moines and Raccoon rivers. Here O'Connor completed his term of service and was honorably discharged as a private on November 28, 1844.

After his discharge, O'Connor returned briefly to New York City to engage in some sort of "mercantile" business, and then moved on to Texas early in 1846, hoping to make a name for himself in the impending conflict with Mexico. Here, at Point Isabel on May 6, he enrolled as first lieutenant in Company A of a three-month volunteer regiment of Texas Foot Riflemen being organized by Colonel Albert Sidney Johnston.[4]

With a new commission and status, the young officer evidently felt it was time to rid himself of some of his more noticeable Irishness. Perhaps he just wanted a name that sounded more suitable for an officer, or maybe the intense anti-Catholicism of many volunteers had something to do with it. For whatever reason, he signed on as "P. Edward Connor," shedding the "O'" from his surname and shriveling "Patrick" to a mere initial, so that no one could be tempted to call him "Pat" or "Paddy." This is how he would be known for the rest of his life.

Finding them somewhat of a liability, General Zachary Taylor decided to send home those short-term volunteers who wouldn't extend their enlistments to the full year as had been recently provided for by Congress. In early August, Colonel Johnston's Texans were faced with this decision to extend their enlistments and, in spite of the appeals of their colonel, the regiment voted to disband. Only about 150 men chose to remain with the army, and P. Edward Connor was one of these — he evidently not ready to leave the fight until he had made his mark. Connor re-enrolled at Point Isabel, on the same day the regiment was disbanded, as first lieutenant of Captain Seefeld's independent company of Texas volunteers.

Seefeld's company was assigned to General John E. Wool's Army of the Center, which consisted of two Illinois infantry regiments, one of Arkansas horsemen, and a small contingent of regulars. Wool's army invaded Mexico starting from San Antonio,

Texas and, after a long and difficult march, joined Taylor on December 17 near Saltillo, Mexico, to meet a threat posed by General Antonio López de Santa Anna and his army of over 15,000.

As far as is known, Patrick Connor fought in only one battle of the Mexican War — Buena Vista — but it was a fierce one in which he fought with courage and tenacity, leading what was by then known as "Connor's Company." The young volunteer had been promoted to that position a mere ten days earlier.

The battle was fought February 22 and 23, 1847, just south of the Hacienda San Juan de la Buena Vista, where 4,500 Americans had taken up an excellent defensive position. Here the road passed north and south through a narrow valley. A number of impenetrable arroyos protected the Americans to the west and, on the east, a two-mile-wide plateau rose steeply from the road, cut by a series of deep ravines that ran at right angles up into the mountains of the Sierra Madre.

The fighting the first day at Buena Vista was desultory and inconclusive. By darkness, the Americans and Mexicans, in an attempt to outflank one another on the American left, had extended their lines nearly to the summit of the mountain. Before daybreak the next day, Mexican forces on the slopes were reinforced and succeeded in gaining the left rear of the Americans. General Wool, noting this development, sent Major Xerxes F. Trail with two companies of the Second Illinois and Captain Connor's company to assist.

The Mexicans attacked in force on the American left the morning of the second day. The initial assault on the mountainside slowly forced the Americans back but, although outflanked and greatly outnumbered, they held. Then came a strong attack on the plateau by two Mexican divisions. According to Wool's report, the enemy's artillery concentrated on the American left, while Santa Anna's main force advanced "in admirable order, crossing one deep ravine after another . . . deploying out of them into line with a regularity that excited our admiration."[5]

The assault on the plateau eventually caused the American left to collapse. A gap was opened that left the Americans on the mountains unsupported and under strong pressure. They were able to withdraw to the plateau, but only after fighting their way out at great loss.

The Mexicans now fought toward the enemy's supply point at the hacienda. Taylor sent in Jefferson Davis and his Mississippians, who had been held in reserve, and they and the survivors of the battle in the mountains anchored the American left at Buena Vista, using the thick walls of the hacienda to hold off attacks by Mexican cavalry. Here they held, and by late afternoon, with the artillery batteries of Braxton Bragg and others taking a severe toll of Santa Anna's forces, the field still remained in possession of the Americans. His confidence badly shaken, Santa Anna marched his men southward that night after being pelted by a cold rain.

Captain Connor's company had fought with conspicuous gallantry, and was said to have suffered the greatest casualties of any on the field. Two subalterns, Lieutenants Campbell and Leonard, and thirteen men died in the bloody battle, in which no quarter had been given by the Mexicans. They received the surrendered sword of Lieutenant Campbell, and then "plunged it into his bosom."[6]

Connor himself was wounded in his left hand by a musket ball early in the engagement, but remained on the field. General Wool is said to have come upon him at the height of battle and asked: "Captain Connor, where are your men?" Connor then pointed to fifteen dead Americans strewn about him and said: "General, there!" and pressed forward.[7] Wool's report mentions that Connor "was attacked by three lancers and saved himself by his skill with the sword."[8] When darkness came, the young captain had lost so much blood that keeping him warm this cold and rainy night on the battlefield was essential to keeping him alive. Two of his comrades are said to have huddled close to him on either side throughout the night.[9]

After a period of recuperation, Connor left Taylor's army on May 24, 1847, receiving an honorable discharge while in camp at Monterrey. Rheumatism was recorded as the reason for his separation. The war would go on without him, to end the following February. Connor is thought to have lived for a time in Santa Fe and then, a bit behind the "Golden Emigration" of the summer before, he traveled overland to arrive in Stockton, California, on January 22, 1850.[10]

The great central valley of California at that time was still largely in its virgin state. The town of Stockton had not even existed a mere three years before. It was Charles M. Weber, a member of the Bartleson overland party of 1841, who had first begun attempts to develop the town, but only after the discovery of gold on the south fork of the American River in January 1848 had it begun to flourish. The town's location was ideal, served on one side by easy water communication with San Francisco and on the other by direct roads to the mines, used by a constant stream of wagon and pack trains.

Our Mexican War veteran had arrived driving a band of mules bought for resale in California. Once in Stockton, he changed his plans and used the mules in a business of his own. He purchased a ranch on Waterloo Road and here, while excavating to construct a small adobe house, he found deposits of gravel. Noting that Stockton's streets presented the year-round problem of dust in summer and mud in winter, the enterprising Connor went into business on Weber Avenue selling gravel to the town, hauling it with his own mules to increase his profits.[11]

In the spring of 1850 the cry heralded in California was "Ho for Trinidad!" The previous summer, overland expeditions had returned from the Trinity River headwaters in the northern part of the state, having found gold in paying amounts. Patrick Connor got caught up in the excitement and joined three young military officers in a short, abortive expedition by sea to locate the mouth of the Trinity. Five men were drowned — and Patrick Connor nearly so — when their small boat broached in heavy surf while trying to land near present-day Crescent City.[12]

Undaunted, Connor made further attempts to gain his fortune in northern California. In May, he led a group of some forty men on an arduous overland trek from Sonoma to the Trinity diggings. Apparently dissatisfied with what he found there, the restless captain moved on for a time to the Humboldt Bay region. Here, near Eureka, he went to work cutting and shipping pilings to supply a rapidly-growing San Francisco. Connor is also said to have served as the first pilot for ships in and out of Humboldt Bay.[13]

A drop in the price of pilings quickly put an end to Connor's ventures in northern California, and he returned late in 1851 to Stockton. In 1853 he joined a group of kindred spirits known as the "California Rangers" in a summer manhunt authorized by the state legislature for the mythical bandit known as "Joaquin Murieta." Under their leader, Captain Harry Love, Connor and the others — mostly former Mexican War veterans — managed to produce a bloody, severed head, said to be that of Murieta, just before their term of service expired. Each received $150 per month for three months' service, and may also have shared an additional $5,000 awarded for the "relief" of Harry Love by a grateful legislature.[14]

In the eight years between the "Joaquin" affair and the outbreak of the Civil War, Pat Connor achieved the wealth he had sought so incessantly. Most of the stake that allowed him to get into business seriously in Stockton came from a surveying contract that fell into his pocket in the summer of 1854. Connor surely knew nothing of the science of surveying, but he thoroughly understood the patronage system and its uses. He and his partner, William Howard, obtained the contract from the newly-appointed surveyor-general of California, Colonel John C. Hays — Indian fighter, Texas Ranger, and commander of the First Texas Mounted Regiment in the Mexican War.

But first, the young entrepreneur found himself a bride. In a frontier state where women were extremely scarce, he managed to find a certain Johanna Connor, an attractive woman who shared not only his surname but also his birthplace of County Kerry, Ireland. Johanna had come to California with her parents by way of Valparaíso, Chile in the winter of 1848, and when Connor found her she was living in Redwood City. At the time, he was owner and master of a small freight boat, the "Water Lily," using it in the lumber business between there and San Francisco.[15] The captain was thirty-four years old and Johanna a mere eighteen when they exchanged vows on August 14, 1854, at St. Francis Xavier in San Francisco.

From Stockton a few days after the wedding, Connor wrote William Howard concerning plans for the expedition:

"I have seen a surveyor, and he tells me it will be necessary to have all white men to act as chain bearers, axe-men, etc. We will have to give a Surveyor $200 a month. You could take two or three Indians along and make them useful — one for hunting, one for hauling wood and water, etc. . . . Schofield [*sic*] arrived from San Francisco the night before last, and says he would like us to start for the Tejon as soon as possible, as he expects Brown, the Secret Agent of the Department, may pay us a visit. . . ."[16]

Johanna Connor, ca. 1863. (Courtesy Utah Historical Society)

"Brown" was J. Ross Browne, special agent of the Treasury Department, operating out of San Francisco, who in September toured the San Joaquin Valley. James M. Scofield, the collector of customs at Stockton, had good reason to fear him, as Browne was a noted believer in economy and honesty in government. In writing of the Stockton customs house, Browne was later to say:

"I never knew a collector there to have any thing at all to do, except to keep the run of his office — rent and salary . . . yet this officer is expected to pass the time agreeably year after year on a miserable pittance of three thousand dollars, without even the hope of ever seeing a dutiable cargo landed upon the wharves of the city. I don't believe the most sanguine gentleman that ever held that position aspired to anything of greater commercial value than a flock of sheep supposed to be on the way from Mexico, and for the capture and confiscation of which two inspectors were stationed for many years at the Tejon Pass about three hundred miles from Stockton."[17]

It seems very likely that Pat Connor and William Howard were the inspectors thought to have been waiting for sheep at Tejon.

The Connor-Howard surveying party worked until late that year in the Kern River and Buena Vista Lake areas. Connor's young bride accompanied her husband on the expedition. When it was completed, the couple returned to Stockton, by now grown to a city of over 5,000, and took up residence on a ranch about two miles from town, near the racetrack on Mariposa Road. Here, two years later, their first child, Thomas Jefferson Connor, was born.

Connor became postmaster of Stockton in 1855, but resigned in less than a year, preferring a "more active life."[18] His gravel business flourished, but major financial success didn't come until early in 1859, when he founded the Stockton waterworks. At that time, city and county authorities gave him the exclusive use for twenty years of the water from a large artesian well, in return for which he was to pay $700 per year and furnish free water for all governmental uses such as fire hydrants and cisterns.

Always the innovator and individualist, P. Edward designed and built his family a unique new home on Sutter Street in 1858. It resembled more than anything else a fort, being of an unusual octagonal design, with a flat roof and walls of large lime-concrete blocks, and with an observation tower perched on top. Its proud owner considered it "quite a swell house," and so it was, becoming a Stockton landmark until being demolished in 1954.[19]

Connor, who was also something of a "joiner," now became totally involved in community activities. He served as an executive officer and treasurer of the State Fair Board in Stockton; as a trustee of a private seminary, and in various offices of the San Joaquin Agricultural Society.

In 1859, when he was president of the Board of Trustees of the State Insane Asylum, a letter to the editor of the *Sacramento Bee* labeled the institution a "sink of iniquity." It was alleged that the board members were "innocent tools in the hands of a bold, wily speculator like Captain Connor."[20] The captain was accused specifically of charging the state for 100 tons of sidewalk gravel at the asylum, when only forty had been furnished from his "gravel mine," and of awarding himself the contract to plow a field surrounding the institution without having first obtained competitive bids. A joint committee of the legislature spent a month investigating matters at the asylum before concluding that all was well. Bids were found to have been awarded competitively, and the trustees were commended for their service, which they had performed without recompense.

Connor had also been involved since January 1855 with several quasi-military and militia organizations in Stockton. He was briefly captain of the "Anniversary Guards" until its dissolution. In 1856 he was elected first lieutenant of the "Stockton Blues," later becoming its captain, and regularly drilling the company at its armory.

II

As the Union began to unravel, a great deal of political uncertainty, fear and suspicion existed in California. The San Joaquin Valley, with its thousands of Southerners who had come in the Gold Rush, was a particular hotbed of secessionist activity. Confederate flags were boldly flown in such towns as Stockton and Visalia, and many newspapers unabashedly proclaimed the Southern cause.

A close friend, C. C. Goodwin, writing of the days when war drew near, said that Patrick Connor "lived a very rugged life," and

Unusual octagonal home built of concrete by Gen. Connor in Stockton, California in 1858. (Courtesy Utah State Historical Society)

there was a group of very determined Southern men who detested him. "No one who was not in the West," Goodwin wrote, knew "how troublous were the times, on how slender a thread at last the Golden State hung in the Union, or how much one such a spirit as that of General Connor counted." For two or three years, Connor's life was "a hundred times threatened," but he was, nonetheless, "always resolute for... the Union, and courted rather than avoided danger."[21]

No one was above suspicion of secessionist sympathies in those days — especially high-ranking military men. Captain Gardner, the commander of the Mare Island Shipyard, was removed from command on the grounds that he wasn't a sound Union man, even though nearly all his officers and employees refuted the charge. The commander of the army's Department of the Pacific was Brigadier General Albert Sidney Johnston, who had for a short time been Patrick Connor's colonel in the Mexican War. Johnston was a Southerner whose loyalty was in doubt, and on April 1, 1861, Brigadier General E. V. Sumner sailed from the east coast under secret orders to relieve him of the Pacific department. Sumner arrived in San Francisco without advance notice twenty-four days later, and promptly assumed command from Johnston. He found everything in good order, but wasted no time in reinforcing the batteries at Alcatraz, Fort Point and Benicia, and preparing for a six-month siege. Johnston would later be killed at the bloody battle of Shiloh while in command of Confederate forces.

Sumner's initial impression of the situation was that, while the majority of Californians might be loyal to the Union, a plot was afoot to draw California into the Confederacy — initially as the "Republic of the Pacific." In spite of just having arrived, the new commander begged his superiors to relieve him so that he might get into the war. Sumner thought his job would be done in two weeks, after which he could safely be spared.[22]

Early in May, after President Lincoln had called for 75,000 militiamen, volunteers began coming forward in California as martial spirit ran at a peak. State law was revised to organize the militia into six divisions and twelve brigades, with a full staff of officers for each, and provisions were made for equipment, drills and for muster into the nation's service.

In July Connor was appointed a brigadier-general of the First

Brigade, Third Division. He resigned his command of the Stockton Blues, and within a month North-South dissension in the organization was so great it ceased to exist. As commander-in-chief of the area militia, Connor approved the decision to disband and then took steps to see that the company's arms did not fall into secessionist hands. Within a few days of the "Blues'" dissolution, a large contingent of Union men met and formed a new militia organization, to be called the Stockton "Union Guard." "General" Connor was elected its captain.

The turmoil continued throughout that long summer. In June both the Republican (Union) and Democratic political parties held conventions in Stockton and took the opportunity to bitterly denounce one another for bringing on the war. In early August a Stockton theatre presented a piece called "Life Scenes in New York and Virginia," which included a song called "Dixie" and its rousing chorus. A local newspaper deemed it a delightful piece of music and expressed the hope that "neither North or South, who are both grabbing for it, will be allowed to take it from California."[23]

As the national situation worsened, and it became evident that a few thousand militia would not suffice, the states were asked for volunteer regiments. Two levies were made on California in July and August, within several weeks of one another, asking the state to provide a total of four regiments of infantry and two of cavalry, to be placed at the disposal of General Sumner.

As the state elections drew near that turbulent summer, fear of a Southern takeover grew epidemic. In mid-August General Sumner was directed by the War Department to prepare to lead personally an expedition into Texas, using all of the California regiments. Hearing of this, sixty-five businessmen of San Francisco hurriedly wrote Secretary of War Cameron urging him to cancel such plans, so as not to leave the state at the mercy of the Southerners. In their somewhat hysterical letter, the San Franciscans claimed that the majority of state officers were avowed secessionists and the rest advocated peace at any cost. The large, closely-knit secessionist population — some 16,000 of whom were supposed to be "Knights of the Golden Circle" — was said to be working full time at rebellion. The businessmen were particularly concerned about possible civil strife should there be a loss in the September 4 elections, since loyal voters were divided between the Union and Douglas Parties.

In receipting for the orders to lead the Texas expedition, Sumner added to the general fears by pointing out that since the Bull Run battle in July, the secessionists had gotten ever bolder. He said that he had been forced to take strong repressive measures, and that he too was concerned about the outcome of the election. Hoping to avert the planned expedition, Sumner threw more cold water on the idea by pointing out that raising the regiments would take some time since there were so many rebels among prospective volunteers.

Apprehension was reduced substantially when, within a few days, Leland Stanford and the Union Party triumphed in the election. General Sumner was now able to tell his superiors that the situation seemed safer, although he still intended to send reinforcements to the southern part of the state where the rebels were said to be organizing and gathering supplies. Colonel James Carleton's First Regiment of California Infantry, which had been intended for service on the overland mail route the coming winter, was promptly dispatched southward to the Los Angeles area.

The day before the state election, P. Edward Connor was mustered in as a colonel and began recruiting his Third Regiment. It, like the other volunteer infantry regiments, would be organized into companies containing 83–101 men. Each company was to have a captain and first and second lieutenants. After the rolls had been mostly filled, the men were to select their own officers by voice vote in the presence of a regimental staff officer. The officers would then be placed by grade, based upon an examination before a Department of the Pacific military board.

The new colonel appointed six temporary captains, the first of whom, Thomas Ketchum, opened his recruiting roll books in mid-September at Agricultural Hall, just east of the courthouse in Stockton. Like Connor, Captain Ketchum had been an officer in the Mexican War and was a well-known San Joaquin County pioneer. Other recruiting offices were soon opened in San Francisco and the mining region. Arrangements were made for free transportation to bring recruits down from the mountains, but a number of potential soldiers refused to quit working the riverbeds and enlist until such time as they were driven out by the rains. Ultimately, the rolls of the regiment would show enlistees from a variety of such colorfully-named mining camps as Comanche

Camp, Poverty Bar, Fiddletown, Chili Camp, Chinese Camp, and Campo Seco.

The pay of the volunteer soldiers was thought to be fair by the standards of the time. A private received an advance bounty of $27, $13 per month, food and clothing, and $75 at the end of his service. An additional $5 per month was to be paid by the state after the soldier was mustered out. Besides this, there was the usual 160 acres of bounty land, and the soldier's family would receive a certain amount of financial assistance during his absence. The period of service was to be for three years.

Governor Downey's letter to Connor, which tendered command of the regiment, assigned Robert Pollock, a Douglas Democrat from San Francisco, as Connor's second in command, Pollock having been a Mexican War veteran who had also rendered favorable service to the state militia. Others who became Connor's principal officers included another militiaman, Major Jeremiah Moore of the San Francisco Police Department, and Major Patrick A. Gallagher, who was a former member of the Stockton Fire Department and who had been a senator from Calaveras County for the previous three years. Doctor R. K. Reid, new resident physician at the insane asylum, was appointed regimental surgeon.

Colonel Connor traveled to Sumner's headquarters in San Francisco to make the necessary logistic arrangements and, on September 19 the steamer *Cornelia* arrived in Stockton with 683 packages of goods from the army commissary department for the regiment's use, with more to come. Tents were also soon forthcoming, along with one thousand Minie muskets and the same number of United States Infantry uniforms.

Newly-recruited men were quartered in Agricultural Hall until arrangements were made for their new camp. A site was chosen near French Camp Slough and, a few weeks later, one hundred new men of Company A marched to the music of fife and drum, led by Major Pollock, to their quarters at Camp "McDougal." Colonel Connor brought up the rear riding in a buggy. Once there, tents were pitched and the soldiers made their beds by covering the ground with tules. A guard was established and the army routine began. Each man had been issued a regular uniform, a fatigue uniform and a soldier's overcoat, and soon the new infantrymen were to be seen in town wearing their best kit.

The locals were of the opinion that the soldiers had been very well dressed indeed by their Uncle Sam, and commented favorably on the handsome dark blue frock coat, the brass eagle buttons and collars trimmed with light blue cord. The officer's uniforms were thought to be very rich with the handsome epaulette straps and custom tailoring. But not all Stocktonians were enthused about Union soldiery and their new uniforms. A strong "hanging excitement" was created one night when diehard Rebels ran up Confederate flags at the courthouse, the Weber Engine House and atop Captain Weber's flagstaff.[24]

About the same time as the Third was being organized, another California unit, the Second Regiment of Volunteer Cavalry, was recruiting and training at Camp Alert, San Francisco, located on the ground now enclosed by Mission, Folsom, 24th and 26th streets. A number of companies of the Second would soon come under Connor's control and figure significantly in events along the overland route.

Up until now, Connor was expecting his regiment to be used in the expedition into western Texas, but General Sumner received orders to suspend plans for that invasion, perhaps because of the San Francisco businessmen's fears. The War Department now told Sumner to send all regular troops via steamer to New York as quickly as possible, leaving only three companies of artillery at San Francisco and one at Fort Vancouver, Washington Territory. The new California regiments were to be held ready for use on the Pacific coast or wherever else they might be required.

In late September, on General Sumner's recommendation, plans were cancelled for sending Carleton's troops out on the Overland Trail that winter. Sumner wanted Carleton left in southern California and Arizona to ward off the threat that was perceived there. Carleton could be sent out in March but, for now, the overland route seemed safe from Indian attack.

Although they weren't yet trained, in mid-October 1861, the first company of the Third was dispatched to duty. Captain Ketchum with Company A left Stockton to take up Indian-watching duties at Fort Seward, Eel River, Mendocino County. It wasn't long before Ketchum had forty of his sixty men in the guard house for failing to salute non-commissioned officers, and for refusing to work on the fort and its quarters. This unhappy news all came in a report from a correspondent who, in all likelihood, was a disgruntled soldier. One can imagine the discontent at this lonely post, particularly among men who had visualized themselves winning glory fighting Rebels. Major Edward McGarry and Company E of the Second California Volunteer Cavalry were also at Fort Seward with Ketchum's company. McGarry, a former senator from Napa-Solano and Yolo counties, was adjudged by the correspondent to be the best of a poor bunch of officers.[25]

General Sumner finally got his wish to go fight Rebels in the East. He was relieved on October 21 by Colonel George Wright, who until that time had been commander of the Ninth Infantry Regiment. Wright had served in the Seminole and Mexican Wars and was an old hand in Western affairs.

In November, plans changed again and Wright, now a brigadier, was directed to send Carleton out on the Overland as soon as possible, in spite of the continued objections to removing him from southern California. Carleton was to place troops at Simpson's Park and Ruby Valley in Nevada and at Camp Floyd near Salt Lake City. Wright grumbled about the bad weather which would probably make it impossible to get men and equipment across the Sierra Nevada, and stated his belief that the Indian problem could be solved that winter by simply feeding them. He maintained that if they hadn't been starving in the first place, there probably would have been no depredations the past season. Wright thought that $20,000 worth of provisions, distributed annually to the tribes along the route in Nevada, would in the long run save money.

Wright was able to convince his superiors that Carleton should make a move that winter to retake the forts the Rebels had captured west of the Rio Grande, and that he then could move to Utah to protect the Overland in the spring or summer after the Rebel threat was contained. He arranged for Governor Nye of Nevada to buy government supplies and distribute them to Indians along the trail; this action proved successful in quieting things all that winter.

The recruiting of Californians was going well by late fall. The two cavalry regiments had filled quickly, since that was the type of service most popular with Westerners. The First Infantry, nearly full, was on duty at Fort Yuma and elsewhere in the Southwest, with Carleton in charge of the District of Southern California. Companies B, C, and D of Connor's regiment had been filled and then dispatched to the Humboldt region to relieve regular troops at Forts Bragg, Gaston and Ter-Waw. The Second Cavalry had also been considerably dispersed, with two of its companies at Fort Churchill, one each at Fort Crook, Benicia and Fort Seward and the remaining seven still at Camp Alert.

With four of its companies deployed, the Third Infantry was moved to the Benicia Army Barracks on upper San Francisco Bay on November 25, 1861, to train and to continue recruiting the remaining six companies. Before the regiment left, the citizens of Stockton presented Colonel Connor with a horse, dragoon saddle, pistol, holster and bridle, all valued at over $600. The gift was said to be highly prized and well-merited. The unfortunate foot soldiers of the regiment had to content themselves with a kit containing a towel, handkerchief, comb, thimble, needles and thread, presented to each of them by the ladies of Stockton. It was always thus.

The last of the regular troops on the Pacific coast who were scheduled to do so shipped out on December 11, leaving the West in the hands of volunteer troops and only four companies of regular artillery. General Wright could report at this point that everything in his area of concern was quiet. He took pains to remind army headquarters that the volunteers would gladly serve in the East if asked, and said he believed they would be excellent for that service. General George B. McClellan endorsed the idea, suggesting that two regiments of Californians be formed for the purpose, but nothing ever came of it.

Wright held an inspection of the Third at Benicia in early December, reporting that the troops were "in high order, well clothed and presented a handsome appearance," and were progressing rapidly in discipline and instruction.[26] He was impressed from the start with Colonel Connor and his way of doing things, and while in command he was to support Connor's every action and recommendation.

The rains in northern California during the winter of 1861–62 were some of the heaviest ever recorded. At Benicia, with nothing to live in but tents for a time, frequent complaints on various subjects were heard from Connor's private soldiers. They groused about their paltry thirteen dollars per month pay, recalling that they had been promised fifteen dollars on the printed recruiting bill signed by Connor. A larger aggravation on this score was the fact the men hadn't been paid since entering service some four months earlier. Grumblings continued throughout winter and early spring but, by March, the volunteers were reported to be a comfortable and happy lot, content in their barracks.[27]

Connor and his staff, along with the regimental band and twenty officers, took a break and journeyed to San Francisco on March 17 to take part in the Saint Patrick's Day parade. Forming behind Connor's men at Union and Powell streets were the McMahon Guard, French Guard, Montgomery Guard, Shields Guard and other militia units, followed by a host of Irish organizations such as the Irish American Benevolent Society, St. Patrick's Brotherhood, and the Sons of the Emerald Isle. A high mass was said after the parade at St. Mary's Cathedral and, that night, a grand ball was held at Haye's Park. Here, Colonel Connor was among speechmakers that included newly-inaugurated Governor Leland Stanford of California and Governor Nye of Nevada.

Colonel Connor's family was with him at Benicia Barracks during the entire training period. Johanna had borne her husband two more sons, Edward Maurice in 1859 and Maurice Joseph two years later. Edward Maurice died in infancy while Connor was on an encampment in Sacramento with the Stockton Blues. Now, at Benicia, little Thomas Jefferson Connor, the first-born, died at age six. He was the second of three offspring who would die in early childhood.

The waiting was over at last when, in late March 1862, General Wright assigned Connor's regiment to protect the Overland and directed him to ready his troops for movement at an early date. Plans for sending Carleton's regiment on the trail had been scrapped because of a continuing need for him in the Southwest.

On May 26, with training completed, the Third sailed on the steamer *Helen Hensley* back to Stockton. Connor and his men were received in a rousing fashion despite their 5:00 a.m. arrival. Salutes were fired as the steamer proceeded up the slough, and Connor's friends hurried to the wharf, accompanied by the Union Guard, the Cornet Band and a throng of cheering citizens. Observers said the troops presented a fine appearance as they lined the upper and lower decks with their knapsacks and blankets on their backs.

While the band performed and the Union Guard kept an open space on the landing, Connor's soldiers unloaded and a delegation

Patrick E. Connor and his son Thomas Jefferson Connor, taken in 1860. Connor is wearing his uniform as the captain of the Stockton Blues. (Courtesy Haggin Galleries, Stockton, California)

boarded the steamer to welcome the colonel and escort him to a waiting hack. A procession was then formed with Connor, in fatigue dress, riding in the rear of the Guards, followed by the regimental band and all seven companies, numbering about 650 men. With the band playing "Hail to the Chief," the soldiers marched up the levee to Hunter Street and through town to their new encampment at the fairgrounds.[28]

Connor was taken by his friends to the Weber House for breakfast. Never one to mince words, he undoubtedly ruined the digestion of a few with this response to his welcome:

"I am surprised to find many of my old Democratic friends disloyal to the Government. They are now my enemies, and the enemies of every loyal man; and let those within the sound of my voice look well to the ballot box at the coming election, as it will be necessary to beat the traitors by such an overwhelming majority that they never again will rear their heads in California."[29]

"Camp Halleck" was established at the race track near the Stockton fairgrounds and here the regiment began assembling supplies and making preparations for the long trip to Utah. The new camp was named for Henry Wager Halleck — known as "Old Brains" in army circles — who was then serving as commander of the Department of Missouri and who would soon become Lincoln's military advisor with the title "General-in-Chief." Halleck was a pioneer Californian, having been secretary of state during the period of the military government. He had also been a successful lawyer and businessman and had served as senior officer of the California militia. It is probable that Colonel Connor had known him in this capacity.

The Third was much better disciplined than most volunteer regiments of the time and was at least as well-officered as many regular units but, with departure for Utah imminent, Connor had a good deal of trouble with desertions. There were reports that he had issued an order that future deserters would be shot, but these were without basis in fact. Connor did, however, issue a scathing circular warning rebel sympathizers to refrain from attempting to influence his men.[30]

Courts-martial were held on a number of deserters and other offenders in late June. The punishments, published later, indicate that it was a tough life in 1862 for soldiers gone astray. Of eight men found guilty of desertion, several received six months' hard labor at Fort Alcatraz, one forfeited pay and allowances and received a dishonorable discharge, and the remainder got hard labor for the balance of their enlistments and were to wear a ball and chain on their left leg. Upon expiration of their sentences, all the offenders were to have their heads shaved and their left hip indelibly marked with a one-and-one half inch long letter "D"; they were then to be drummed out of the service.

Plans were now firm for the deployment of seven of Connor's infantry companies and three companies of the Second Cavalry along the overland route. Wright already had three companies of the Second in Nevada, one of which — Captain George F. Price's Company M — was off distributing provisions to the Paiutes near Pyramid Lake. The commander of the Second, Lieutenant Colonel Columbus Sims, was told to abandon Camp Alert and bring his headquarters and Companies K and L to join Connor. These two companies, plus one of those already in Nevada, would constitute Connor's cavalry. A post would be established in Ruby Valley and garrisoned with two cavalry companies under Sims, after which Connor and the remainder of the command would advance to Salt Lake City.[31] The three companies of the Third serving in California's Humboldt region were to be sent along to Utah as soon as they could be spared. All that spring they had engaged in bloody little skirmishes with the Indians in attempting to stop repeated thefts and minor depredations in that area.

General Wright's intentions had been for Connor to leave about June 20, as soon as the road over the Sierra Nevada was passable, but that date came and went and still the regiment remained in Stockton, waiting for better travel conditions and for the cavalry detachment to arrive. Wright inspected the regiment once more and was able to comment on the fine appearance it presented — the obvious result of Connor's zeal and energy. This zeal and energy must have been contagious. On July 4 when the regiment participated in a parade in Stockton and the raucous festivities afterward, the committee for the celebration was required to pay substantial bills for wine, lager and crockery breakage.

Finally, on July 5 Wright issued instructions for the regiment to start as soon as practicable. Sims and his overdue cavalry were now to join on the other side of the mountains. On the twelfth, Connor's order for taking up the line of march was read to his eager and restless Volunteers.

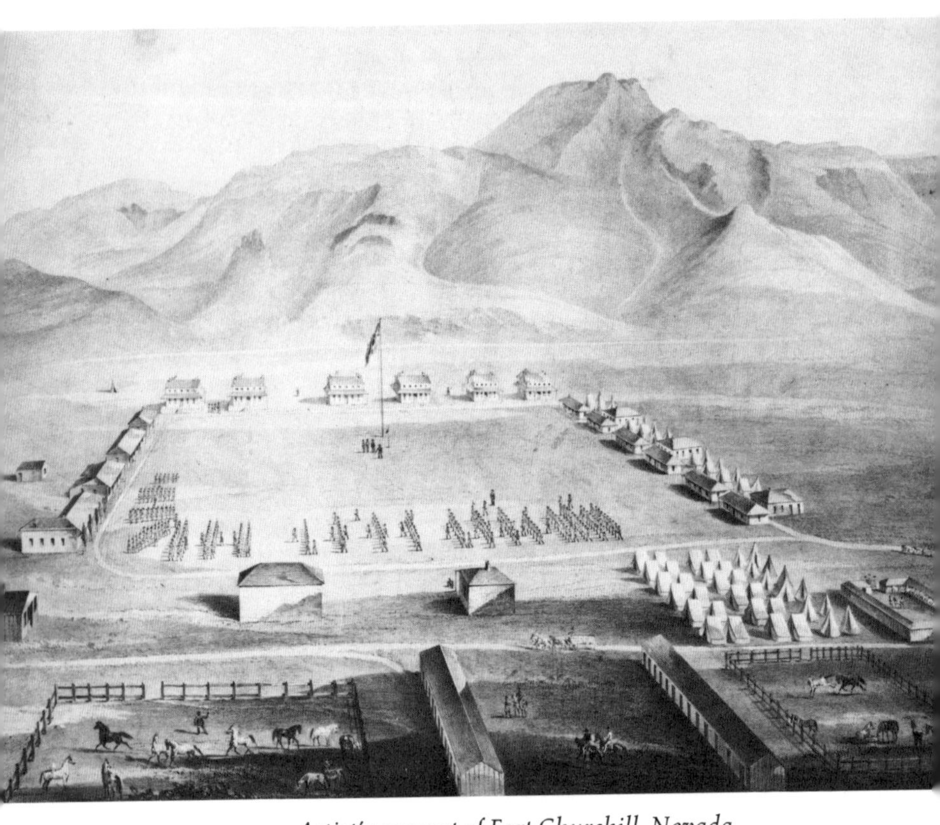

Artist's concept of Fort Churchill, Nevada.
(Courtesy Bancroft Library)

Off For Utah 2

"It never rains here, and the dew never falls. No flowers grow here, and no green thing gladdens the eye. The birds that fly over the land carry their own provisions with them."[1]

— Samuel Clemens, writing of the Washoe country of Nevada

I

News of the desertions and subsequent courts-martial in Patrick Connor's regiment had brought forth pious scorn from the Salt Lake City *Deseret News*, an organ of the Mormon Church and sole newspaper in Utah Territory. In several vituperative articles appearing just before their march was to begin, the Californians were dubbed "evil," and notice was taken of supposed difficulties in filling the rolls of the regiment due to the "unattractive nature of the service." Claiming that the regiment's destination gave it "great celebrity," one disdainful writer said many Californians considered the expedition the most important government movement to be undertaken that summer. He was sure that the "pompous procession" would both tremendously scare the Indians and "wondrously" attract "horse-thieves, gamblers and other pests of the community."[2]

That the movement of Colonel Connor's regiment to Utah might result in "celebrity" and produce such articles was only to be expected. This was, unhappily, an era of almost universal mistrust of the Mormon Church by the rest of the nation. A general belief existed that church leaders were disloyal to the Union, and there were even suspicions that the Confederates might gain Mormon support in return for a promise of Utah statehood. Thus, though the motive at first remained unstated in official correspondence, Patrick Connor and his men were being sent out along the line as much to ensure Mormon loyalty as to protect against Indian depredations.

The mail route, emigrant trails and recently-completed transcontinental telegraph line were all considered at risk, passing as they did squarely through the heart of Utah Territory, remote and isolated from the rest of the nation, inhabited almost entirely by Mormons and with Brigham Young its uncontested master. When the final link-up of the telegraph with the East occurred on October 21, 1861, in Salt Lake City, Acting Governor Frank Fuller had sent a congratulatory message to President Lincoln, stating that Utah citizens "strenuously resist all imputations of disloyalty." Brigham Young also sent a wire on the occasion declaring that Utah was "firm for the Constitution and laws of our once happy country."[3] Very few non-Mormons believed either statement.

The people of the Church of Jesus Christ of Latter-Day Saints had been at odds with most of the rest of the nation almost since the church was founded in 1830 by a young self-proclaimed "prophet" named Joseph Smith. Known as "Mormons," after Smith's *Book of Mormon* — the principal document upon which the faith is founded — the "Saints" were persecuted and driven from one locale to another in the Midwest. Those responsible for the expulsions saw the Mormon people as over-acquisitive, irritatingly self-righteous and clannish. They perceived a threat in Smith's claim to be a "prophet, seer and revelator," in his creation of the large militia known as the "Nauvoo Legion" and, later, in his aspirations for the presidency.

After Smith had been killed and martyred at the hands of a mob at Carthage, Illinois, in June 1844, Brigham Young assumed leadership of the church over the objections of Smith's first wife Emma, and thereafter led a successful exodus to the desolate Great Basin. In 1846, as the Mormons were starting west, Young swore that he would not return until the American nation had been scourged by the hand of Almighty God. This was to become his persistent theme.

In March 1849 a first attempt was made by Young and his followers to gain statehood. A "Provisional Government of the State of Deseret" was formed, taking its name from a word supposed to mean "honeybee" and intended to symbolize the industry of the Mormon people. A constitution was adopted and a huge state defined, encompassing much of present-day Utah and Nevada and parts of California, New Mexico and Colorado.

This first appeal for statehood was rebuffed, as would be many others. Instead, the Territory of Utah was created in 1850 and Young was appointed its first governor. Then, the following year, when the first set of "Gentile" (non-Mormon) judges and lesser officials arrived, a clash began which would last forty years.

The establishment of a theocracy on earth is a principal tenet of Mormonism and, as interpreted for most of the 19th Century, no distinction was perceived or applied in Utah between church and state. The only true earthly government was the "government of God, or the holy Priesthood"[4] — that is, all worthy men from Brigham on down to the newest deacon. The bishops of the wards (parishes), the presidents of the stakes (counties) and those above them ran the business of church as well as that of the community. They settled most disputes without recourse to courts; they controlled the militia; they decided where people were to settle, what was to be their employment, who and how many times a man might marry — in short, all aspects of a true believer's life. Gentiles, not unreasonably, thus believed they could never receive justice from Mormon courts, and the Mormon-controlled territorial legislature was seen as obstructing the work of the federal judiciary, executive and army.

While the quality of federal officials often left much to be desired, Brigham Young and his people were determined not to be ruled by any class of carpetbaggers — good or bad. The first group of Gentile officials soon left in dismay, setting a pattern of "runaway judges" and governors that would persist until the coming of Patrick Connor's Californians.

The most serious breach with the nation had come in 1857 during the so-called "Utah War," prompted by the resignations that spring of Justice Drummond of the territorial supreme court and other officials. Drummond accused the Mormons of complicity in several murders, and claimed knowledge of secret, oath-bound societies of Mormon men that existed to "resist the laws of the country" and to take the lives and property of persons who might question church authority. These were the so-called "Danites," or sons of Dan.[5]

With Drummond and others representing Utah as being in rebellion, President Buchanan replaced Brigham Young as governor with Alfred Cumming of Georgia and sent a force to the territory to sustain his authority. Advance elements of a 2,500-man army took up the march from Fort Leavenworth in late July, even though the Mormons had revealed in May that Judge Drummond was living in Utah with a prostitute.[6]

A sure result of Mormon hysteria at the coming of the army was the infamous massacre of the Fancher immigrant party at Mountain Meadows in southern Utah. There, on September 11, 1857, a combined force of Ute Indians and Mormon militiamen disguised as Indians murdered an entire train of over 120 persons, sparing only eighteen small children. Mormon participation in the affair would be covered up by the church for years to come, including the period when the California Volunteers were in Utah.

On September 15, 1857, Brigham Young declared martial law and mustered the Nauvoo Legion to resist the oncoming troops. A force of raiders under Lot Smith was sent eastward to harass the army and to burn Fort Bridger and nearby Mormon-owned "Fort Supply." Delays caused by organizational and command problems and the burning of several supply trains by the Mormons forced the army to halt for the winter at Fort Laramie and an improvised "Camp Scott," near the ruins of Bridger.

This respite allowed cooler heads to prevail. A truce was agreed upon and a presidential pardon for the inhabitants of Utah was issued on April 6, 1858. In an obvious bid for the nation's sympathy, Brigham Young had already begun moving most of the population of Salt Lake City and the surrounding areas southward, leaving the city virtually deserted and ready to be torched. Brigham accepted the pardon on June 12, but he and his people remained in the south until the army had marched through Salt Lake to the site agreed upon for their encampment forty miles beyond the city. Here, near present-day Fairfield, Utah, they established Camp Floyd.

To the Mormon people, the Civil War came as God's punishment on the evil nation which had rejected them, and was the sure fulfillment of a prophecy given during the "nullification crisis" of 1832 by Joseph Smith, regarding the "wars" that would "shortly come to pass" in which the Southern states would be divided against the Northern states and slaves would "rise up against their masters."[7] During the first years of the war, Sunday sermons described how the nation would be used up, after which the Saints would step in and rescue the Constitution — the only thing worth saving — and then establish the Kingdom of God, first in the ruined country and then throughout the world.

Polygamy — reviled by non-Mormons — was the means by which the kingdom would be established in the wake of the war. According to the prophet Brigham, widows in the ruined nation would eagerly marry Mormon men. Speaking in 1861, Young said God had introduced a plurality of wives for the express purpose of bringing a "royal Priesthood upon the earth" and "not to gratify lustful passion in the least." The Mormon leader was "almost daily sealing young girls to men of age and experience" and he asked Mormon women to love their duties because they were to be the mothers of "kings, princes and potentates" who would come to "govern and control the nations."[8]

There were few, if any, abolitionists in Utah. Certainly not Young, whose feelings were well known to his followers. Slavery was "always so and would be. The inferior would always be in subjection to the superiour."[9] Brigham said he would never fight "one moment" in a war in which "one portion of the country wish to raise their negroes as black slaves, and the other portion to free them, and apparently almost worship them."[10]

The federal presence in Utah had begun to evaporate in 1860. Most of the troops stationed at Camp Floyd had departed in May, leaving only a few companies to perform garrison duties. Their commander, General A. S. Johnston, also left that spring without ever meeting Brigham Young, and without ever entering Salt Lake City again after his arrival. The new commanding officer, Colonel Philip St. George Cooke, renamed the post "Camp Crittenden" in February 1861 not long after Secretary of War Floyd — a loyal Southerner — was asked to resign.

Another who departed with the war's advent was Governor Cumming, who left Utah quietly in May 1861 to return to his native Georgia. Then, in August, the last of the troops at Camp Crittenden left for the East, abandoning one of the best-equipped military posts in the West after holding public sales to dispose of huge amounts of provisions and stores of every kind. It was estimated that four million dollars worth of goods went on the block for about $100,000.

With the army gone from the territory, Brigham seems to have decided he could safely reassert his authority. There followed what was perhaps the most flagrant challenge yet to the federal government when Governor John W. Dawson — newly appointed by Lincoln — was driven out of Utah, in a most ignominious fashion, only a few weeks after his arrival.

Dawson's alleged mistake was making improper advances toward his housekeeper. One faithful Mormon confided to his diary that the governor had met with "voilent [*sic*] resistance" from the widow of T. S. Williams while trying to practice "some of his Devilish Gentiles civilization" on her. After offering the widow a large sum of money and being refused, the "poor mean curse" had feigned sickness and then left for the states.[11] This was confirmed by the *Deseret News* which spoke gleefully of the "novel and peculiar" circumstances of the governor's sudden departure on the Eastern stage, after being confined for ten days to his room, "very sick" and "distressingly *insane*."

While this may have been so, Dawson had given greater offense to the Mormon hierarchy. In an irritating speech to the territorial legislature just three days after his arrival, he had hinted at Mormon disloyalty and made recommendations for radical change in Utah. The legislature had recently been making one of its periodic attempts to gain statehood, and Dawson managed to give further offense when he vetoed a bill providing for a constitutional convention.

Dawson and his doctor were soundly beaten and robbed at the mail station in Parley Canyon by four roughneck "bodyguards" the Mormons had assigned to "prevent his being killed or becoming qualified for the office of chamberlain in a King's palace."[12]

Anti-Mormon authors Catherine Waite, John H. Beadle, and T.B.H. Stenhouse all were to insist that Dawson was entrapped by the Mormons into a compromising situation. In any case, on January 16 he failed to win confirmation for the gubernatorial appointment after Mormon representatives presented an affidavit from the offended woman to the Senate.

After Dawson's departure, and with two federal judges having fled as well, Brigham and the legislature went ahead with their plans to again apply for statehood. With only two compliant and sympathetic federal officers remaining — Secretary Frank Fuller, the acting chief executive, and John F. Kinney, the chief justice of the territory — there were now no problems. The convention met in late January to produce another "Constitution of the State of Deseret," and an election was subsequently held in which Brigham ran for governor and his principal advisors for other important offices. With numbered ballots and only one slate, the vote was predictable: of the 9,880 votes cast, 9,880 were in favor of Brigham, his advisors and the State of Deseret.

On March 17 Young, as "Governor-elect," issued a proclamation convening the legislature of his proposed state and ordering the election of "senators" to Congress.[13] After William H. Hooper and George Q. Cannon were chosen for these positions, Acting Governor Fuller gave his sanction to a statehood memorial to the Congress, and Hooper was sent off to Washington where he would join Cannon and congressional delegate Bernhisel in lobbying.

This statehood petition, like the others, would be denied. But, undaunted, for each of the next eight years the "Deseret" legislature — a ghost government consisting of the same men as the territorial legislature — met, listened to "Governor" Young's annual message and adopted for "Deseret" the territorial laws they themselves had recently enacted. Congress was routinely petitioned for admission to the Union and, just as routinely, it denied the requests.

II

The overland mail road and emigrant trails had never been a very safe proposition but, by 1862, as Indian bands became more and more pressed, attacks and depredations became frequent and intense. When spring came that year, Shoshoni raiders struck the mail line between Bear River Station (near what is now Evanston, Wyoming) and Platte Bridge (Casper, Wyoming), captured nearly 150 head of company stock, and burned nearly every station between Fort Bridger and the North Platte. A number of men were killed; mail coaches were destroyed and the mails pilfered or abandoned. Mail service was interrupted for better than a month.

These were the attacks which had helped force the decision to assign Colonel Connor's command to the line. But with the Third Infantry still months away from arriving in Utah, other measures became necessary. In early April, volunteer troops under Brigadier-General James Craig were ordered to protect the eastern stretch of road, but these arrangements would likewise take some time to implement.

By 1862 the entire Overland Mail Company system was owned and run by Ben Holladay who, as chief creditor, had taken over the financially distressed Central Overland, California and Pike's Peak Express Company. The eastern end of the route ran from Atchison, Kansas along the North Platte River and through South Pass to Fort Bridger and Salt Lake City, following the established emigrant trail. For nearly a year the "Million Dollar Mail" — so called because it was the first time such an amount had been paid for a mail contract — had been running six times a week, and going through in 20-23 days, depending on the time of year. Tri-weekly service was being provided to Denver by a branch line from Julesburg.

On April 11 Acting Governor Fuller, Chief Justice Kinney and six others representing the mail and telegraph lines wired Secretary of War Stanton that the Indians were robbing the mail company of its horses and provisions and destroying its stations, and had declared that the "paper wagons" would be stopped within two months. This alarming message further related that the natives were stealing the cattle of settlers and demanding provisions of them and of the mail company superintendent in a threatening manner. Two thousand Shoshoni were said to be entering the northern settlements demanding food and clothing. Pleading for immediate military protection, the officials recommended that Superintendent of Indian Affairs James Doty be authorized to raise a regiment of mounted rangers from the inhabitants of the territory.[14]

Quick to see an opportunity to head off the coming of Connor's California troops, Brigham Young reinforced the plea of the Gentiles by sending a telegram to the Utah delegate to Congress, stating that "the militia of Utah are ready and able, as they ever have been, to take care of all the Indians, and are able and willing to protect the mail line if called upon to do so."[15]

Young took it upon himself to order Lieutenant-General Daniel H. Wells, commander of the Nauvoo Legion, to provide a detachment of twenty men under Colonel Robert T. Burton, to escort an east-bound mail coach leaving Salt Lake City on April 24 which contained precious cargo — Judge Kinney and William Hooper, who was carrying with him the recently-prepared memorial for statehood. Burton and his men were to continue with the stage as far as Hooper and Burton deemed necessary and then guard the line until it was considered safe, or until they were relieved by some troops expected to be coming from the East. It was a full day after Burton left before Young's actions were confirmed by Frank Fuller, when he finally sent an official requisition for the men to Daniel Wells.[16]

Secretary Stanton drug his heels but finally, on April 28 the adjutant general of the army made a request for troops. It was made directly to Young instead of to Acting Governor Fuller, in spite of the fact that Young was not a government functionary in the territory. But, instead of a regiment, the Mormon leader was asked to raise, arm and equip one company of cavalry for up to ninety days service. This militia was to be used to protect the property of the telegraph and mail companies in the vicinity of Independence Rock, only until such time as U.S. troops could reach that point. The requisition specifically stated that no other types of offensive operations were authorized.

Stanton's decision was most likely based on the need to get some armed men onto the line immediately and the knowledge that a small Mormon force could be raised quickly and dispensed with just as quickly when troops whose loyalty was not suspect arrived from the East. It was said to have also taken into account Young's personal interest in keeping the telegraph line operating and his "well known influence over his people, and over the Indian tribes around."[17]

Brigham Young had Judge Kinney swear in the officers and, by May 1, he could report that General Wells had a company of seventy men on the road for Independence Rock. The officer in command was Lot Smith, the same who, during the Utah War, had led the Mormon raiders in burning United States Army wagons along the road he was now to protect.

Brigadier General Craig proclaimed martial law on the plains on

May 15. About the same time, Burton arrived at Deer Creek and reported that the Indians had apparently disappeared, since he had encountered none on the whole trip. He had, however, found all the mail stations from Green River to Deer Creek deserted, sacks of mail scattered over the prairie, stock either stolen or removed, and property abandoned on every hand. Burton's company was relieved within a few days, after several companies of the 11th Ohio Volunteer Cavalry arrived at Deer Creek and Fort Kearny. By May 31 he and his men were home and had been discharged. Lot Smith and his men also failed to see the elusive Indians. After being sent for a while to Fort Bridger to guard the line from Green River to Salt Lake City, Smith's company was mustered out on August 14.

Thus ended the total Mormon contribution to a Gentile war. Indian troubles flared up again almost immediately, but when asked to reenlist his Utah militia company, President Young refused. By now, he knew that Patrick Connor's arrival in Utah within just a few months was inevitable and that, therefore, the place for Mormon militiamen was at their prophet's side.

III

Absence of any federal presence in Utah may also have contributed in June 1862 to the ruthless suppression of the most recent of the many offshoots from the Mormon religion. The Californians were still making final preparations for their march to that territory when the denouement was reached in this major clash between religious authority and apostate. They would arrive only in time to help pick up the pieces.

For several years past, an impoverished drifter named Joseph Morris had preached the message among Mormons that he was the true successor of Joseph Smith. Morris had bombarded Brigham Young with letters and revelations making this case, much to the Mormon leader's irritation. Morris had organized his "Church of Jesus Christ of Saints of the Most High" by baptizing nineteen apostate Mormons on April 6, 1861. Before long he had attracted—by prolific prophesying and his disapproval of polygamy—over 400 believers from surrounding areas.[18]

The "Morrisites" took up residence at South Weber, or Kingston Fort as it had once been called, on the south side of the Weber River about thirty miles north of Salt Lake City. Upon joining, new members were required to give up most of their property to the church for the common good of all. Believing the second coming to be close at hand, Morris's people laid most work aside and spent their days in religious activity. In some cases crops were trampled underfoot to make the point that they would not be required.

About the time the army was withdrawn from Camp Floyd to fight in the conflict in the East, troubles began to grow between Morrisite and Mormon. They were brought on, in part, by the increasing size of Morris's church, but also by Mormon suspicions of the sect and by the seeming desire of Morris to bring on the conflict called for in his revelations, in which the Mormons would be destroyed by God. When Morrisite men refused in September to drill with the Nauvoo Legion they were court-martialed and fined. Subsequently, the sheriffs of surrounding counties began coming to Kingston Fort to attach Morrisite possessions to satisfy these claims as well as some for delinquent taxes. From the Morrisite viewpoint the Mormon lawmen had come to harass and steal, and force was used to turn the interlopers away.

Morris and his followers, impoverished and lacking adequate food and fuel, suffered intensely during the winter of 1861-62. They lived from day to day on Morris's promises of Christ's imminent return. Ultimately, the hardship brought dissension. A few left — at first peacefully — with permission to take most of their remaining property, but those who left later in the winter were permitted to take only their clothing.

The departure of a certain William Jones in April gave the Mormon authorities an opportunity to act decisively against the struggling new cult. When the disillusioned Jones left, his family chose to stay behind, and Morris refused to return his possessions. Jones subsequently threatened Morrisite men at gunpoint several times in an attempt to regain his belongings. Finally, an armed Morrisite posse captured Jones and two other defectors in a barn in which they were living in nearby Kaysville. The three men were trussed up, thrown in a wagon and taken back to Kingston Fort, where they were put in a small log "calaboose."

Joseph Morris became increasingly more militant. He openly called Brigham Young a blasphemer, deceiver and an insult to God, and reviled the Mormon leader in public meetings. Such militancy demanded an army, and on May 16 the "First Division of the Soldiers of Israel" — some eighty or so men with an assortment of old shotguns, muskets and pistols — was organized at Kingston Fort for the revealed purpose of "cutting off" all who might apostatize.

The full force of Utah law soon began to be focused on Morris and his adherents. On May 22 Chief Justice Kinney issued a writ of habeus corpus for the imprisoned men, based on complaints by their friends and relatives that they were being held unlawfully. The marshal attempting to serve the writ was coldly rebuffed at Kingston Fort by armed Morrisite men.

Three weeks later Kinney issued another writ of habeus corpus, along with a warrant for the arrest of Morris and four others, citing them for contempt and false imprisonment. These were given to Deputy Marshal Robert Burton to execute, inasmuch as Territorial Marshal Lawrence was absent from Utah when they were issued. Burton had just returned from leading the expedition on the overland road. He asked Acting Governor Fuller for a large posse and, when Fuller passed the request on to General Daniel Wells of the Nauvoo Legion, two hundred eager troops were produced overnight from the different Mormon wards in Salt Lake City.

Gentiles would maintain that Brigham Young "bulldozed" Kinney into issuing the second writ and told him that a posse strong enough to serve it would be provided. According to one account, Brigham had "fastened a hook in the jaw" of the chief justice by pandering to Kinney's "lusts of the flesh."[19] That Young was involved in the proceedings there can be no doubt. Kinney later told Apostle Wilford Woodruff that he hadn't taken any steps without Young's approval.[20]

So it was that on Thursday, June 12, 1862, Burton and his "posse comitatus" left Salt Lake City to serve the writs. All along the thirty-five mile route to South Weber the force was augmented by other men wanting to take part in quelling the Morrisite apostasy, until its numbers had swollen to about 500 or 600 armed men.

On the morning of June 13 Burton sent a note into Kingston Fort demanding surrender. Then, unwilling to wait long for an answer, he opened fire with his cannons from the bluffs above, just as the Morrisites were gathering to consider his demands. Two women were killed and another had her jaw carried away by this opening cannonade. The Morrisites then took up arms and for three days successfully resisted the Mormon militia before their ammunition and faith gave out and Morris's lieutenants convinced him to surrender. Two militiamen and several more Morrisites were killed in the fight.

With the Morrisite arms stacked, Burton entered the camp on horseback with about seventy-five men backing him up. When Morris urged his people to further resistance, Burton shot him dead. In the ensuing confusion, Morris's second in command, John Banks, was mortally wounded and two more women were killed — all by Burton according to some witnesses. The excited Morrisites were then ruthlessly suppressed by Burton's men, and their property confiscated.

Next morning, the bodies of Morris and Banks were thrown into a wagon and ninety-three male prisoners followed it on the two day trek to Salt Lake City. One observer remembered the prisoners marching into the city as "about the most forlorn, mud-bespattered procession that ever tramped the earth, the wretched victims of maximum faith and minimum brains."[21]

The leaders' corpses were put on display for several days at City Hall, with Morris's robe, crown and rod lying beside him in mockery. Most of the many Mormons who came to see the remains of the notorious apostate apparently felt that Morris had received his rightful due for daring to "set himself up to teach heresy in Zion, and oppose the Lord's anointed."[22]

The prisoners were brought before Judge Kinney for arraignment the day after they arrived in Salt Lake City. Kinney placed most of them under bonds of $1,500 each for their appearance at the next court session in March 1863. Only five of the men would sign the bonds, and the rest, many of them Danes who could speak no English, protested vehemently against the whole proceeding. But since the five who had signed still owned considerable property, Kinney ruled that they could bind all the rest as their representatives. Two militia leaders, Peter Klemgard and Christian Neilson, were sent to prison to await trial.

After the battle, the Morrisites were a lost people. Some left for the East and a few went to Nevada and California to avoid trial in March. With Banks and Morris dead, and the apostles either imprisoned, indicted or leaving the territory, they had neither a strong leader nor a prophet. A few of the survivors tried to go back to Mormonism but Brigham Young preached to his people that the Morrisites were to be ignored and not to be baptized or given shelter.[23] Any significant help for the numerous outcasts who stayed on in Utah would not be forthcoming until Colonel Connor and his Californians arrived in the fall.

IV

Early in the morning of Saturday, July 12, 1862, the Third Infantry departed Camp Halleck — at long last starting toward Utah and the task at hand. Leaving Stockton, the Volunteers marched proudly through the center of town and out American Street to the insane asylum, escorted by the Stockton Light Dragoons as the regimental band played "John Brown" and "The Girl I Left Behind Me." Near the asylum they halted to imbibe some lager provided by the city, and then marched a beery seven miles farther to their first camp at Waterloo House on Stockton's outskirts. Here the regiment remained over Sunday, entertaining families and visitors.[24]

On Monday morning, tents were struck and the large column got moving in earnest, the men marching at route step and carrying only their weapons. The command consisted of about 700 men in seven companies of infantry, accompanied by a train of fifty-five wagons, each of which was heavily laden with a ton and one-half of supplies, company equipage and baggage. There were three ambulances and a number of "handsome turnouts" carrying officers' families, including Connor's wife and his small son Maurice. Three artillery pieces and a contractor's large herd of cattle completed the train.

Left behind were wagons, mules and property for the use of Companies A, B, and D, still on duty in the north, but expected to arrive in Stockton within a fortnight. Captain Jeremiah Moore was to keep the three companies a few weeks at Camp Halleck before following the regiment to Utah.

Most of what is known of the march to Utah comes from two soldier-diarists and from the articles of the Reverend John A. Anderson written for the San Francisco *Bulletin*. Anderson, age twenty-eight, had been pastor of the Stockton Presbyterian Church from 1858 until joining the Third early in 1862. He was a graduate of Miami University of Ohio, where he had been the roommate of future president Benjamin Harrison. Like Connor, Anderson had served as a trustee of the state insane asylum at Stockton. The soldier-diarists were Private Van DeLashmutt of Company G, and Richard Condy, the regiment's principal musician and a former mayor of Stockton.

That first day of the serious marching was chaotic, with a great deal of shouting and disorder as companies competed to gain the front of the column. During the day the regiment passed a man who gave an audacious three cheers for Jeff Davis — and who was promptly beaten by several soldiers for his trouble. The drum major of Condy's band won the apparent race to be first in camp by reaching Athern's Ferry on the Mokelumne River early that afternoon. The rest of the command dragged in behind him over the next several hours. It was a pleasant place, overlooking the river, and many of the overheated infantrymen took the opportunity to bathe in the cold stream.

In the evening Connor had a teamster named Fiske, a deserter from another regiment, drummed out of camp. Then when he learned of the man who had cheered Jeff Davis, the colonel sent a squad back along the road to fetch the unfortunate fellow and put him to work "packing sand" until the next morning. This delightful punishment of the era consisted of strapping a sixty pound bag of sand on the back of an offender and making him pace back and forth for hours under its weight.

The entire next day was spent crossing the Mokelumne. The teams and wagons all had to be ferried, which proved to be slow work, made even slower by disruptions. The crossing was first interrupted by a whiskey-inspired fight among the members of a fatigue party on the far side of the river. Later a man driving a two-horse team came into camp selling liquor. He was ordered out but, rather than leave, went across the river and began dispensing his product to the teamsters and soldiers. Colonel Connor had the man seized and brought back into camp, where his "grocery" was demolished. Then, before being sent on his way, the would-be peddler was tied across a log and horsewhipped by Captain Samuel Hoyt "in a most workmanlike manner."[25]

The column made it to Buckeye Branch by the evening of July 16, where an extra day was spent repairing wagons and resetting tires. Here the soldiers enjoyed themselves bathing, washing clothes and entertaining the many visitors who came to see them perform guard mounts and other military evolutions. One obviously impressed woman was heard to remark, "Why dog um, it's so good as a circus!"[26]

Two more hard days of marching brought the Third to Camp Number 6 at Weaver Creek, about a mile west of Placerville, where the regiment remained over Sunday. Next morning, with the band playing to buoy their spirits, Connor's men marched through Placerville and made camp in the foothills a mere three miles beyond. Here, the drum beat called assembly and the men formed into line for an inspection of their canteens for liquor. Some of them, it seems, had robbed a whiskey shop while resting at Smith Flat and, according to Condy, Connor said he would give $50 to find the ones responsible. When a few were found with whiskey — and after it had been poured on the ground — the parade was dismissed. Nothing is said of what punishment awaited the offenders.

By now, the men were in better condition and able to make ten to twenty mile marches. Subsequent stops on the steep climb up the Sierra were made at Mountain View House, Webster's Ranch (Sugar Loaf Station), and Strawberry Valley. The road the men traveled generally parallels present-day Highway 50. At that time, the entire road from Placerville to Genoa, Nevada Territory, was known as the Johnson cutoff of Carson Pass. It served as the principal wagon route across the Sierra and was likewise the path of the overland mail and telegraph.

Traffic on the trail was heavy because of the many teams involved in the Washoe and Carson Valley trade, but the heat and dust of the day could be forgotten each evening in camps cooled by mountain air and tall trees. Water and grass for the animals was plentiful and, after supper, Condy frequently rehearsed his band, much to the delight of the soldier audience. At Sugar Loaf, several men climbed the mountain to erect a flag on the summit and this was hailed as quite a feat.

On July 26 the regiment crossed the summit to behold a glorious view of Lake Tahoe — or Lake Bigler, as it was then known. Although the lake seemed close at hand, the soldiers had to march another ten miles before camping along its shores. After Sunday services the next morning, Condy, his band and other soldiers embarked for a sail on the lake, returning in time for guard mount and a parade observed by many visitors. On Monday the band entertained Connor, his staff and the ladies during a schooner excursion on the lake. A dance was held on board, and near the end of a pleasant day, the chaplain led a rendition of "John Brown's Body."

In a five hour march on July 29, the regiment struggled up the grade past what is now an area of plush condominiums called "Heavenly Valley," and then down onto the Carson Valley floor via the Kingsbury or Daggett Pass Trail. This road debouched at the foot of a very steep incline close to Van Sickles's Station, a now-historic stage station that is still standing. The regiment camped here on the Carson River near some warm springs. Connor made "quite a speech" regarding the thievery of vegetables from a nearby garden by some of his men and he threatened to make a terrible example of the first man he found out in it.[27]

On August 1 the regiment arrived at Fort Churchill after marching almost three more days along a gnat-infested road that followed the Carson River through Genoa (Mormon Station) and Carson City. The fort was located on a rise about 200 yards from the river, on its north bank, and consisted of twenty-one substantial adobe buildings and two of wood, without benefit of any surrounding defensive wall. The adobes were painted a gleaming white and, set against the green cottonwoods lining the river, were a welcome sight to Connor's dusty troops.

By the standards of the day, it was a comfortable post. The buildings were roomy, with twenty-inch thick walls, high ceilings and wide porticos. Bandsman Condy thought the adobe houses were the best of their kind he had ever seen, and that the fort had "everything required for the comfort and accommodation of troops."[28] It was nonetheless a stark place, with unbearable heat, disagreeable winds and blowing sand. Timber was scarce and the water, which had to be drawn from wells, was considered by soldier tastes to be generally unpalatable.

Churchill had been established as a direct result of the opening of the Washoe silver mines in nearby Gold Canyon. The huge influx of fortune seekers, that began in 1859, quickly raised the white population of western Nevada from a few hundred to over five thousand, and brought on inevitable conflicts with the Washoe and Paiute Indians of the area. After defeating the Indians in the

"Pyramid Lake War" during the spring of 1860, Captain Joseph Stewart was directed to establish a permanent post, and it had been completed within a year.

The fort was now under command of Major Charles McDermit of the Second California Cavalry, whom Connor found to be a competent officer. Companies M under Captain George F. Price and H under Captain Daniel McLean, also of the Second California Cavalry, were at Churchill under McDermit's command when Connor arrived. Company A of the Second was nearby at Adobe Meadows.

At Churchill, Connor told General Wright that he had found many Rebel sympathizers along the entire route in Nevada; and that while they were "loud-mouthed brawlers"[29] before the regiment's arrival, they were now "very careful in the expressions of such sentiments." The colonel assumed command of the Military District of Utah — comprised of the Territories of Utah and Nevada — and then, on that same day, issued his first order, directing disbursing officers to be economical, and to purchase nothing from persons known to be disloyal. Those who uttered treason were to be arrested promptly and held until they took the oath of allegiance.[30]

Nevada was part of Utah Territory when the war broke out, and its only government was the one dominated by the Mormon Church in far-off Salt Lake City. Congress was quick to pass an act creating a separate territory, and, after Lincoln was inaugurated, he appointed James Nye of New York as governor and Orion Clemens — brother of Samuel — as secretary of state. In the four months it took Nye to reach Nevada, it was nearly lost to the Union. The Washoe area was already full of Southern sympathizers and more came over the mountains as California became solid in the Union. When the federal loss at First Bull Run caused rioting and Secessionist displays in Virginia City, the danger was thought to be so great that more troops and ammunition were sent from California to Fort Churchill, and an officer and twenty dragoons were dispatched to Virginia City to organize a 400-man militia. Governor Nye was still very apprehensive about the problem when the Third arrived.

Colonel Connor had planned to remain at Churchill only long enough to repair his wagons and allow the animals to recruit. Sims and his cavalry had been expected to join a few days after the Third arrived. But the wagon repairs took longer than expected, Sims did not appear, and the column couldn't move. The men made the best of the delay, spending a lot of time swimming blissfully in the heavily-polluted river. Upstream, several large "Washoe pan" amalgamators and stamp mills, which used quicksilver, salt and copper sulphate in the reduction of Comstock Lode silver ore, dumped their wastes unchecked into the stream. On one outing, Van DeLashmutt and his friends swam across the river to see eight "dromedaries," which likely were some of the Bactrian camels used at the time to haul large quantities of salt from the Rhodes Salt Marsh in Mineral County to the silver reduction mills.[31]

Sims, with companies K and L, his staff and the band, finally arrived on August 11, with Captain Samuel P. Smith of Company K under guard, and the men and the majority of the officers in a state of insubordination. Sims had lost thirty men by desertion enroute and his officers had threatened to march their companies to Churchill without him. On the night of the tenth, when the cavalrymen were camped near Virginia City, Sims had dispatched an officer to Connor, asking for help in suppressing a possible mutiny and expressing fears that the citizens of Virginia City were going to demonstrate to get Captain Smith released from confinement. This was the first Connor had heard from Sims, and he must have been very disturbed. Instead of sending any more men to him, Connor instructed him to make a forced march on the eleventh to Churchill.[32]

Major Edward McGarry and other officers informed Connor that if the cavalry companies had to garrison Ruby Valley with Sims in command, most of the troopers would soon desert. In reporting the incident, Connor gave assurance that things were now all right and would remain so while the cavalrymen were under his immediate control. Within a week, the disgraced Sims would be ordered by General Wright to turn over command of the Second Cavalry to Major McGarry and, after facing a board of inquiry in October, Sims would resign from the service.

Finally, on the twelfth, Connor issued orders to continue the movement to Utah. After another "grand review and inspection," the infantry and Company M of the cavalry under Captain Price left Fort Churchill in late afternoon on the fourteenth for the hot

Fort Ruby, Nevada, late 1860s. (Courtesy Bancroft Library)

march across the Churchill Valley and onto the alkali flats. Colonel Pollock commanded the battalion for this march, while Connor remained behind to straighten out the cavalry situation.[33]

Within a few days, Connor had convinced General Wright that Ruby Valley was a bleak and inhospitable place with little forage, and that it would be best to let him take all the cavalry along to Salt Lake City where he could instill some discipline in them. The new post at Ruby would be garrisoned for the present with two infantry companies. Wright ordered Captain Edwin A. Rowe's Company A and Daniel McLean's Company H to take up the march to Utah as soon as Rowe could be recalled from Adobe Meadows. Major McGarry, with Captain Smith and Company K, was told to leave Churchill and join the advance column without delay. Captain Albert Brown's Company L would be the only unit to remain at Churchill.

The part of the overland road the column was now traversing between Fort Churchill and Salt Lake City had been first examined by Mormon pioneer Howard Egan in 1855, and was later explored by Captain James Simpson during an 1859 government survey. George Chorpenning, the first to hold the Salt Lake City to California mail contract, adopted this more direct route in November 1858 in lieu of the established Humboldt River route. The new 558-mile trail went in a northeasterly direction from Churchill to Hastings Pass in the Humboldt Mountains, and then followed the 40th parallel closely until passing to the south of Great Salt Lake.

In crossing the Carson Lake area, Pollock marched the men fast and hard, taking only one meal a day, so that they might reach good water, wood and grass as quickly as possible. The column crossed the Carson River about a mile from the fort and reached Desert Station nine miles farther on at 9:00 p.m. There, an already strained Condy received a tongue-lashing from a soldier's wife for not providing a better place in his company's wagon for her and her children. After a rest, the command was off again at 4:00 a.m. for an eighteen-mile march without water, reaching Carson Lake at 11:00 a.m. in 102-degree heat. Since the water at the edge of the lake proved to be "quite green,"[34] the only way to get a drink was to walk into the middle of the lake before sinking the canteens and barrels.

After a brief layover the men marched on another twenty-five miles, through Sulphur Springs to Sand Springs, where they finally made camp on August 16. Private DeLashmutt was dismayed to learn on arrival here that all the dogs had died from the heat. Wagons had to be sent back with barrels of water to meet the many stragglers who had fallen out of the companies, and Richard Condy reported that "the mirage was so strong in some places we could see the whole command reflected in it."[35]

After laying over a day to wait for all the teams to come up, Pollock's foot-sore troops marched yet another twenty-six miles to arrive at Middle Gate at four in the morning of August 18. There Connor rejoined his command. From this point, for a time at least, the going was easier. Good water was plentiful, refreshing rains fell, and grass for livestock was abundant. The column was encountering numerous large emigrant parties along the road and, at Cold Spring, a sizable band of Paiutes was seen, supposed to be that of a chief called Buffalo Jim.

The layover at Cold Spring had raised the morale of Connor's regiment. Chaplain Anderson was able to report to his *Bulletin* readers that "all are in good health and spirits rejoicing tonight that McClellan has lifted from off each heart a weight of uncertainty by his junction of forces with Pope. The band is playing 'Glory Hallelujah' with a luscious vengeance."[36]

The weary trek continued now, through Edwards Creek and Smith's Creek to the Reese River, thence via Simpson's Park to Dry Creek. Farther on, at Camp Station on the evening of the twenty-seventh, it was necessary to obtain water for the entire command from one well. Since this took such a long time the men settled themselves in and, when called upon to traipse another twenty miles, they were extremely difficult to get moving. A few hid in a haystack and came up the next day, but most of them plodded on wearily on all that cold night, building fires during rest periods to keep warm. At every new start the infantry regiment grew smaller and officers and men alike began to growl about the necessity for such long marches.

The column halted at Roberts Creek, at an elevation of over 6,500 feet, just at daylight of August 28. The exhausted men made fires to keep warm until the wagons came up with their blankets and, when these arrived, most of the troops flopped on the ground without bothering to put up tents. Bandsman Condy slept all day until required to play for mounting of the guard. He awoke to see men still dragging into camp, some arriving just in time to answer their names at retreat. About this time Private DeLashmutt complained to his diary: "Oh, golly! how sore my feet are."[37] Connor found it necessary to give the troops a lecture on grumbling.

McGarry and cavalry Company K joined at Diamond Springs while the column rested there over Sunday. Then on September 1, in a long twenty-seven mile march, Connor and his men ascended the passes over the Diamond and Ruby ranges and arrived in Ruby Valley late in the evening. After laying over a day, Connor moved everyone several miles to another location near a large spring and pond, and here the work of building Fort Ruby was begun. The fort was officially established by Connor's Order Number 8 of September 4, 1862. It would be situated on the southwestern side of the Ruby Valley, two or three miles southeast of an existing Overland Mail Company station. A six-mile-square military reservation was proclaimed in what is now White Pine county, its northern boundary coinciding with the present northern boundary of that county.

The Volunteers were by no means the first white people to inhabit the valley. The first settler is supposed to have been Colonel William Rodgers, or "Uncle Billy" as he was known, who had served a few years beginning in 1859 as agent to the Shoshoni Indians. A telegraph station had been there for a time in the fall of 1861, when it was the eastern terminus of the new line. But the most significant activity in the region was that of the mail company, and had been since Ruby was designated as a major station in July 1861.

Working parties were sent to gather stone and timber from nearby canyons and the task of building the new post was begun. Cabin-style quarters were fashioned of hand-hewn logs, while stables and storehouses were started using vertical logs set in a trench in stockade fashion. A few corrals were also made, using adobe bricks. As if to speed Connor's men in their work, heavy rains now began falling in the valley and snow appeared on the surrounding peaks.

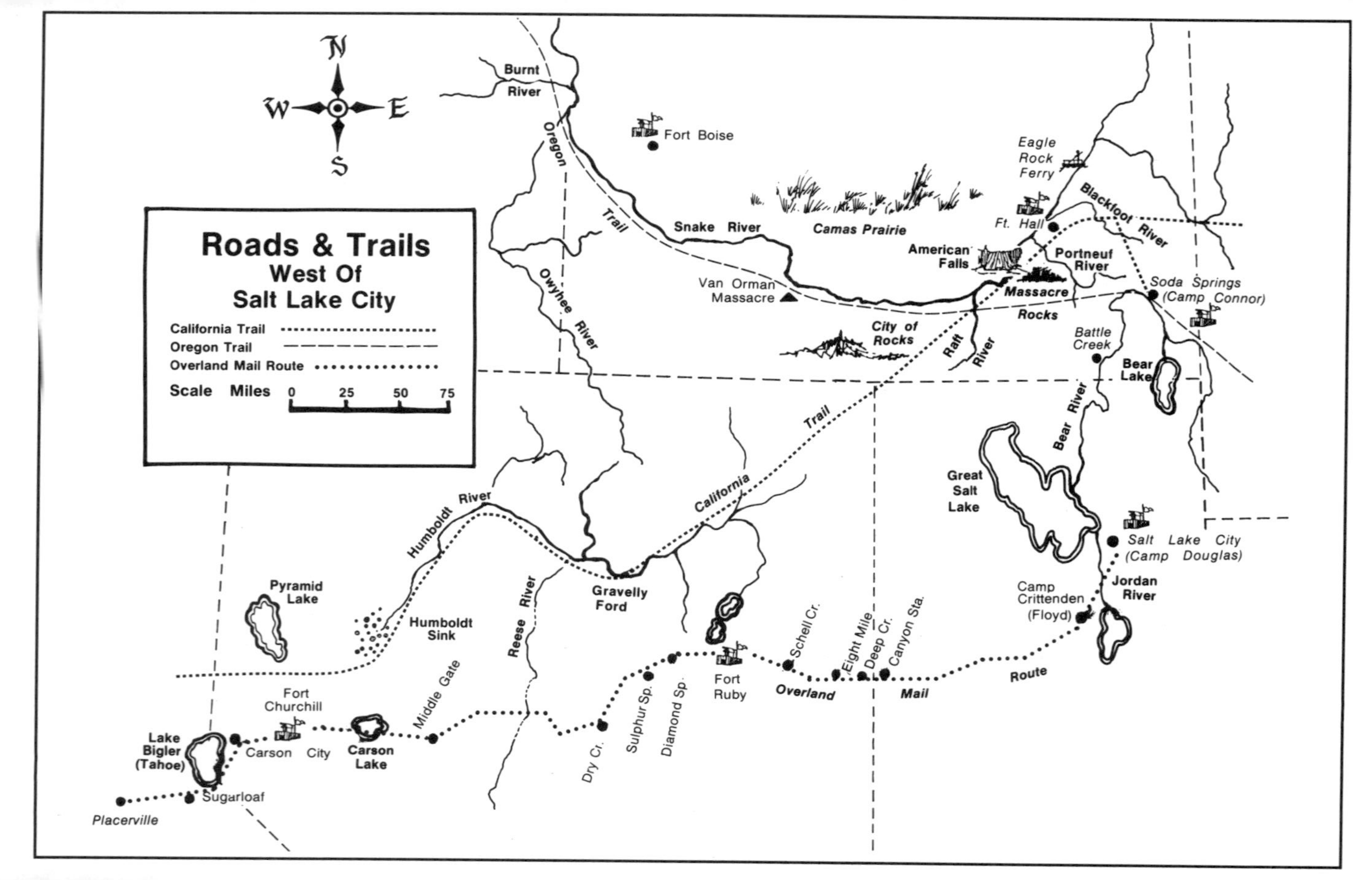

Roads & Trails
West Of
Salt Lake City
California Trail
Oregon Trail
Overland Mail Route
Scale Miles
0
25
50
75
N
S
E
W
Burnt River
Fort Boise
Oregon Trail
Snake River
Camas Prairie
Eagle Rock Ferry
Ft. Hall
Blackfoot River
American Falls
Portneuf River
Massacre Rocks
Van Orman Massacre
Soda Springs (Camp Connor)
City of Rocks
Raft River
Battle Creek
Bear Lake
Bear River
Owyhee River
California Trail
Great Salt Lake
Salt Lake City (Camp Douglas)
Jordan River
Camp Crittenden (Floyd)
Humboldt River
Gravelly Ford
Reese River
Pyramid Lake
Humboldt Sink
Fort Ruby
Schell Cr.
Eight Mile
Deep Cr.
Canyon Sta.
Overland Mail Route
Middle Gate
Dry Cr.
Sulphur Sp.
Diamond Sp.
Fort Churchill
Carson City
Carson Lake
Lake Bigler (Tahoe)
Sugarloaf
Placerville

Entering Zion 3

"If armies are again sent here, they will find the road up Jordan a hard road to travel . . ."

— Brigham Young,
Salt Lake City,
January 19, 1862.[1]

I

Colonel Connor left his troops building Fort Ruby and took the stage to Salt Lake City on September 4, 1862, to have a firsthand look at the desert crossing to that city and the situation that awaited him there. But the primary purpose of the visit was to find a suitable location for his new camp. While there he would spend some time with the governor and other federal officials, then visit the city and old Camp Crittenden. In acknowledging his presence, the Mormon newspaper noted that he had strolled about town and "looked around with an air of familiarity that indicated that after all Salt Lake City was something of a place and might not be unpleasant, notwithstanding its desert surroundings."[2]

However, in his report to General Wright after his return to Ruby Valley, Connor minced no words in giving his real opinion of the Mormons and their capital. From what he had seen and heard he labeled them a "community of traitors, murderers, fanatics and whores." He told Wright the people were publicly rejoicing at Union reverses, while their prophet and bishops preached treason from the pulpits. Federal officers were entirely powerless and were forced to talk in whispers, for fear of being overheard by Brigham Young's spies. Brigham, Connor said, "rules with despotic sway, and death by assassination is the penalty of disobedience to his commands."

Camp Crittenden was found in ruins except for a few buildings, for which the owner wanted $15,000. Connor told Wright that to make it a permanent post once again, nearly everything would have to be rebuilt. Furthermore, the location was a poor one, lacking timber and sawmills, and adjoining as it did a village which was inhabited by "a class of persons of questionable character."

Wright was told of a preferred location on a plateau about three miles from Salt Lake City, more accessible to building materials, where Connor thought that hay, grain and other produce would be cheaper than at Camp Crittenden. The federal officers — particularly the governor — urgently desired that Connor locate near them. But, most significantly, the site commanded the city, and was located "where one thousand troops would be more efficient than three thousand on the other side of the Jordan." Connor said that if Wright approved, he intended to quietly entrench his position, "and then say to the Saints of Utah, enough of your treason." If, on the other hand, it was intended that he merely protect the overland mail and allow the Mormons to continue to "act and utter treason,"[3] then he might just as well locate at Crittenden. As can be seen, Connor had made his proposal difficult to refuse, and it was quickly approved, Wright praising all the while the job the commander of the Third was doing.

As for "powerless" federal officials talking in whispers, Connor undoubtedly was referring not to Judge Kinney or Secretary Fuller, but rather to the new governor and two new federal judges, all recent Lincoln appointees, who had arrived in Salt Lake City two months earlier. It had been six months since Governor Dawson had been driven out of the territory when the new man, fifty-year-old Stephen S. Harding of Indiana, arrived by mail coach on July 7. Judges Charles B. Waite and Thomas J. Drake came a few days later, their stage escorted from Fort Bridger to Salt Lake by Lot Smith's Nauvoo Legionnaires who were returning from duty on the plains.

In noting the judges' arrival, the *Deseret News* revealed a major concern of most Mormons regarding the new outsiders, and also communicated an obvious warning: "Judge Waite is accompanied by his family — a very sensible arrangement . . . Drake . . . has never taken to himself a wife, and is emphatically an 'old bachelor.'"[4]

All appeared to be sweetness and light during Governor Harding's first few weeks in Zion. He was thought to be a friend of the Mormon people and he made much of the fact that, as a boy, he had been given the first proof sheet of the *Book of Mormon* by a certain Mr. Tucker, who was involved in its printing. Soon after his arrival in Salt Lake City, Harding presented the sheet to the church historian.

Independence Day had already been observed in Salt Lake City before Harding arrived but, in those early days even as now, the Mormon people were more enthusiastic in celebrating "Pioneer Day" — the July 24 holiday marking the arrival of the first pioneers in the Salt Lake valley. Harding was taken to the festivities in Brigham Young's entourage and was invited to address the assembled people. With a speech full of platitudes and flowery compliments, the new governor was successful in making a most favorable first impression. Religious freedom was vigorously defended: "Religion is a matter between man and his Maker, and not between man and the Government." Compliments were made on Mormon industry in making the desert bloom: "Wonderful progress! Wonderful people!"[5]

So great was this first gush of amity that Brigham Young is said to have declared himself for the first time satisfied with United States officials.[6] Unfortunately, the honeymoon with Harding was soon over. By August 3 the new governor was writing to the secretary of state to inform him of the treasonous preaching of Brigham Young and others.[7]

During the same month that Harding arrived, the first anti-polygamy statute was signed into law, and defiance of it was a major factor in bringing Harding and other officials to believe that Mormons were blatantly disloyal to the nation. This harsh bill, initiated by Justin S. Morrill of Vermont, made polygamy a felony subject to a $500 fine and a five-year imprisonment. It also annulled those acts of the Utah territorial legislature which tended to establish or support polygamy — the ones that incorporated the Mormon Church, provided for the control of church property, and gave the church the power to make laws with regard to marriage. Morrill's bill further provided that no religious organization in a territory could hold real estate of a greater value than $50,000.

Just the day before Harding had come to town, Brigham delivered a threatening sermon in the Bowery defending the "peculiar institution." This diatribe, which Harding must have read in the *Deseret News* in early August, ripped into the new law. The Congress, Brigham said, had "undertaken to dictate the Almighty in his revelations to his people, and those who handle edged tools, unless they are skillful, are apt to cut their fingers . . ." Little wonder that Governor Harding was disenchanted, frightened and anxious to have Colonel Connor's regiment close at hand.

II

The intense Indian activity along the Overland mail road and the emigration routes, which led to the use of Mormon militia in the spring, had continued throughout the summer of 1862. When the forward edge of the annual emigration reached Fort Hall and beyond, major attacks were reported to the north and west of the Great Salt Lake, while sporadic activity also continued to the east near Fort Bridger and in the counties adjacent to Salt Lake City.

Early in August rumors abounded that the Shoshoni had repudiated their chief Washakie, a peace advocate, in favor of Pashego, "a bloodthirsty warrior," who, it was said, "would like to inaugurate a war with the whites in conjunction with the Bannocks." Little Soldier, a supposed friendly Weber Ute Indian, confirmed this information in a visit to a prominent Mormon militia leader. He told of an alliance the Bannocks and Shoshoni in northern Utah and southeastern Washington Territories had formed for an all-out campaign in the fall against emigrants and settlers, and said they were attempting to recruit other Shoshonis, Goshiutes and Weber Utes for the plan.[9]

Indian Superintendent James Doty, alarmed by these reports and by recent depredations in the Tooele and Rush Valleys, urged the commissioner of Indian affairs to get Connor to speed up his march. This plea was followed by one from mail company owner Ben Holladay, who informed the postmaster-general that a war with nearly all of the nearby tribes was about to occur. Holladay recommended stationing soldiers every hundred miles along his line.[10]

Unfortunately, no protection was forthcoming against the attacks then taking place. Colonel Connor's command was still in western Nevada. The Mormon militia had been mustered out and Brigham would not allow their use again. There was an army expedition in the area beginning in July, sent out from Fort Walla Walla under Lieutenant-Colonel R. F. Maury for the protection of the emigrant road, but it would prove of no use. Maury went only as far as Salmon Falls on the Snake River, camped there and, amazingly, saw absolutely no trace of unfriendly Indians, although a large band of them was hard at work pillaging train after train only sixty miles away.

One stretch of the emigrant trail to the west of Fort Hall was, that summer, a particular type of hell for those traveling it. This deadliest section ran from the American Falls of the Snake River to the junction of the California and Oregon roads at Raft River, and just beyond that to the City of Rocks on the California trail. From August onward it was littered with burned wagons and emigrant possessions and was marked with the graves of their former owners. Here, one band — probably that of the Shoshoni chief Pocatello — attacked one train after another, prompting the *Deseret News* to express the opinion that the Snakes and Bannocks appeared "to have unreservedly seceded from the rest of mankind and made themselves particularly disagreeable and dangerous."[11]

The worst of the killing began August 9 when, in two separate incidents on the same day, a party of five emigrants was set upon near Fort Hall, and another company enroute from Denver to the Salmon River mines was attacked and five of its men killed and scalped. But this date would be remembered more for the attack on the Hunter and Adams emigrant trains which occurred near what has come to be known as "Massacre Rocks," a few miles westward of the American Falls.

The A. J. Hunter party, in advance of that led by Captain George W. Adams, was first to be hit by the Indians. Only eight wagons and seventeen men, mostly former Iowans, were in this leading group. Five of the men had stopped to fish in the river while the train moved slowly along. About one-half mile east of Massacre Rocks, the Shoshoni swooped down out a ravine to the left of the road and attacked a wagon trailing 300 yards in the rear. With one of their mules shot and their wagon overturned, the two drivers abandoned it and ran to overtake the rest of the train, which had moved ahead a short distance into a better defensive position.

The attack lasted two hours, during which Captain Hunter was killed by a bullet in the neck. The Indians tried first — unsuccessfully — to find a weakness by riding in circles around the train, and then withdrew to the overlooking sagebrush hills to sharpshoot. When they finally left with the plunder from the abandoned wagon, the train moved forward another half mile to a still better position and made camp. The fishermen soon came in to report that one of their number had been killed in their attempt to regain the train.

Captain Adams's party was surprised a bit later the same day, when the wagons were scattered along the road for some distance. First to be killed was Charles Bullwinkle, a wealthy bachelor from New York. Later there would be secondhand reports that Bullwinkle had drunk whiskey with some whites and Indians who were in the habit of loafing at the ferry near American Falls, and that he had been free in showing his money and expensive firearms to these people. Whatever the case, after the train left the falls, Bullwinkle, who had a lightly loaded wagon, became impatient. Disregarding warnings, with his sole companion — a large St. Bernard — he traveled on in advance of the train. When he was nearly a mile ahead, the Indians struck. They put eight balls into Bullwinkle and four into the dog, after which they looted the wagon.

The remainder of Adams's train then came under fierce attack. In spite of having corralled for defense, they were soon nearly overwhelmed by the 75 to 100 well-armed, mounted Indians whose tactic was to ride up near the wagons and fire, and then ride off some distance to reload. The emigrants quickly decided to retreat and abandon their wagons; in doing so, two men were killed and several persons wounded.

Hamilton Scott, a member of the Kennedy train immediately behind the Adams party, recounted the tragedy in a letter to a friend a few days later. He recalled that, at dinner time, a man came riding back with the news that Indians were robbing another outfit four miles ahead. Some of the Kennedy men started immediately, while others hitched up, then drove as fast as they could punch their teams along. Before they could arrive to help, however, the Indians had finished their work and left, taking along all the emigrants' stock, provisions and clothing — even the covers from the eleven wagons.

Only twenty-five men and a few women had been in the Adams party. Of these, two men had been killed and the captain's daughter, Elizabeth, critically wounded in the neck. Kennedy's men took the shocked survivors to a place four miles farther on where they joined the equally-traumatized Hunter party.[12]

The Kennedy train, along with others that came up to the scene during the afternoon, made it possible for over 100 wagons to join together that night for mutual defense. The next morning, August 10, a company of forty men under Captain Kennedy rode eastward in an attempt to recover the stolen livestock. After traveling five miles, they stumbled upon a camp of nearly 300 Indians. The startled Shoshoni, led by a chief wearing Bullwinkle's best suit, reacted quickly, firing a salvo that killed Captain Adams's son and at least two others, and mortally wounded Kennedy. Some of the whites ran, and the rest had to fight a dogged retreat for three miles before the Indians finally broke off the attack.[13]

Captain John Walker's company of about forty-five wagons came up later that day. A strong guard was posted during the night, campfires were put out and the wounded cared for as well as circumstances would permit. The next morning, a company of volunteers went back to where the initial attacks had taken place and were able to find five bodies. The young man who had been fishing — an Indian from St. Paul — was found scalped. Several others had been chained to juniper trees with their own log chains and burned to death. Everything abandoned by the emigrants had been carried off or destroyed. The contents of Bullwinkle's six trunks were gone, including six thousand dollars. The only evidence that could be found of his four fine horses was some silver harness lying on the trail where it had been cut from the animals. The stock of one of his silver-mounted guns was found among the rocks, and was taken to camp where it was auctioned off for the benefit of the survivors. The dead were buried near Massacre Rocks.

The Hunter and Adams survivors were taken along by Captain

Walker. On the morning of August 12, at Raft River, young Elizabeth Adams died of her wounds. Her loss caused one westering woman to commiserate to her diary: "Poor father and mother lost one son and one daughter, all of his teams, clothing, and four thousand dollars, is left dependent on the bounty of strangers."[14] After burying Elizabeth in a wagonbox coffin, the California and Oregon-bound companies which had temporarily banded together split once again. Those for California appointed Walker as their captain. Enroute to Carson City with their defenses still up, they came across the wrecks of many wagons, with emigrant bodies strewn by the roadside. In one instance, twelve corpses were found; in another, four; and in still another, two—all minus their scalps. The train was attacked several times before reaching the Humboldt, but suffered no serious losses.

Assaults continued against other companies. Near City of Rocks on the morning of August 26, the Smith train from Warren County, Iowa, was overwhelmed by Indians in the canyon that the emigrant road took in leaving that place. Theirs was a small company of only about forty people and, after an hour-long fight, they abandoned their wagons and cattle, and most of their horses and mules, to attempt the remainder of the journey with only one wagon.

Before sundown of the same day, the Indians, about 100 in number, attacked them again, this time killing three men. A fourth man—a Mr. Waterhouse—turned up missing and wandered into another emigrant camp four days later to report that he was the only survivor.

The rest of the party had only about forty pounds of flour amongst them for food, and in their destitute condition they set off southward. Three of them were able to find the Mormon settlements on Bear River and obtain help, which eventually reached the rest of the company about ten days after the attack. Captain Smith had been shot through both legs and the right arm, and his wife and small daughter both shot through their bodies. The little girl died on the journey to the settlements and, at the time the incident was reported, the captain and his wife were thought unlikely to recover.[15]

Yet another late August attack was made by the same band of Indians against the Louis Swarens–Thomas Craig party from Linn and Hardin counties in Iowa. This train consisted of twenty-nine wagons and forty-five men, some with families. About noon the Indians hit them just as they entered the City of Rocks canyon. Teams were corralled and ditches thrown up. Some forty head of loose livestock had to be left outside and, after two attempts, the Indians were able to run them off. The war party then retired a short distance away and "had a grand dance over it," after which they once again surrounded the train and kept up a brisk fire until dark, and thereafter at intervals throughout the night.[16] Next morning, when the Indians were gathered on a nearby bluff, part of the men in the train went out on horses, followed by some on foot, and drove the Indian band over the ridge. The train then came on, having lost about fifty head of stock and with two persons wounded.

Just a few weeks later an eastward-bound pack train of fifteen miners was attacked near the same spot, reportedly by the same band once again. These men, from various places in California and the Washoe, were destined for Colorado and Missouri. Well-armed, they had traveled without incident up the Humboldt and arrived at the junction of the roads, near the City of Rocks, on the evening of the 11th. Here they camped for the night.

Next morning they took the Salt Lake road, and had only traveled a few miles when they heard the lowing of cattle. Thinking there were emigrants camped nearby, and sighting smoke from campfires a short distance from the road, several men rode toward it to find out if much-needed meat could be purchased. Much to their surprise, they found Indians, not emigrants.

The Indians who came out to meet them appeared friendly enough and, seeing a large herd of 400 or 500 head of cattle, the whites made their needs known to the man who seemed to be the chief. They were told that if they all would come into the camp they could buy all the beef they wanted.

The miners returned to their friends, but suspected treachery. Instead of returning to the Indian camp they hurriedly started on toward Salt Lake City, trying to increase their distance from the red men. They hadn't gone far before they were fired upon from the roadside and, at this, they took off at full speed, followed by thirty-five to forty Indians on horseback and by many more on foot. A running fight continued for several miles, during which all of the miners' horses were wounded, but only one man received a slight injury.

On reaching Cassia Creek, with two of their party dismounted, the whites were forced to take up into a canyon and try to gain a position in the rocks from which to defend themselves, since to proceed would have meant certain death to anyone without a horse. But the Indians anticipated their movement, and before they reached the rocks three white men were killed. From that time until after dark a fierce fight ensued, during which another miner was killed and four wounded — two mortally.

The Indians gained possession of all the whites' animals at about eight o'clock in the evening, after which they withdrew, "whooping and singing hideously."[17] Soon after they had gone, the seven men who were unhurt, and two men who each had a broken arm, left their position just as the moon was rising. They carried their two mortally wounded companions down to the bank of the creek, where they placed them side by side, life in each being nearly extinct, and then left them and moved slowly and cautiously in the direction of the settlements in Box Elder. They were five days without food before finally obtaining help from a large company of emigrants they met some six miles beyond Bear River.

III

Colonel Connor and his command had not been in a position to prevent the raids along the road west of Fort Hall, nor did these attacks even take place within his district, but he undoubtedly had received news of the Adams-Hunter attack, and the brutality of it surely influenced his later actions. Now, in the Ruby Valley, he was available to enter the fray.

On September 15 Major McDermit at Fort Churchill received information that twenty-three emigrants had been murdered at Gravelly Ford, some 200 miles up the Humboldt River, near present-day Beowawe, Nevada. The residents along the lower Humboldt had urgently requested McDermit's assistance and, since Ruby Valley was only seventy-five miles from the location of the assault, McDermit passed the information to Connor, informing General Wright and Governor Nye of his actions. Connor told Wright on the sixteenth that he would attend to it. In a dispatch the same day from Ruby Valley, Chaplain Anderson told *Bulletin* readers that the Indians thought to be involved were White Knives, Shoshoni and Bannocks.[18]

In Governor Nye's mind, most of the troubles along the Humboldt were being caused by Rebel guerrillas he believed had joined with the Indians to rob and plunder loyal citizens. He claimed that the Rebels had first organized in the Carson City area under the pretense of going East to join the Confederate army, but were in reality "lurking about the country" in the Ruby Valley area. In a letter to Wright the same day he received the news about Gravelly Ford, Nye urged the general to station troops from the lower Humboldt to Ruby Valley, including some at Gravelly Ford.

Captain Albert Brown of the Second California Cavalry, who had conversed with Nye, wrote to General Wright a few weeks later. In his letter he pooh-poohed the extent of secessionist activity and laid the blame for inciting the Indians upon Mormons keeping ferries on the Humboldt, and on a few other white men who were "rebels to all governments."[19]

It is apparent that Connor and his men also disbelieved the stories of secessionist activity but the colonel nonetheless sent out Indian interpreter Butterfield and Sergeant Newton of Company G on September 17 to Gravelly Ford. They reported no trace of either a massacre or of Rebel guerrillas, but had found everywhere "convincing signs of hostility upon the part of the Indians."[20] Connor therefore made "arrangements for putting several grains of very hot corn in the ears of the Indians who committed the late butcheries." Said Chaplain Anderson:

"For two or three days he has been holding patent pow-wows with red painted, buffalo-robed, longhaired chiefs. I can never look at their heads without being reminded of the hymn which speaks of a narrow road 'with here and there a traveler.' But that is not to the point; the point is that the Shoshones are divided into numberless bands or cliques. These chiefs profess to know exactly what band did or did not commit the murders. The Colonel . . . offers the chiefs aforesaid $50 for each live corpus produced in the camp, of the Indians who participated in the late slaughters. In the event of the chiefs claiming the reward — and they started off exceedingly filled with the idea that they would be millionaires in a week at the farthest — the Colonel proposes to hang said live corpuses to a tree and leave them as a warning to other Indians who have a penchant for murdering white men and ravishing emigrant girls."[21]

Besides attempting to turn Indian against Indian, Colonel Connor had other plans for dealing with the natives. He knew the guilty parties would likely never be identified — but no matter, for he seems to have decided to deal with the problem of depredations in a cold and deliberate manner. After the arrival of a contractor's supply train on September 29, he dispatched a large cavalry expedition under command of Major McGarry. The main thrust of this sweep would not be made toward Gravelly Ford, but rather would follow to the north of Connor's intended path to Salt Lake City; its goal would not be just to punish a few offenders, but to make a long-lasting impression upon all the tribes.

IV

Toward the end of their stay in the remote and lonely Ruby Valley, Colonel Connor's frustrated Volunteers concocted a scheme, typical of the age in its naiveté and unabashed patriotism. The incident was reported like this:

"The Third Infantry wants to go home — not for the purpose of seeing the old folks, but for the purpose of tramping upon the sacred soil of Virginia, and of swelling the ranks of the brave battlers for the brave old flag . . . the glory which awaits the California regiment that first lands on the Atlantic coast combined to make seven hundred hearts camped in Ruby Valley pulse vigorously with the patriotic desire to serve their country in shooting traitors instead of eating rations and freezing to death around sage brush fires, which two are the only military duties to be performed here."[22]

Committees were formed and, amazingly, about $25,000 was pledged by the men in Ruby Valley, on the condition that the regiment be ordered east. Captain John B. Urmy's Company G alone pledged $7,431, including a promise of $5,000 from a certain Private Goldthaite. How Goldthaite planned to do this on $13 per month was not explained. Colonel Connor sent both a dispatch and a letter to General Halleck on behalf of his men, authorizing the paymaster to withhold the money subscribed, and urging that the regiment be allowed to fight the Rebels. If the sum pledged was deemed insufficient, Connor said, the regiment would also pay its own passage from San Francisco to Panama.[23]

Chaplain Anderson pointed out to his readers that infantry was of no use against Indians, and that there were enough of the Second Cavalry to handle the problems. Why the Californians had been sent was a mystery, Anderson said, since Brigham Young had offered to protect the entire line with 100 men. He was sure the Volunteers had not been sent to keep Mormondom in order, since Young could "annihilate" them with the "5,000 to 25,000 frontiersmen always at his command."

Anderson hoped that Halleck was in good humor when the regiment's dispatch reached him; that he might have just eaten the biggest kind of a good dinner, just have lit the best cigar in all America and might have just heard of the greatest Union victory of the war. Only if he said yes to the Third would they "have a chance to shoot seceshers, and pat Uncle Abe on his long back for that slavery proclamation!"[24]

But all of this unbridled enthusiasm went for naught — the offer was ignored. This would be only the first of several pleas made by Connor to try to get his regiment out of Utah and sent east or back to California. T. B. H. Stenhouse, who after leaving the Mormon Church came to know Connor well, said the colonel was "mortified to find himself sent to 'watch Brigham Young,'"[25] and that this was a major cause of the initial ill feeling of the Volunteers toward the Mormon leader.

The Californians stayed at Ruby a month before resuming their march to Utah. The delay was caused by failure of contractor James Street to provide, until September 29, what Connor considered adequate supplies for so large a command about to enter unfriendly territory. The regiment left the fort on October 2, just a few days after McGarry had been sent on his Indian expedition. Major Pollock had gone back to California to take charge of the three missing infantry companies only to learn they were to be retained there for the time being. In other changes, Companies A and H of the cavalry had by now joined from Fort Churchill, and Richard Condy and his regimental musicians had been discharged and sent home as an economy measure.

Departure from Ruby Valley evoked strong feelings in the Volunteers. Being left behind to garrison the inhospitable new post were the 161 men of infantry Companies C and F under Major Patrick A. Gallagher. Three men had died while there and one, Sergeant McQueen, had just been buried. After the battalion bound for Salt Lake saluted and marched past, Colonel Connor rode in front of the men remaining at the fort and told them he hoped to see the regiment together again in the spring. To this everyone collectively uttered a hearty "amen." The thoughts of the soldiers moving down the trail were not only of the living left behind, but also of those "who heard not the column's tread as they rested stiff and cold in their graves." The chaplain hoped the Secretary of War would speedily abolish Fort Ruby, and create instead one nearer the scene of the Indian "massacres," and on a spot that was not a "fever breeder and a natural hospital filler."

The march was another hard one, and Connor kept his men moving, even breaking his usual rule about resting on Sunday. He realized now how urgent it was to get his men into winter quarters. More patches of desert had to be crossed, making dry camps at night. Several times water was hauled in barrels from miles away so a route could be taken that would allow better grazing. Then came the unbroken, white alkaline dreariness of the western Utah desert.

On Saturday, October 11, the regiment arrived at Fish Springs after a twenty-two mile march. Anderson, whom the sun had "well nigh broiled most of the vigor" from and whose "pantaloons were tired," found the springs excessively tantalizing. He was disappointed to find that, "like a seat in the California Legislature," the sulphur brine of the spring was "excruciatingly nauseous."

After crossing two more desert valleys, a distance of twenty-four miles, camp was made for a few hours beyond Dugway Hill. As the command was preparing to march once again at midnight one of the "infants" — that is infantrymen — on being aroused, announced in a rich Irish brogue "that this was the best country he ever struck, where they called a man at midnight to eat." That afternoon, at Indian Springs, the column halted for a day of rest and Anderson could report that "the great bugbear was safely passed . . . winter quarters were not many miles distant, and the march virtually over."

Arriving at Rush Valley, Connor and his troops were only twenty miles from old Camp Crittenden. From there, Anderson reported that he still didn't know what their final destination was to be, since Connor had "a fashion of keeping his own counsel." The only certainty seemed to be the inevitability of death. With the sounds of a carpenter making a coffin still ringing in his ears, the chaplain reported that Private Cooper of Company G had died of typhoid during the day and that his body would be placed "in the bosom of this quiet valley." "Not stranger than are the comings and goings of the gentle breeze which causes the canvas walls of the tent to rustle against the tall grass," Anderson mused, "is the coming and going of the spirit; and . . . the mysteries of the life beyond the grave."[26]

On October 17, from Camp Crittenden, Colonel Connor sent an ominous telegram to General Wright informing him that tomorrow he would "cross the Jordan."[27] The troops sensed the tension and were surprised to learn that they were to spend the winter at a point nearer to the Mormon capital. Connor, who rarely made speeches, had made two that day within half an hour. After halting the column, he had first told the cavalry not to take a cent's worth of property from the Utahns without paying. They were coming among a people whose customs were different, Connor said, but they were to be treated with the same courtesy and justice as people elsewhere. He, the colonel, would not suffer a few bad men to plunge the government into a war, and would punish all offenders severely. Then, riding down to the infantry, Connor told them he had no complaint to make but was heartily proud of them and he spoke now only because circumstances required that strictest discipline be observed. As he departed, the "infants" gave their colonel three rousing cheers.

A twenty-mile march northward on October 18 brought the column to a point on the west side of the Jordan within twenty-five miles of Salt Lake City. There, from a slight rise, the men thought they could make out some of its buildings. Apprehension heightened further, and rumor ran unchecked through the companies. Great excitement was said to prevail in Salt Lake City; Mormon leaders were meeting to decide what action to take; force would be used to oppose the crossing of the Jordan; the "Chief of the Danites" was said to be riding through the streets offering to bet $500 that the Volunteers could and would not cross the river Jordan.

Anderson disclaimed any knowledge of what was actually true. He did say, however, that a prudent Connor had arranged for each soldier to receive thirty rounds of ammunition and had seen to it that the two six-pound cannon and the mountain howitzer had ammunition. He noted also that the night's camp had been well chosen from a defensive standpoint. Full of shameless emotion and patriotism inspired by the war, he also reported that Connor had "sent word to the chief of the Danites that he would 'cross the river Jordan if hell yawned below him,'" and that "the battlefields of Mexico testify that the Colonel has a habit of keeping his word."

The chaplain thought it disgraceful that United States troops, acting under lawful orders, might be forcibly prevented by the Mormons from executing those orders. While everyone in the command was disposed to treat Brigham and his people with courtesy and strict justice, the moment they became traitors, the Jordan would "be as acceptable . . . as the river Potomac" since the Volunteers, like their "eastern brethren," would be fighting for the same exact principle — "the flag and national existence." And, if they were annihilated, the Union men of California "would swarm forth by the thousand" to wreak vengeance.

Anderson seemed aware that the source of the rumors might turn out to be the speculators who had purchased the buildings at Camp Floyd for a song, and mentioned that his colonel had been solicited a number of times to repurchase them. The chief of the Danites was reported to be the principal owner of the buildings. Whatever the truth might be, our reporter knew that Colonel Connor was "a blessed hard man to scare."[28]

The chaplain closed this latest dispatch with a juicy tidbit for his "lady readers":

"As we came into camp, a middle-aged lady, dressed in homespun, a yellow sun-bonnet, nature's stockings, and *no* hoops, was espied sitting near the spring engaged in sock-knitting. Scarcely any power extant could have restrained the embodied and hooped female curiosity of the regiment from paying a scouting visit. We learn that the visitee was married in the states; that her husband became a convert to Mormonism and moved hither . . . that in the course of time he proposed to take a second wife, whereupon she 'reared, kicked, plunged,' but finally consented; that he also took a third wife . . . and that by her he had a daughter . . . that said daughter grew into maturity [and] . . . he made said mature daughter his fourth wife, and has by her a child one year old.

Whether or not he will also marry his third wife's granddaughter has not yet transpired, but if he should, and his third wife's granddaughter should have a daughter, what relation will that daughter be to each wife and the whole concern?"[29]

In a later article, Anderson would spoil the full pungency of the anecdote when he admitted he had learned that the daughter married by the polygamous Mormon was a daughter by marriage, not by blood.

At reveille that Sunday when the expedition crossed the Jordan, the soldiers awoke expectant of battle, each wondering how he would perform under fire and which side would "whip." Colonel Connor was seen seated upon a log, calmly loading his revolvers and playing with his toddling son Maurice. The popping of muskets and the thud of ramrods could be heard as some men tested their pieces. Others vigorously polished already-glittering muskets, determined to "die according to regulations, if die they must." Surgeon Robert K. Reid, while arranging his knives, saws and probes, was able to convince twenty-eight of the forty-one men reporting for sick call that this was a day when every man able to carry a musket should do so.

Soon after beginning the march, a courier arrived with information that no resistance would be made at the bridge and, fifteen miles farther on, the Jordan was crossed that afternoon without incident — in fact not a soul could be found on the eastern bank of the river. Anderson claimed all were glad to have avoided conflict, but he nonetheless noted that "it was a magnificent place for a fight . . . with a good sized bluff upon the eastern side from which splendid execution could have been done."

While camped that night near the bridge below the mouth of Little Cottonwood Canyon, it became clear that all the excitement about crossing the river had been instigated by parties interested in selling the Camp Crittenden buildings. But when the line of march resumed the next morning — Monday, October 20 — for the final day's trek, the chaplain still was unsure of what awaited them and what was to be their final destination:

"That it was to be near the city we knew; that the leading Mormons objected to its proximity because of the danger of difficulties between the soldiers and citizens, we knew; that in 1858 they had resisted the now traitor Johnston's 10,000 men, and . . . had . . .

forced him . . . not to locate within forty miles of Salt Lake, we knew; that they were far stronger and better armed now than they then were, we knew . . . the precise animus of the people and the treatment that would meet us, we did not know. . . . All these certainties and uncertainties conspired to create the same excitement that passengers in olden days felt when two Mississippi steamers lapped guards, burned tar, and carried the engineer as a weight on the safety valve. We had generally supposed, and the people had universally supposed that the command would pass around the city, or at the most but through the outer suburbs, which of course, under the circumstances, was considered decidedly bold."

A few miles outside Salt Lake, the Volunteers were met by the governor and Judges Waite and Drake. Here Connor ordered a halt to realign his column, putting the cavalry, its brass band, and a makeshift infantry field band near its head. Arriving at the city's edge, the troops were astonished when they were turned onto one of the main thoroughfares and marched slowly and deliberately toward the center of town. Every crossing they passed was occupied by spectators, as were many windows, doors and roofs. Anderson reported that not a cheer or jeer greeted their arrival, nor were there any flags flying or other manifestations of loyalty, save one instance in which three ladies in a carriage sang "John Brown" as they drove by. One little boy, running alongside Connor's staff, asked "You are coming, are you?" — to which an officer replied that "we thought we were."

After passing Emigration Square and the theater the column halted at Governor Harding's mansion. As an inquisitive crowd of people packed the sidewalk to watch, the infantry was formed in two lines with the cavalry behind them. Connor saluted the governor and introduced him to the Volunteers, after which Harding rose in his buggy and addressed the troops and assembled Mormons.

Hedging and pontificating, Harding didn't sound at all like the same man who, several weeks before, had urged Connor to locate near the city. While expressing pleasure to see the soldiers, he took pains to assure everyone that the mission of the troops was one of peace, and that they hadn't been sent to cause trouble or mischief. He told the soldiers to behave themselves — twice admonishing them not to "run wild in the riot of the camp." The colonel must have listened in disgust as Harding said he was somewhat disappointed that the Volunteers had come to the city, and that he, Harding, knew nothing of the disposition to be made of the troops or where exactly they would establish camp.

Anderson commented on the speech by pointing out that the Mormons were known to fear that the soldiers would drink to excess and bother their women and "be naughty generally." He thought it proper that the governor should have warned the troops to be good boys, since this was reassuring to the Mormons.

At the end of the harangue, Connor led his men in three cheers for country and flag, and — dutifully — three more for the governor. Then, bands playing and flags flying, he marched his column through more of the city, and up the hills to the east onto the sloping plateau between Emigration and Red Butte canyons, to the place where he intended to establish his post. Anderson noted that the Volunteers could have reached their destination by a much shorter route, but that Connor had purposely marched them roundabout. The chaplain expressed no objection, since he was "curious to see rosy cheeks and sparkling eyes." An amazing comment from a pastor, let alone one who had just received a lecture on morality from the governor and, before that, from his colonel.[30]

Thus ended the long trek begun more than three months earlier in Stockton. No blood had been shed, but a new era had begun for Utah, in which all hopes of an isolated "Kingdom of God" would be lost forever. As the weary soldiers made camp above the city, the countersign for the nightly guard was given as "rest" — which more than one footsore soldier must have agreed was the most appropriate choice possible.[31]

Camp Douglas, Utah Territory, ca. 1865. Photograph taken from the hills to the east, looking westward toward Salt Lake City. (Courtesy Fort Douglas Museum)

Among the Saints 4

"We had a fine supper . . . and . . . walked about the streets some, afterward . . . and there was fascination in surreptitiously staring at every creature we took to be a Mormon. This was fairyland to us . . . a land of enchantment, and goblins, and awful mystery. We felt a curiosity to ask every child how many mothers it had . . . and we experienced a thrill every time a dwelling-house door opened and shut as we passed . . . for we so longed to have a good satisfying look at a Mormon family in all its comprehensive ampleness . ."[1]

— Mark Twain, describing his first visit to Salt Lake City, 1861.

I

By 1862, when the California Volunteers arrived in Utah, the "City of the Saints" had matured into an attractive community, surrounded by a desert valley, now somewhat tamed and beginning to flourish after years of Mormon hard work and industry. Although the houses were for the most part small, one-story adobe affairs, "Great" Salt Lake City had been laid out on a grand scale. It was built — like most Mormon towns — using Joseph Smith's "Plat of the City of Zion" as a model. Set square with the cardinal directions, streets were a generous eight rods wide. Each block contained ten acres, divided into eight lots, which allowed a quarter of an acre for buildings, and an acre for garden and fruits to each owner. A ditch running down every street provided a stream of clear, fresh mountain water for use in gardens, and for irrigation of the cottonwood, locust, acacia and poplar trees which had by now grown tall enough to provide ample shade against the desert sun. Ever since Gold Rush days the city had been a welcome way station for most travelers in the West.

Salt Lake City's population in 1862 was about 10,000, and was almost entirely Mormon. A few "Gentile" merchants — including, ironically, some of the Jewish faith — were doing business on East Temple Street. They, along with representatives of the mail and telegraph companies, federal officers and a small population of miners and emigrants, had been living in virtual social isolation.

On October 22 Colonel Connor moved his men a bit farther northward from his initial halting place to a point near the mouth of Red Butte Canyon, and there began establishing his camp in earnest. Mormon observers thought the selected location might be all right for summer use, but that it would be a bit exposed and cold in the winter.[2] Of course the colonel hadn't chosen the spot either for its comfort or its magnificent view of the lake and city. To him, it was a defensible position in close proximity to the Mormons. Brigham Young knew this and would soon begin to complain bitterly.

A reserve was declared, two miles on a side, with the camp flag staff as its geometric center. Several months later, Connor would deem it necessary to expand the original reservation to four miles on each side, for the reported reason that "some whisky establishments had begun to take root outside the former lines, and another institution forbidden by Moses was threatening to grow up in the same quarter luxuriantly."[3] The establishments and institutions were notified to quit the area.

The new post was named Camp Douglas, in honor of the "Little Giant" — Senator Stephen Douglas of Illinois — who had died just the previous year. The choice of names was undoubtedly a deliberate jab by Colonel Connor at the Mormons. There had been a long history of encounters between the Saints and Douglas, most of them disagreeable. As a member of a commission appointed by Governor Ford of Illinois, he had helped find a peaceful solution to the Mormon question in that state after Joseph Smith's assassination. The harsh but realistic terms developed by the commission required the Mormons to leave the state, in return for which their safety would be guaranteed.[4]

For a time, Douglas became a particular favorite of the Saints because of his belief that inhabitants of the territories were just as capable of regulating their internal affairs as people of the states. After he began to aspire to the presidency, however, Douglas had sounded more like a candidate from the state that had banished the Mormons. Speaking in Springfield, Illinois on June 12, 1857, during the "Utah War" excitement, the senator called Mormonism "this pestiferous, disgusting cancer which is gnawing into the very vitals of the body politic," and recommended that it be "cut out by the roots." Douglas declared himself in favor of repealing the 1850 law which had authorized the territory, on the grounds that most of the inhabitants were aliens and outlaws, "unfit to be citizens."[5]

Mormon leaders were incensed. Douglas was reminded that he was once "but a country judge," and that Joseph Smith had prophesied he would some day become president if he continued to be a friend of the Mormons, but if he ever lifted his finger or voice against them, such would not be the case.[6] Unwilling to defy such potent prophecy, the nation would never allow the "Little Giant" to achieve his dream. Patrick Connor thus could hardly have chosen a better name than Douglas for his new post if his object was the daily chafing of a few Mormon sensibilities.

With winter so hard upon them, the Volunteers were forced to work fast to ensure adquate housing. Only rudimentary shelters would be thrown up that first year, and even all of these would not be completed until mid-January. For enlisted men, excavations were dug four feet deep, covered by canvas tents and provided with a stone and adobe fireplace. Each of these crude shelters — laughingly known as "Connor tents" — was meant to house twelve men. They were touted as being warm, comfortable and well-ventilated. One can be sure of the latter.

The officers' thirteen small quarters were built over the same sort of excavations but these particular holes in the ground had adobe or log walls, and roofs of boards, straw and earth. Each contained three to five rooms and was heated by a fireplace. The post commander was provided with a five-room adobe house, which he shared with the several adjutants. Colonel Connor and his family took up residence this first winter in the house of a certain John Long, near the center of town on Second East Street.

The Volunteers also began building a guardhouse, to contain

three rooms and a cell, and a bake house — both of which were entirely above ground. For a hospital, a small log structure was erected and three tents pitched nearby, the latter warmed by fireplaces and packed round with boards and earth to provide additional protection. Finally, to provide shelter for the soul, Chaplain Anderson erected the chapel tent which had been donated by the First Presbyterian Society of San Francisco. It undoubtedly was the first non-Mormon "house" of worship in the territory.

Substantial numbers of those "pariahs of the plains" — the Morrisite exiles who had remained in Utah — began to gather and take up residence at or near the new military post, seeking refuge and employment. Colonel Connor put many to work and fed them freely from government stores. A few of the Morrisite men enlisted in the infantry companies.

The chaplain submitted a lively report about this time that wonderfully describes the mood of the men and their activities. Salt Lake City, he said, was not at all like San Francisco, "where the weather is so cold, blustering and abominable all summer that it is ashamed to get any worse during the winter," and where winter was regarded merely as a "philanthropic, magnitudinous squirt-gun which washes the sand from your eyes." Here in Utah, Anderson said, "the approach of January with its four feet of snow, is a chilling affair."

Fifteen miles up in the hills a work party was cutting trees faster than fifty teams could haul them and, two miles distant, another force was quarrying sandstone. The chief engineer was described as being "flat on his belly, sighting over a stake and yelling in the most approved topo-graphical style" while staking out quarters around three sides of a parade ground. While a force was molding adobes, another fifty "police" were executing the pick and shovel drill on a trench ten feet wide and ten feet deep that was to bound the camp as a drain. The "masonic fraternity" was building a huge regimental bake-oven and the quartermaster and commissary were "up to their elbows in bills, boxes, and barrels" from contractor Street's supply trains, which had been arriving from the West.[7]

The first Sunday after their arrival, a large party of inquisitive officers and their wives accompanied Governor Harding to the Salt Lake City Bowery where they attended a Mormon worship service. This place of outdoor worship and meeting was constructed in the usual Mormon fashion, being simply a large expanse of ground covered by a roof of interwoven boughs and leaves, and furnished with the requisite pews and platforms. The pulpit rostrum extended the whole width of the front end, and was occupied that day by Brigham Young, his apostles and other dignitaries. In front of them was a lower platform for the choir and a string orchestra. The Gentile visitors joined a huge congregation of about four thousand Mormons, and were ushered to seats reserved especially for their use.

The fiery John Taylor preached the following message to an attentive audience: that no sure knowledge could be received by man except through direct revelation from God; that the Mormon Church was the only channel of correct communication and that it must finally govern the world; all nations would be overthrown by it; God had preserved the modern Saints amid their persecutions, and always would "put a hook in the nose of their enemies, and lead them to destruction." At this last statement, the people said "Amen!" vociferously and numerous persons gazed intently at the Gentile visitors, "doubtless to admire our moustaches," Chaplain Anderson wrote.[8]

It can't be determined if Colonel Connor was present at this service—probably not, since he is supposed never to have met Brigham Young, and he would have found it difficult to avoid doing so had he attended. Of a certainty, however, is that no converts were made of any of Harding's party of visitors that day.

Connor's men behaved themselves quite well in Salt Lake City, considering that a good proportion of them had been rugged, individualistic miners. Only two men from each company were initially permitted daily to visit the town, and then only until sunset. Most of the men who went on pass looked at the sights in the "New Jerusalem," as they termed it, paid for what they bought, and returned on time. When one cavalry trooper subsequently made a fool of himself by getting drunk, riding furiously through town insulting people, and shooting at a local citizen, it became front page news in the Mormon paper. Upon his return to Douglas from the rampage, the errant soldier was turned over to city officers for trial.[9]

II

In late October, soon after the Volunteers had begun digging holes for their new quarters, Major McGarry and his two companies of cavalry arrived at Camp Douglas, having completed the expedition against the Indians which had been prompted by news of the Gravelly Ford "massacre."

When he started his sweep from Ruby Valley nearly a month earlier, McGarry had been instructed to proceed with Company H of his regiment to the confluence of the Humboldt River with its south fork, and wait there for Captain Sam Smith and his Company K, sent out the day before on reconnaissance. After Smith joined, the command was to proceed along the northern emigration route, via the City of Rocks, to a point about ten miles north of Salt Lake City. Here, McGarry was to leave his troops and report personally to Colonel Connor — if Connor could be found. If not, McGarry was to wait in that place for further instructions. By ordering such a cautious approach to the Mormon city, Connor showed just how concerned he was at Ruby Valley for the safety of his command as he was about to enter Brigham Young's fief.

McGarry was told to examine every valley and place that could harbor a band of either "traitors or guerrillas," or hostile Indians, that might have been involved in the Gravelly Ford incident. Connor undoubtedly included mention of "traitors and guerrillas" in the orders as a sop to Governor Nye's fears. If McGarry found any such Rebels or Indians, he was to capture them — unless they resisted, in which case they were to be "destroyed." Women and children were not to be harmed, but every male Indian found in the vicinity of the massacre was to be killed. Suspects found in other areas would be taken prisoner and brought to Salt Lake City — unless they resisted, in which case they also were to be destroyed. Connor conceded that his orders might be considered harsh and severe, but he wanted them rigidly enforced, since he was satisfied that, in the end, this tactic would prove the most merciful.[10]

Connor had found in Major McGarry a cavalryman to his liking, fully as tough and uncompromising as himself. The post-expedition report makes it strikingly clear that the major wouldn't be found coddling any Indians. After the rendezvous and several fruitless days searching Pine Valley, the combined force had set out for Gravelly Ford. At that crossing, the frustrated McGarry sent Smith and Lieutenant Darwin Chase with one party of men down the Humboldt, and ordered Lieutenant George D. Conrad and another troop upstream on the south side, with instructions to thoroughly scour the country. McGarry and the balance of the command then rode up the north side of the river to a place designated for rendezvous and camped there.

The evening of October 9 a few of McGarry's men somehow enticed three Indians into the camp. Their rifles and other weapons were taken, and the natives were placed under a strong guard while awaiting the arrival of the interpreter who was with the detachment under Lieutenant Conrad. According to the major, a short time after their arrest, the Indians succeeded in regaining their weapons. When they broke and ran, they were fired upon and disabled by the guard. Afraid that the Indians would escape, and "not wishing to hazard the lives of . . . [his] men in recapturing them alive," McGarry coolly ordered his men to continue firing, and the crippled Indians were killed on the spot.

On the tenth, Captain Smith rejoined the command, empty-handed, to report that he had seen no one. The next day, as McGarry resumed the march, he once again sent out his officers with instructions to bring any Indians they could find into camp. Smith's company, traveling in advance, had not ridden more than ten or twelve miles when they came upon a party of about fourteen or fifteen natives, who were armed with rifles, bows and arrows. Smith surrounded them and took their weapons, and once again the obliging Indians attempted to escape. They dove into the river, were fired upon, and nine were killed.

Now, a veritable potpourri of red men was rounded up. Lieutenant Conrad and party brought in three with a child in tow. Captain Smith returned in the evening with two women. Next day — October 12 — Captain McLean captured a man and his wife; Lieutenant Clark returned with a male prisoner, and still another man was captured nearby during the evening.

On the thirteenth, McGarry told two of the Indians, through the interpreter, that they would be released if they would go and bring in warriors who were guilty in the emigrant massacre but, if they failed to return that night, he would kill all the prisoners he held in camp. The next morning, having heard nothing from the Indian messengers, McGarry executed his four male prisoners. The women and the child were then sent on their way to tell "all the Indians" that the soldiers had been sent amongst them to punish those who were massacring emigrants and, if they did not desist, McGarry would return next summer and destroy them.

The indiscriminate killing continued the next day when Lieutenants Chase and Conrad, with a detachment, came upon a party of Indians camped in the hills just south of the Humboldt. This band was also surrounded, their arms taken from them and eight of them killed while "attempting to escape."[11] After this last incident — and not at all surprisingly — no further natives were to be found, and by the afternoon of the twenty-ninth the troopers were safe in Camp Douglas. None of McGarry's men had been injured on the expedition, and in his report he remarked that all had performed their duties well. Indeed.

The horses of McGarry's men were hardly unsaddled before the controversy over his actions began. A news dispatch telegraphed to San Francisco the day of McGarry's arrival erroneously reported that he had shot twenty-four Indian hostages, when, in fact, that number was the total killed, of which only four had been — strictly speaking — executed "hostages." The *Bulletin* of October 30 contained a scathing denunciation of McGarry's barbarity, and the *Deseret News* declared that he had gotten the wrong Indians.[12] Chaplain Anderson, a descendent of two generations of clergymen, but himself sounding less and less like one, was quick to defend what had been done. After straightening out his editor regarding how many Indians had been killed, and in what manner, Anderson told his readers that one had only to look in the recent newspaper files to see that the Americans were in a full scale war with the Indians.

Anderson conceded that, before leaving California, he would have agreed with the *Bulletin* editorial, but having seen the victims of Indians had changed his attitude. He pointed to "hundreds" of "well-authenticated stories" of atrocities committed by the tribe over the last nine years upon "thousands of American citizens." Each male Indian killed by McGarry, whether he was engaged in the Gravelly Ford massacre or not, had at some time or other participated in other murders. As proof of this, all had been found dressed in the bullet-riddled clothes of their previous emigrant victims. Thus, Anderson reasoned, "the killing of any male Humboldt by Government's order is but simple and justifiable retribution . . . since each male is a guerrilla."

Anderson offered a trip to Nevada for the editor and San Francisco's Reverend T. Starr King, which he thought might change their minds about Indians. He then preached them a lengthy sermon, using as a text, "human nature must be prescribed for just as human nature actually is."[13]

Reading these stinging comments on the Indian problem by a man of the cloth, one can well imagine how most ordinary soldiers and settlers felt. While the Easterner might believe the Indian to be a noble and simple creature whose pristine state was being changed by the imposition of white men on his culture, to the Westerner all this was hogwash. To most, conflict was inevitable. It was "them or us," right against wrong, kill or be killed, if civilization's march was to be unimpeded.

As one well-educated California soldier explained, men gave their lives in the suppression of aborigines so that the "denizens of these mountain vales might enjoy the blessings of peace; . . . that the sturdy emigrant, the fragile woman, the helpless babe might traverse the continent in search of new homes . . . and . . . ne'er fear the war-whoop of the Indian brave, or dread at each lingering step his gleaming scalping knife."[14]

Mormon attitudes regarding the Indian peoples are different still. They are believed to be the "Lamanites" spoken of in Joseph Smith's *Book of Mormon* — lost brothers who, along with the "Nephites," were once part of a great American civilization. In spite of having heard the gospel directly from Jesus Christ when He visited the peoples of America shortly after the resurrection, the Lamanites had become a fallen people who had rebelled against the "truth" and who could, and must, be redeemed by the Saints so that they might once again become "white and delightsome."[15]

The Saints naturally held a fairly pacifistic attitude toward these errant brothers. Following Brigham Young's imperative that it was cheaper to feed them than fight them,[16] the pioneers were liberal in dispensing what food was available. As is still done today, the ordinances and principles of Mormonism were preached at every opportunity and those Lamanites who agreed were baptized and converted to the faith. Hundreds of Indian children were brought into homes of church members and, beginning as early as 1831 when Joseph Smith claimed to have his first revelation regarding plural marriage, Mormon elders were urged to help speed prophecy a bit by taking a few Indian wives.

One must suspect, however, that the relatively kind treatment given to the "Lamanites" by the Mormons — greatly outnumbered and living in isolated settlements — was as much an expedient taken to save their property and scalps as it was to make the Indians once again a great people. For in spite of the benevolent actions required by scripture, Indian problems had always existed in Utah. As early as 1849 expeditions had to be sent out to recover stolen cattle and to mete out punishment for depredations in remote areas. And the settlers were always glad to see the Lamanites take a vacation. In 1861 Chief Bear Hunter and some of his Shoshoni band were issued gifts in Salt Lake City and the chief was decked out "in a complete suit of citizen's clothing with boots and hat" which made him "look much like an 'American'" and feel "first rate." But afterward, when Bear Hunter announced that he would return to Cache Valley and then go immediately into the mountains to hunt, and not return until the wheat harvest, the departure was hailed as "a great blessing"[17] to the whites in that valley.

Another important Mormon belief of that time — the one that led to the Mountain Meadows massacre — was that Indians were allies who could be used as an instrument of retribution against enemies — a "battle ax of the Lord"[18] which might be loosed against the "Americats" who had persecuted and exiled their Mormon brothers.

General Wright at Pacific Headquarters was quick to support McGarry's actions in the Gravelly Ford affair. He thought such punitive action was the only way to deal with "savages" and prevent a repetition of their barbarities.[19] Although Wright only a year earlier had arranged to send food, rather than soldiers, to the Indians along the road in Nevada, perhaps he can be excused in view of the tragedies that had taken place that summer. And of course he had, in his time, done more than his share of Indian campaigning. It was he who — in a hanging mood — had completely broken the power of the tribes of the inland Northwest in retribution for the attack on Colonel E. J. Steptoe and his detachment of soldiers in May 1858.

That the natives killed by McGarry were the ones responsible for the Gravelly Ford affair is doubtful, and they certainly weren't the ones involved in that summer's activities in the City of Rocks area. All those he gathered up were apparently unmounted since they were so easily surrounded, and no mention is made by the major of having captured any horses. The Indians who were the objects of McGarry's revenge most likely belonged to small, isolated bands, which were probably not strong enough to have attacked a sizable white party. In all probability they were so-called "digger" Indians of mixed Shoshoni blood — either White Knives or perhaps Goshiutes.

III

It took just a few short days for overt signs of Mormon hostility to appear in reaction to the arrival of the Gentile soldiers. In late October, Brigham Young and his councilors formed a trade committee, consisting of one or two persons in each ward, and ordered that the people do all of their business through it. A new, standard church price was fixed for commodities. In order to "look after the interests of the people," Young recommended that the number of teachers in each ward be increased to thirty-six, that they be constituted into a police force and that any church members suspected of dealings with the camp be watched "day and night until it could be learned what they were doing and who frequented their houses. If they found any of the sisters going to Camp Douglas, no matter under what pretense, they should cast them from the church forthwith."[20]

Very few farmers were noted visiting the camp after issuance of the decree and many prices were raised, including that of the hay so necessary for winter forage. The price of flour jumped overnight from three to six dollars, in gold. One of Connor's officers, Captain Albert Brown, was later to recall that the merchants were glad to find a moneyed market for their produce, but that a few weeks after the troops arrived, Brigham preached that the military post was a public nuisance that should be abated and that those who traded there would go straight to hell, and "the 'sisters' who went there would have their names published in the streets and be 'cut off' from the church." Brown said that Brigham soon turned the trade into the church, where "by some mysterious process, it was purified."[21]

Brigham's "recommendations" regarding Mormon women were in perfect keeping with previous policies of the Mormon leadership. Since the earliest days of polygamy, Mormon men had been almost paranoid about advances by outsiders toward their women, and had frequently sanctioned violent retribution against any who were foolish enough to attempt a seduction. One early incident that drew national attention was the 1851 murder of Dr. John M. Vaughn in the Utah town of Manti for his dalliance with the wife of a certain Madison D. Hambleton. Brigham Young, at that time governor of the territory, personally represented the offended husband in a court of inquiry, and his speech justifying the shooting was more than enough to get Hambleton released.

The attitude of the Mormon priesthood — which includes all males who have reached the age of puberty — was fairly accurately shown in an article appearing in the *Deseret News* of September 21, 1854. In response to this question posed by an outsider — "Can a gentleman of good reputation not of your religious creed, associate with your females?" — the editor replied:

"If a gentleman wishes to associate with our females, let him repent and be baptized for the remission of his sins. . . . Let these gentlemen go forth and preach the gospel to the nations, like the Mormon Elders, without 'purse or scrip.' Let them be mobbed, tarred and feathered, and whipped a few times for Christ's sake, not for their own follies; return after a few years' labors, clear in conscience, pure in heart and unspotted from the world. If they can do these things, and endure; they may begin to associate with our females . . . but . . . there is no female in our Church that stands upon her good name and honor as a Saint . . . that will freely mingle in the society of any, except those who are soul, body, and spirit, devoted to the cause of the Latter Day Saints."

Soldiers were considered to be particularly bad influences on the Mormon ladies, and had been so classified ever since Colonel E. J. Steptoe and a detachment of dragoons had spent the winter of 1854-55 in Utah. The question posed above may, in fact, have been that of one of Steptoe's ardent and panting men. While Steptoe's conduct was above reproach during the stay, some of his officers and men had a glorious time arranging assignations with bored wives and daughters. One young lieutenant, Sylvester Mowry, even had the temerity to lust after Brigham's daughter-in-law, Mary Young, whom he characterized as being "as hot a thing as you could wish."[22] Mary, whose husband was on a mission at the time, was apparently about to surrender her charms to the lieutenant when Brigham found out about the affair and Mowry was forced to turn his attentions elsewhere.

But Brigham Young was not to be satisfied with merely imposing trade and social restrictions on this new wave of Gentiles in the Kingdom. He wanted them clear out of the territory or, failing that, as far away from Salt Lake City as possible. And from the beginning, Patrick Connor suspected the Mormon leader of inciting Indian depredations as a means of removing or severing his command.

From the east, reports were received in November that the telegraph stations at Big Sandy and Pacific Springs had been attacked. Judge W. A. Carter, the sutler at Fort Bridger, also alleged that Indians had run off one hundred horses which had been grazing on the Fort Bridger reserve. Carter expressed fears that the Indians might attack some of the stations of the Overland Mail Company, and is believed to have urged Connor to move his entire command to the Bridger vicinity.

Colonel Connor took the initiative and dutifully sent forth enough troops to ease the apprehensions. Ten men were assigned to protect the station at Big Sandy, even though it was out of Connor's area in the Military District of Oregon. In a larger move, infantry Company I, under Captain M. G. Lewis, was sent on its way to garrison Fort Bridger, 112 miles to the east, from which place detachments could be sent as required to protect individual stations. Since Pacific Springs was in the area controlled by the Department of the West, it was manned by troops from that command.

Fort Bridger had been completely rebuilt and manned by General Johnston's men in the months following its burning during the 1857 "Utah War." In December 1861, with a Civil War to fight, all the regular troops departed except a small caretaking detachment under Ordnance Sergeant John Boyer. Judge Carter, who had come as sutler with Johnston's army, also is said to have taken the precaution of organizing a volunteer company of mountaineers from the surrounding country, should they be needed against the Shoshoni. Now, a year after the regulars had departed, Captain Lewis and his California infantrymen arrived to find only enough serviceable quarters for a few officers and four companies. Other buildings still in use in the fort's vicinity included Judge Carter's store, a post office, and the facilities of the telegraph and mail companies.

In early December, a rash of communications was received by the War Department from the mail company, the Post Office De-

Drill with mountain howitzers, Camp Douglas, Utah Territory, ca. 1868.

partment and the Department of the Interior, all urgent in the desire that Connor's entire command be removed to Fort Bridger and Ham's Fork. General Wright quashed these attempts by assuring General Halleck that Bridger had already been garrisoned, and that other places would be manned as necessary. Wright recommended against the entire abandonment of the position now occupied by Connor and, in fact, told Halleck on December 9 that "prudential considerations require a force in that country strong enough to look down any opposition." The Pacific commander thought that about 2,000 men in the Salt Lake Valley, commanded by a "firm and discreet officer," would do nicely.[23] Wright reaffirmed his plans to send Connor's three missing infantry companies along to Utah as soon as the roads became passable.

Connor was incensed at the pressure to scatter his command and, having had a chance to do some investigating, and listen to a few rumors, he now had strong ideas of where to lay the blame for the attempts. Judge Carter was one who was extremely interested in manning Bridger and establishing more posts, so as to line his pockets by selling more of his surplus goods to the government.

But Brigham Young — the "real Governor"[24] of the territory — was the true villain. On December 20 Connor reported to Wright that Young wanted the command scattered along the Overland because he was making active preparations — even at that moment mounting cannons — to oppose the United States in the spring, should Utah not achieve statehood or should there be a foreign war or a reverse in Union arms. Furthermore, it was Mormons who had instigated the Indian attack at Pacific Springs, in order to draw Connor's forces to that point, and Mormons also who were encouraging depredations to the north of Salt Lake by trading powder, lead and produce with the Shoshoni in exchange for plunder taken from massacred emigrants. The colonel, however, believed himself able to defeat Brigham's intentions since he now occupied every necessary position on the entire line from the Ruby Valley to Ham's Fork and — most importantly — Camp Douglas, commanding Salt Lake City and all roads to it.

Always supportive, General Wright sent the acrimonious report on to General Halleck, assuring him that Connor was a "man of observation, undaunted firmness and self-possession under all circumstances," and that his views of the state of affairs in Utah could be relied upon. Halleck was further assured the policies to be followed in Utah would be prudent ones until Connor's small force could be augmented in the spring. After that, the flag *would* be respected and United States laws observed.[25]

Stephen Harding was having no easier a time than was Colonel Connor in dealing with Brigham Young. Toward the end of the year, in an attempt to assert his authority and do his job as governor, he came face to face with the realities of his situation. There had been minor insults to his dignity, such as the night someone tossed a live cat through the window of his residence, and the failure of the territorial militia commander to make an annual report as required by law. But now, the new governor was to be completely and thoroughly ignored. It began with his Thanksgiving Day proclamation. The following year, Lincoln would proclaim a national day of Thanksgiving which would evolve into the one we now celebrate each November, but in 1862 there was no such observance. In early December, Harding issued a document which declared that January 1 was to be "a Day of Thanksgiving and Praise to Almighty God."[26] The people of Utah were told, in effect, that they should give thanks that they had been allowed to prosper while the rest of the nation was catching hell in a bitter war. When New Year's Day came, this attempt to impose a day of religious dedication would go unheeded throughout the entire territory. But before that could happen, Harding misstepped a second time in his attempts to Americanize the Saints.

A few days after the Thanksgiving proclamation was issued, Harding delivered the governor's address to the first session of the territorial legislature for the coming year, and he spared no words in telling that entirely Mormon body what was wrong in the Kingdom of God. He called for a thorough revision of the statutes, warning that Mormon isolation was about to end and that it would be the right of the many new inhabitants to claim the protection of "just and wholesome laws." One of the things that must be changed, Harding said, was the practice of requiring that a voter's name be recorded alongside the number of his ballot.

But Mormon loyalty and polygamy were the subjects that Harding had really come to talk about. He told the now-sullen lawmakers that since coming to Utah he had heard no sentiments expressed, either publicly or privately, that would lead him to believe that much sympathy was felt by the Mormon people in favor of the government of the United States, now struggling for its very existence "in the valley and shadow." The legislators were reminded that, in July, the Congress had enacted a statute which prohibited polygamy in the territories, and annulled certain acts of the legislative assembly of Utah. "I am aware," the governor said, "there is a prevailing opinion here that said act is unconstitutional and therefore is recommended by those in high authority that no regard whatever should be paid to the same. . . . I take this occasion to warn the people of this territory against such dangerous and disloyal council."

Although Harding attempted to ameliorate the effect of his words regarding polygamy by delivering them in a cloud of polite Victorian language, it didn't work. Poking through were phrases whose message was painfully clear: "Anomalies in the moral order cannot long exist in a state of mere abeyance . . . religious opinions . . . must not outrage the opinions of the civilized world, but . . . must conform to those usages established by law."

The legislators sat silently as polygamy was compared to other barbarisms such as human sacrifice and suttee, and as the marriage of one man to a mother and her daughter was referred to as "no less a marvel in morals than in matters of taste."[27]

T. B. H. Stenhouse, who listened to the address, later called it "the tocsin of war," and said that the manner of delivery was even worse than the content. "Probably no Legislature," he said, "ever felt more humiliated and insulted."[28] Harding, in turn, saw the failure to respond to his message and to his Thanksgiving proclamation as a personal insult as well as a scoff at federal power. When the legislature refused to have the address printed, he angrily sent copies of it to newspapers in California and New York. Later Harding would say that his speech marked the end of his social contact with Brigham Young.[29]

And so by year's end the battle lines had been clearly drawn. There was no longer any doubt in the minds of leaders on either side — accommodation was impossible. The holiday season that year was to be a forbidding and gloomy one for Gentiles in Salt Lake City. As a gesture of good will and as a means of raising spirits, the Camp Douglas Band serenaded a number of Salt Lake City homes — Gentile and Mormon alike — but this was to be the extent of any sanctioned interaction.

On Christmas eve, a "Grand Ball" was held by the officers at

Camp Douglas. Everyone in the small group of Gentile leaders and their ladies was there, including Colonel Connor, Governor Harding, the officers of the mail and telegraph companies and others in government service or engaged in trade in the city. But across town a much larger party was taking place at the Salt Lake City Theater. This was an exclusively Mormon affair, attended by Brigham Young, his first presidency, the city council, the legislature, and the bishops — all undoubtedly glad to be temporarily free of worries about threats to the Kingdom of God and corrupting outside influences on wives and daughters. A sumptuous dinner and some lively dancing was theirs to enjoy, but the best part of the evening must have come when the Saints watched Brigham's wife, Ann Eliza Webb Young, starring in a new play — a "mirth-provoking Irish farce" entitled "Paddy Miles' Boy," or "Irish Mischief."[30]

The Battle of Bear River 5

"Comes the message to the Colonel: "Indian warriors dare
your guns.
Camp'd for murder and for battle where Bear River's channel runs.
Just one year ago that message. It was January then.
Frost and snow and storm and tempest sentinel'd the Indian den.
California's sons are ready, and their Colonel brave commands;
'Soldiers, march! Your foe awaits you; meet him boys, with steady
hands.'"[1]

— From "An Anniversary Lay," recited
on the first anniversary of the
Battle of Bear River

I

It would be late January 1863 before Colonel Connor found the opportunity he was seeking to severely punish the Shoshoni Indians of the region and to make an impression on them strong enough to stop attacks like those of the past few years against the emigrants who traveled the Oregon and California Trails. Of the several circumstances that would lead to this decisive collision of Californians and Shoshoni, one had had its beginnings in a massacre on the emigrant road more than two years earlier.

Colonel Connor was visited in November 1862 by a certain Zachias Van Orman who asked assistance in recovering his young nephew Reuben from Bear Hunter's band of Shoshoni in the Cache Valley. The little boy and his three sisters had been captured in the September 1860 attack on the Otter–Van Orman emigrant party west of the Salmon Falls of the Snake River. Van Orman had since located his nephew, but was certain the little girls had died.

Of all the Indian depredations of the period, this one attack did more to harden the hearts of Western whites against the Shoshoni than any other. The Otter–Van Orman train had consisted of forty-four persons, mostly from Wisconsin, traveling in eight wagons and escorted for six days by twenty-two dragoons who were stationed near Fort Hall that summer.[2] Unfortunately, the soldiers had turned back on the morning of September 8, just before the train came under siege.

First the Indians attempted to stampede the livestock trailing behind the caravan as it moved across the sage-brush-covered plain. The emigrants managed to form a corral in an excellent defensive position, but at some distance from any water. After the attack had been repulsed, the Indians threw down their arms and made signs of friendship; eventually the gullible whites were persuaded to let them inside the corral. Some of the Indians were even fed in the hope that this would satisfy them.

After assurances that they wouldn't be further molested, Van Orman moved his people out of their strong position and headed the wagons for the Snake River. The Indians struck again and, this time, two men were killed before a corral could be formed and the cattle chained inside it. The renewed struggle continued well into the next day, with two more whites killed at a reported cost of about twenty-five Shoshoni lives. In the fierce fight, young Charles Otter was said to have killed five Indians as fast as he could load his rifle after his father had been wounded and entirely disabled.

The extremely warm weather made people and cattle alike uneasy after two days and one night of being hemmed up. About sundown of the ninth, the train again started for the river. Leading the way were four mounted men and two young boys on foot — the four on horseback being recently-discharged soldiers who had joined at Fort Hall. When the Indians closed in again, and the forward guards fled for their lives, the train had to be stopped for lack of sufficient men to keep it moving while fighting.

The beleaguered whites made another attempt to strike a deal with their attackers, but were rejected. They decided at last to leave everything and steal away on foot in the darkness. Mrs. Otter refused to leave her wounded husband, so she, two daughters and a

Reuben Van Orman and his uncle Zachias Van Orman (at the boy's right) with Zachias's scouts and Indian fighters, taken after Reuben's recovery from Bear Hunter's band of Shoshoni. (Courtesy Edith Farmer Elliot, Granddaughter of Zachias Van Orman and author of her family biography, "Look Back in Love.")

small son were left behind to a sure fate while the rest departed to face the uncertainties of a journey across the barren plain. With only the clothes on their backs, the survivors traveled rapidly throughout the first night. On subsequent nights they moved in a northwest direction, resting during daylight hours.

With their attackers behind them, the survivors now had to struggle to avoid starvation. Their only food was a loaf of bread — grabbed by someone from a wagon as they left — and two dogs which had faithfully followed along. The people caught what fish they could; they ate rosebuds, berries, snakes, frogs, lizards and, occasionally, a few ducks and geese. One stray cow was found and promptly consumed. After nine days, the worn-out group reached the Owyhee River, about ninety miles from their abandoned wagons. Here they stopped and built rude shelters out of willows and grass.

After three weeks in this primitive camp — about October 8 — the seven-member Van Orman family and three other men decided to leave and travel on as best they could. The seventeen who remained at the river were now forced to trade all the possessions they had, except their weapons, to a group of Indians who began hovering around the camp. Needles, pins, and even some of the few clothes they wore were exchanged for salmon. A certain Mr. Chase died after eating too much salmon at one meal and contracting a persistent case of hiccups. One young man named Trimble volunteered to go with the Indians to see if he might make friends and obtain some food. He was fed and treated kindly, and every few days would return, with the Indians, with salmon for the whites. One day, after someone happened to mention "soldiers" in the Indians' presence, they went away with Trimble following and never returned. Later, a lock of the white boy's hair was found near the river.

The emigrants eventually were reduced to eating weeds. Then when children began to die, three of them were cut up and eaten. The widowed Mrs. Chase, mother of two of these youngsters, helped the others consume her offspring. One of the survivors claimed that her children had died in the first place because she had starved them in order to feed herself. After the Indians dug up Mr. Chase's body to steal the clothes from the corpse, the whites decided that they might as well eat him also. They had just cut Chase into small pieces — a day's ration in each piece — and were about to roast part of the ten-day old body when help arrived just in time to save them that ordeal. Captain F. T. Dent, of the Ninth U.S. Infantry, leading a military expedition from Forts Dalles and Walla Walla, found the survivors on October 25. Only twelve were still alive.

Relief parties had been sent out when two of the men who had fled the train managed to reach the Umatilla Indian Agency. Of the other four who had abandoned their companions, two were killed before they reached the settlements, one was forced to rejoin the other survivors and another — a Mr. Schrieber — reached the Dalles on the first of October. Schrieber claimed that the six men had not left the train until the Indians had complete possession of it, and that from the screams of the women and children, he was led to believe that the whole party had been butchered.

On the Burnt River a few days before finding the survivors, Captain Dent had come across the bodies of the three elder Van Ormans and the other adults who had struck out on their own. Reuben's father Alexis and his older brother Marcus had been slain, and his mother Abigail was said to have been raped before she too was killed. All the bodies were brutally beaten and slashed by knives. No trace, however, was found of Reuben and his three young sisters, leading Dent to think they had been captured.[3]

Several military expeditions attempted to locate the missing children, and a halfhearted effort was even made by "Major" John Owen of the Flathead Agency in Montana's Bitterroot Valley. Owen, whose duties required that he deal occasionally with the Snakes, claimed to know where the guilty Indians were camped, only a few days' ride from the Bitterroot Valley. He said that they had spoken "boastingly" of their foul deeds. The major eventually sent a subordinate to visit the Bannocks and Shoshoni and try to learn of the children, but nothing came of the effort.[4]

By the time Reuben's uncle Zachias appealed to Colonel Connor for help in November 1862, he had been searching for the missing children for two long years. Zachias, an Oregon resident, had recently received information from a relative that the children had been seen living with the Shoshoni in the Cache Valley region of northern Utah. The relative had tried to ransom the captives but could not raise the high price demanded by the Indians. When Zachias heard of Lieutenant-Colonel R.F. Maury's summer expedition to the Salmon Falls region, he obtained permission from the commander at Fort Walla Walla to join Maury and obtain any possible assistance.[5]

After finding Maury and receiving no help, Zachias made his way to Utah and there found the missing boy near Smithfield in the hands of Shoshoni Chief Bear Hunter. From what he learned, the uncle became convinced that the three little girls had died of starvation in the region of the Goose Creek Mountains. Zachias was able to talk to the boy and even had seen an opportunity to steal him away, but apparently had thought it unwise. Before leaving Smithfield, the frustrated uncle threatened the Indians with forceful measures, but this failed totally to impress them.[6]

After hearing Zachias's story, Colonel Conner dispatched Major McGarry and a troop of sixty cavalrymen to Cache Valley. The major was told to encircle Bear Hunter's encampment, capture the Indians and demand that they surrender Reuben. If the boy was not given up, McGarry was to bring three of the principal Indians to Douglas as hostages. He was to find out if Bear Hunter's band had been involved in the massacres that summer and bring in for trial any Indians he thought to be guilty. McGarry was also to search near the Indian camp for a large herd of livestock supposedly stolen the previous summer from murdered emigrants and Cache Valley settlers.[7]

These Mormon settlers had first entered the Cache Valley in 1856. Maugham's Fort (Wellsville) was established, and in 1859, the hamlets of Logan, Providence, Mendon, and Smithfield were founded. These were followed in 1860 by a few other villages, including Franklin — the first settlement in what would later become Idaho. An ever-present concern about Indians caused the settlers to build these towns in the form of a square fort, about 200 yards on a side.[8] Stock was generally driven into stables and corrals within the fort each night. Although the Indians took no concerted action against these Mormon pioneers, they did harass them constantly by stealing horses and cattle, and frequently intimidating individuals for food and gifts. Any settlement outside the fort area had been impossible. By the summer of 1860, the "Cache Valley Militia" had been formed, with Ezra T. Benson as its colonel, to respond quickly to emergencies.

A hard night's journey of seventy miles brought McGarry and his detachment near the village of Providence just before midnight on November 22. Here an eager Uncle Zachias was ready to lead them to where Bear Hunter and his tribe were encamped several miles away. McGarry left his horses in Providence in charge of a guard and started out at one a.m. toward the Indians. The detachment got lost during the dark, cold night and it was almost daylight before they could locate the camp. Once there, McGarry divided his men into three parties, under Captain Sam Smith, Lieutenant George D. Conrad and himself, with instructions to surround the Shoshoni and close in on them at daybreak.

Entering the Indian camp at first light, McGarry found it to be deserted, save for two old squaws. Unextinguished fires in many of the shelters indicated that the remainder had only just recently flown the coop. The irate McGarry marched his men back to Providence and by seven a.m. they had retrieved their horses. Somehow, the ever-diligent Captain Sam Smith had taken an Indian prisoner on the return trip.

At about eight a.m. a party of forty mounted Indians came out of a canyon and onto the bench between Providence and the hills and, McGarry said, "made a war-like display, such as shouting, riding in a circle, and all sorts of antics known only to their race." McGarry orderd his men to mount and he divided them into parties as before. Smith was sent to the right, Conrad to the left, and McGarry himself took the center to begin driving the Indians into the canyon. At its mouth, when the Indians fired on Conrad's party, McGarry unhesitatingly ordered his men to fire, and to "kill every Indian they could see."[9]

The major soon concluded it would be impossible to enter the canyon without severely exposing his men to fire from the hills on each side. He thus reinforced Lieutenant Conrad and gave orders to take the hill on the left of the canyon at all costs. After three braves had been killed, and about the time the reinforcements reported to Conrad, Bear Hunter made his appearance on one of the hills with a white flag. McGarry took the chief's antics with the flag as just another warlike demonstration until a Mormon civilian who had heard the chief's "hallooing" finally came up to McGarry and told him the chief was asking for a truce. After ordering his men to cease fire, McGarry sent the civilian to tell Bear Hunter that if they would surrender and come in they would not be killed.

When Bear Hunter came in with twenty or more of his warriors, McGarry took them into Providence where he questioned the chief and four others, through an interpreter, about young Reuben's whereabouts. Finding that the white boy had been sent away several days earlier, McGarry held Bear Hunter and the four others hostage while Indian messengers were dispatched to bring him back. The next day the lad was brought in and McGarry released his prisoners. Before departing, Bear Hunter told the major that he had been warned of the soldier's approach by an Indian known as "Weber Tom."

The California cavalrymen suffered no injuries in the hour-long affray with Bear Hunter's warriors, and the command soon arrived safely back in Salt Lake City. The mission had not been a complete success, since no trace had been found of the missing livestock, which McGarry believed had been taken to the Humboldt country.

An account in the *Deseret News*, following Reuben's recovery, told of Shoshoni claims that he was a half-breed whose father was a Frenchman, and whose mother was a sister of Washakie, the well-known chief of the Eastern Shoshoni.[10] Several other news stories related that the ten-year-old spoke both English and the Shoshoni dialect fluently, and when delivered up was "dressed and bedaubed with paint like an Indian and acted like a regular little savage . . . fighting, kicking and scratching when the paint was washed from him to determine his white descent."[11] The boy was said to remember the massacre of his parents by the Indians who took him and his sisters captive.

According to another account, "some of the whites in Cache Valley had seen the child with the Indians, and although the latter had painted its face to resemble themselves, its light hair and blue eyes betrayed its race."[12] These Mormon settlers allegedly had tried earlier to get the boy, but the Indians refused to let him be ransomed and finally kept him hidden.

It is not known what became of young Reuben, but Uncle Zachias stayed on for a time in Utah and served as one of Colonel Connor's scouts. As for Bear Hunter, it was back once again to harassing the Mormon settlers. As for the settlers, it was back once again to feeding, rather than fighting, the Lamanites. Just the day after the troops left Providence, Bear Hunter and his band reappeared and began making warlike demonstrations near the village. He accused the Mormons of sheltering and feeding McGarry's troops. Finally seventy men were sent from nearby Logan to assist, and when the Shoshoni saw them they sued for peace, asking that they be given two beeves and a large quantity of flour as a gesture of goodwill. Colonel Ezra T. Benson and the local bishop, Peter Maugham, put their heads together and concluded that this might be the best and cheapest solution to the problem. The supplies were produced forthwith from the bishop's stores.

Still bothered about recovering the missing livestock, Colonel Connor sent Major McGarry on another expedition against the

Shoshoni late on the evening of December 4. The major and 100 cavalrymen left secretly and traveled northward throughout the night toward Empey's Ferry on Bear River, eighty miles distant.[13] After stopping during the day in Willard, the troop rode again the evening of the fifth, passing east of Brigham City, to arrive on the river the next morning. But the deception was for nothing. The Indians had been forewarned once again of his approach, this time by a runner who had been seen hastening through Brigham City.

From the ferry, the Indian camp could be seen on a hill beyond the Malad River crossing a few miles farther on. The Bear was full of ice and the ferry scows disassembled for the winter. To further complicate matters, the rope had been cut on the opposite bank by the Indians. In spite of these difficulties, some troops got across and by the next morning four Indians had been captured. McGarry then sent an Indian boy "belonging" to a certain Jacob Meek to the Shoshoni to inform them that they must deliver up the livestock by noon the next day or he would kill the prisoners.[14] On receiving McGarry's threat, the Shoshoni band broke camp, crossed to the east side of the Malad and then proceeded up into the Bear River canyon.

Having received no word by the deadline, McGarry had the four prisoners executed. An account of the killings, based on the report of a county resident, told of the Indians being tied by their hands to the ferry rope and shot, after which the cords by which they were fastened were cut and the bodies tumbled into the river. It was said that fifty-one shots were fired before life in all of them became extinct.[15]

In its first reports of the encounter, the *Deseret News* chided the Volunteers for not making a real fight of it, saying that the "bold and saucy" warriors were anxious for a fight and that "a better chance for giving them a brush could not well have been had."[16] Later, however, the newspaper began expressing fears that the killings would make the Indians more vicious and vindictive. Indeed, major thefts of horses and cattle continued through late December and early January in Box Elder and Cache Counties, requiring that herds be moved closer to the settlements on the east side of the Bear to ensure their safety. Rumors were received that "the aborigines in the vicinity of the northern settlements" had become more hostile and that they were determined to have "blood for blood," and that nothing but the killing of some of the whites would satisfy them.[17] Colonel Connor would soon afford them the opportunity.

II

The years 1860 through 1862 had seen the beginnings of significant mining activity in the regions surrounding Salt Lake City. Discoveries were made in the Reese River area near present day Austin, Nevada; on the Humboldt River at Unionville, Nevada; in what is now central and northern Idaho and — most important to this history — in southwestern Montana at Bannack City.

The diggings at Grasshopper Creek, or Bannack, were first worked in paying amounts by John White beginning in July 1862, about the same time the Volunteers started their long march across the Nevada desert. A rush to the region began and, by late August, nearly one hundred men were there. "Gras," as it was affectionately known, was 430 miles from Salt Lake City — the nearest settlement of any size — and consequently the price of necessities in the camp soared. All during November and December freighters and express riders shuttled between Salt Lake City and the new bonanza, whose population was then estimated at 500 to 1000 souls.

The route to Montana not only passed through Shoshoni-Bannock territory but, in November, the road was altered slightly, coming within a few miles of a large Shoshoni winter encampment in the Cache Valley, about twelve miles north of the tiny community of Franklin. Here the new road crossed the Bear River. The natural declivity provided by the river's course, some nearby hot springs and abundant brush and willows for protection from the harsh winter winds, had drawn the Indians to the location for years.

About January 12, 1863, express rider A. H. Conover arrived in Salt Lake from Bannack and reported that two men, George Clayton and Henry Bean, who had left Bannack with an express on November 25, had been killed by the Shoshoni near the head of Marsh Valley, not far from the settlements in Cache Valley. Conover, Clayton and partners Ed House and Jack Oliver had recently been given an exclusive charter by the miners at Bannack to run their "Bannack City Express Company" between that place and Salt Lake, because of their bravery in getting the express through in previous months.

Conover told authorities he had learned the fate of Clayton and Bean from some Indians he had met near the Portneuf River. The murders were said to have been committed to avenge the blood spilled by Major McGarry's men, and it was reported that Bear Hunter intended to kill every white man found on the north side of the Bear River until the score was evened.[18]

Following this, on January 19 a miner named William Blevins appeared before Chief Justice Kinney and stated in an affidavit that on the eighth, while on his way from Bannack to Salt Lake City he and seven others had also been attacked in Cache Valley. One of Blevins's party had been killed, and some gold dust, animals and other property had fallen into the Indians' hands. Blevins further stated that another ten men from the mines had been murdered by the Indians only three days preceding the attack on his party.

Chief Justice Kinney issued a warrant for the arrest of several chiefs — Bear Hunter, Sanpitch and Sagwitch — thought to be leading bands presently in the Cache Valley, and gave the warrant to Marshall Isaac L. Gibbs for execution. Gibbs — no one's fool — went promptly to Colonel Connor for assistance. Connor, however, had already commenced his own preparations for a move against the Indians, fully convinced that they were "part of the same band who had been murdering emigrants on the overland mail route for the past fifteen years and the principal actors and leaders in the horrid massacres of the past summer."[19] The colonel informed Gibbs that he was welcome to join the expedition, but that no prisoners would be taken.

Having seen the Indians alerted to McGarry's recent forays against them, Connor resolved to prevent any recurrence by using a well-planned deception. He would lead the chiefs to believe that a mere company of infantry, thought by most to be ineffective against Indians, was to oppose them.

So it was that on the cold, clear morning of January 23, Company K of the 3rd Infantry, under command of Captain Samuel N. Hoyt, left Camp Douglas and headed north. Traveling in company were Lieutenant Francis Honeyman with his battery of two small mountain howitzers, and a train of fifteen supply wagons guarded by twelve cavalrymen. Judging from later events, it seems certain that early intelligence was gained by the Indians on the make-up of this slow moving force.

Orin Porter Rockwell, guide for General Connor and spy for Brigham Young. (Courtesy Utah State Historical Society)

Two days later, on the evening of the twenty-fifth, Connor followed with detachments from Companies A, H, K and M of the Second Cavalry, under the command of Major McGarry. With Connor and the 220 cavalrymen were Marshall Gibbs and two supernumerary officers — Major Patrick Gallagher, the commander at Fort Ruby and Captain David J. Berry of the Second Cavalry. Both went along as volunteers, eager to serve as Connor's aides, just so they could get into the fight. For Berry, it was to be a bad decision. Five or six "irregulars" also went along, either for the thrill or to settle old scores with the Indians. Among them was Zachias Van Orman.

Also joining to help guide the expedition, strange as it seems, was Orin Porter Rockwell, a notorious Mormon mountaineer and alleged assassin of various enemies of the church. Three days earlier he had signed on for five dollars per day and keep. Rockwell, with his long, flowing hair, plaited and gathered at the neck, and his ever-present pistols, looked every bit the part he was said to have played in the Mormon saga: bodyguard to Joseph Smith; Danite and supposed unsuccessful hit man on Governor Boggs of Missouri; pioneer mail carrier; deputy sheriff, and soldier in the Utah War against the federal troops. He was reputed to be a deadly shot with either pistol or rifle and to know the country as well or better than anyone in the area. Since McGarry had already been in the vicinity of the Indian camp, Colonel Connor must have taken Rockwell along as insurance, and to have someone who could effectively deal with the Mormons. On the other hand, there is evidence to suggest that Rockwell may have sought out the job to spy on Connor's activities on behalf of Brigham Young.

Snow had begun to fall in northern Utah on December 17, abruptly ending the Indian summer that had prevailed up until that time. Every few days thereafter a new storm would sweep through the area. By the time the Volunteers left the relative comfort of their holes in the dirt at Douglas to move on the Indians, conditions were deplorable. The march of the cavalry was described thus:

"Those who were there at that time . . . how can they ever forget? that fearful night march. Clear and brilliant out shone the stars upon the dreary earth mantled with deep snow, but bitter and intense was the cold. The shrill north wind swept over the lake and down the mountain sides, freezing with its cold breath every rivulet and stream. The moistened breath freezing as it left the lips, hung in miniature icicles from beards of brave men. The foam from their steeds stood stark and stiff upon each hair, and motion only made it possible for them to endure the biting freezing blast. All that long night the men rode on facing the wintery wind . . . with not a word save that of command at intervals to break upon the monotonous clamp, clamp of the steeds and the clatter of sabres as they rattled in their gleaming sheaths. As morning dawned the troops, stiff with cold, entered the little town of Box Elder [Brigham City]. . . . Many were frozen and necessarily left behind, but the troops after a halt by day, again faced the severity of winter in the mountains and pressed on: the Infantry by day and the Cavalry by night, in order to deceive the wily foe."[20]

Early on the morning of Tuesday the twenty-seventh, Connor's cavalry overtook the infantry and artillery at the town of Mendon. The infantry marched again that night at eleven p.m. followed by Connor's group at four a.m. Wednesday morning.

Bear Hunter and some of his braves came to Franklin on the twenty-seventh to demand wheat of Bishop Preston Thomas. Not getting all they wished, the Indians favored Thomas with an impromptu war dance around his house. Thomas capitulated and, the next day, three of the Shoshoni returned to Franklin armed with an order from him against the community granary for nine bushels. The Indians didn't seem worried when they saw the infantry approaching the town about four in the afternoon, and left only when the soldiers came quite close. An inhabitant of Franklin is supposed to have said to them, "Here come the soldiers. You may get killed." They replied, "Maybe so soldiers get killed too."[21] Once out of town, however, the braves quickened the pace and lightened their load by dumping the sacks of wheat along the way back to their village on Bear River. Hoyt's men went into camp in Franklin that afternoon as though they intended staying a week.

At midnight, Connor's force joined Hoyt's infantry at Franklin. The colonel had intended that the infantry should start toward the Indian camp at one a.m. and that he should follow several hours later. There were difficulties, however, in obtaining a local guide to lead them across the unfamiliar terrain toward the river, and this, combined with an unexplained accident as Hoyt's men set out, delayed the infantry's march until three a.m. An hour later the main body of cavalry set out and overtook Hoyt about four miles south of the Indian village. The approach of dawn caused Connor to push rapidly on ahead of Hoyt and, after a short march, the cavalry reached a point on the bluffs above the river, in full view of the Indians about a mile away to the northwest.

The Shoshoni were in a deep ravine, dense with willows, through which flows the stream now known as Battle Creek. At their encampment, near where Battle Creek then joined the river, the ravine was from thirty to forty feet wide and about six to twelve feet deep. It began in some steep foothills to the north about three-fourths of a mile from the river and emptied into a flat about 300 yards wide that bordered the river. The Bear, at this place, flows nearly east and west and the ravine runs generally north and south. Wickiups had been placed amongst the willows with their lower parts protected by banked-up earth and rocks. About two hundred ponies were tied to the willows in the ravine.

The camp had been skillfully fortified, particularly on the east side, where the Indians had cut fire steps and had woven willows with loopholes through which to fire across an open tableland, covered with two feet of snow, that extended to the Bear River ford about three-fourths of a mile away. To approach the ravine from the east, the troops would have to pass over two slight declivities that would expose them to Indian fire before the defensive position in the ravine could even be seen.

Immediately upon arriving, Connor ordered Major McGarry to advance and surround the camp, without attacking, while Connor himself remained a few minutes in the rear to await and give orders to the infantry and artillery as they came up. The four cavalry companies loaded their weapons and then were led by McGarry, accompanied by Major Gallagher, into the river. The crossing was difficult, the Bear at this point being four to six feet deep and choked with floating ice. Private John S. Lee of Company K recalled in later years that several troopers were thrown by horses reluctant to enter the half-frozen, swift stream. Once across, everyone knew the fight would be a hard one. Lee had never seen so many Indians in his life, all "screaming, dancing, yelling." "Reminded me of a hornet's nest,"[22] he said.

Lieutenant Darwin Chase, with Company K and Captain George

Price, with Company M, were first to reach the north bank. After a short gallop, they reached the base of the foothills to the east of the Indian camp to form a line of battle. Captain Daniel McLean with Company H and Lieutenant John Quinn with Company A soon joined them, but before all the men were dismounted the Indians fired a fusillade which wounded one of the Volunteers. As the troops formed their line, some of the Indians came forward and a chief brandished his spear, from which dangled the scalps of his victims, as the warriors behind him taunted brazenly: "Fours right, fours left; come on you California sons of bitches!"[23]

Thus invited, McGarry advanced his men on foot frontally against the ravine, either having forgotten his instructions to surround the site, or deciding such a course to be impractical. The Shoshoni warriors all retreated into the ravine and began to pour a deadly fire upon the oncoming cavalrymen. When the firing began, Connor hurried across to the battle, leaving instructions for Hoyt to ford the river as soon as he arrived.

The effect of the Indian fire was devastating. A good number of soldiers fell dead or wounded in this opening sally and, in fact, most of the casualties the Volunteers sustained were in the first few minutes of battle. With the good sense of the Western mountaineers that most of them were, they soon threw themselves to the ground and began fighting cautiously, even before being told to do so. Private Lee was shot in the arm by an Indian woman and later also received a hip wound. In the advance, Lieutenant Darwin Chase was wounded, first in the wrist and moments later in the lung, but he fought on for another twenty minutes before reporting himself mortally wounded to Connor and asking permission to retire. It is thought that he drew heavy fire because of the elaborate trappings of his horse, the Indians mistaking him for Connor. Captain McLean was wounded in the hand, but kept advancing until stopped by a bad wound in the thigh. Regimental Surgeon Reid quickly improvised a field hospital in the rear, and even this came under fire for a time.

After half an hour of this intense duel, Connor decided something else must be attempted. He ordered Major McGarry and twenty dismounted men to try to turn the left flank of the Shoshoni, up where the ravine entered the foothills. About this time, Hoyt and the infantry arrived at the ford and eagerly attempted to cross and join in the battle but, after several men tried it, Hoyt sent word to Connor that it was impossible to cross the river on foot. The colonel ordered a detachment of cavalry, leading additional horses, to bring the infantry across. This done, Hoyt's men, some wet and freezing, were sent to support McGarry's flanking movement.

With the cavalry in front still bearing the brunt, McGarry's detachment finally succeeded in scrambling up the hill, skirmishing as they went. Then followed the battle's climax. Hoyt got to the west side of the ravine, and, while part of his men kept up their fire directly in the rear of the Indians, the others stretched out in a cordon over the north end of the ravine, forming, with the cavalry in front, about three-quarters of a circle. By this enfilading from three points, the Indians gradually were driven to the center and southward.

In spite of their untenable position, the Shoshoni fought doggedly and made no attempt to run. To cut off the only remaining escape route, Connor next ordered a detachment of mounted cavalry under Lieutenant Conrad to go around to the west side of the ravine, near its mouth along the river's edge. He posted portions of Companies K and M on the east side. As expected, the Indians ultimately broke and hurried toward the river, and the slaughter began. As described in one contemporary account, they fought bravely:

". . . but now, away from their lodges and places of natural and artificial defense, it was their turn to feel the weakness of exposure. The Indians therefore fell in heaps; some attempted to escape into the river, but the keen eye of the Volunteer in avenging the helpless emigrants, the women and children whose blood had been unatoned, and the fresh flowing blood of his comrade lying at his feet, was in a moment, upon the fleeing form of the savage, and the deadly rifle did its work, and few escaped. Other Indians sought refuge in the thick willows of the ravine, and on the border of the river; but the order to 'scour the brushes' dislodged the sneaking foe. Some of them, counting no doubt, on the fate that surely awaited them, revealed the places of their concealment by the deadly fire they kept up from the willows, and one by one, they were dislodged, and the silence of grim death began to reign where before the hills had reverberated with the incessant crack of the rifle."[24]

Bear River Battleground, looking from Battle Creek toward the west side

In the final few minutes of this bloody melee, one concealed and determined Shoshoni put a ball through Major Gallagher's arm and into his side, then was able to reload and shoot a trooper from his horse close by Colonel Connor before a volley into the brush stilled his gun. Scores of Indians were killed. Probably only twenty or thirty braves escaped, including Chief Sagwitch, who was reported to have been killed, but who in fact had made his way across the river with another warrior holding on to the tail of his horse.

Another survivor was Ray Diamond, the nephew of Sagwitch, who ran toward the river during the fight with several soldiers right behind him. When he reached the river he fell into the water, feigning death, and then floated under the ice and made for an air hole where he clung with his head just far enough out of the water to allow him to breathe. The soldiers spotted him and fired again, wounding him in the thumb. After the troopers gave up their attempts to kill him, Diamond swam to some willows, and lay hidden for several hours in the intense cold. He would later settle on the Washakie reservation and live to be a hundred years old.[25]

Another warrior told how he swam with his buffalo robe upon his back. The soldiers shot at him, but their bullets couldn't penetrate the robe. Soquitch (Lots of Buffalo) Timbimboo, Sagwitch's oldest child, escaped on a horse with his girlfriend behind him. She was killed. He sat at a distance and watched the rest of the battle in safety.

One Indian woman, being chased by soldiers, threw her small baby into the river where the child drowned and floated down the river with the other dead bodies and the bloody red ice. She then jumped into the river herself and escaped by hiding under an overhanging bank.

Yeager Timbimboo or Da boo zee (Cotton Tail Rabbit), twelve-year-old son of Sagwitch, kept running around until he came upon a small grass teepee that was so full of people that it was actually moving along the ground. Inside the shelter, Yeager found his grandmother. At her urging, the two of them went outside to lie among the dead before the soldiers could set the teepee on fire. Near the end of the battle, as the soldiers were searching among the dead Indians, one of the Volunteers came across the inquisitive youngster, who was looking around to see what was happening.

The soldier stood over Yeager with his gun pointed at him. The two stared at each other; the gun was lowered, then raised a second time before finally the soldier lowered it and walked away.

While Lieutenant Quinn was passing among the Indian dead, he noticed a large warrior without any marks of injury. Quinn gave him a dig with his spur, which caused the body to shrug its shoulders. Quinn put his revolver to the warrior's ear, pulled the trigger, and when the gun did not fire, the "dead" Indian leaped up and seized the gun as well as the much smaller lieutenant. Quinn was only saved by the quick action of another soldier whose weapon functioned properly.

The Californians experienced many other close calls during the fight. Captain Price of Company M was hit in the left side by a ball, but it was stopped by a package of pistol cartridges in his pocket. Price was startled to find that he didn't fall and wasn't bleeding, and he continued the fight "much relieved in his feelings."[26] Lieutenant Conrad had a ball tear through his coat; two men of Price's company had skin cut close from their scalps without any further injury; other men had balls flatten against buttons, belt buckles and miniatures in their jacket pockets.

The battle had lasted four hours, from six o'clock in the morning until ten. When it was ended, the troops began the grim task of collecting their dead and destroying the Indian camp. Seventy lodges were burned, some of them covered with canvas taken from wagons, and still bearing the names of their former white owners. When the surviving squaws and children saw that the soldiers did not want to kill them, they came out of hiding and walked to the rear of the troops where they sat down in the snow like a "lot of sage hens."[27]

Huge quantities of provisions and emigrant plunder were found, including powder, lead, bullets, modern cooking utensils, fine rifles and pistols and a thousand bushels of wheat. The soldiers helped themselves freely to Indian souvenirs such as tomahawks, arrows and buffalo robes. Then, after leaving enough provisions to subsist the 160 women and children reported to have survived the battle, the Volunteers burned much of the remaining property.

Observers and historians disagree on the number of Indians who died at Battle Creek. Connor's report puts the number at 224, but he admits his concern over his wounded prevented close personal examination of the battlefield. Edward Tullidge quotes two sources, one putting the number at 200 and the other, William Hull of Franklin, giving the number as 368, including about 90 women and children.[28] Nearly all accounts agree that in places on the field the slaughter was intense. At one location near the river, forty-eight Indian bodies were counted. Chiefs Lehi and Bear Hunter were both killed; Bear Hunter's severely burned body was found lying in a fire near the mouth of the ravine where, according to the Volunteers, he was making bullets.

According to William Hull's account, the morning after the battle the bishop at Franklin dispatched William Head, captain of the local militia, along with Hull and another man to go to the battle site to discover if any of the Indians were still alive. The men found bodies everywhere — in several places, three to five deep. Two Indian women whose thighs had been broken by bullets were found alive, as well as two boys and one girl about three years old. The little girl had eight flesh wounds in her body. Hull and the others took them back to Franklin for care.[29]

Most newspaper reports of the battle agree that some women and children were killed, but insist that it could not be avoided. It seems unlikely that Connor's men set out deliberately to kill women and children. Had such been the case, with so many men at the scene, and with the event so well reported, the truth would certainly have emerged, as it did a few years later at Sand Creek.

Mae T. Parry's "Massacre at Bia Ogoi" is the only document that tells the story of Bear River from the Indian point of view. Parry, the great-granddaughter of Chief Sagwitch, based her story on oral history, legend, and a certain amount of mysticism. In her work, the entire blame for the confrontation is laid to the white man, except for "a few Indian troublemakers."[30] According to Parry, Connor's attack on the Shoshoni camp was precipitated by three minor incidents. In the first, three Indians of Bear Hunter's band stole some cattle from a nearby farmer, drove them north and ate them. In the second instance, some of Pocatello's Fort Hall band killed several miners, but none of the band on Bear River were said to have had anything to do with this affair. In the third instance, a fight occurred between white and Indian boys in which two whites and two Indians were killed. These Indians were also said not to be from the band at Bear River. Parry makes no mention of who might have been killing whites at such a fierce pace on the Oregon and California trails the past few seasons, and she fails to mention that a nephew of Sagwitch later stated that the Indians had planned to raid the white settlements as soon as spring arrived.[31]

Although she blames Pocatello's band for two of the three incidents that she says led to Bear River, and although she tends to disassociate the Northwestern Shoshoni from Pocatello, Parry admits that only a few weeks before the battle, thousands of Shoshoni, including Pocatello and his band, had gathered at the Bear River site to hold the annual "Warm Dance," which was supposed to speed the onset of spring. It is perhaps fortunate for Connor that his attack did not take place earlier that month.

Parry's version of the battle credits Sagwitch and his people as having only a few old guns. Sagwitch is supposed to have told his warriors not to shoot first, thinking Connor would simply ask for the guilty men and, after Sagwitch turned them over, that would be that. The soldiers, however, are supposed to have fired first without asking questions, and the ensuing massacre was what one might expect wherein bows and arrows were pitted against muskets. And, according to Parry, the rifle pits and dugouts used by the Indians in fighting the Volunteers were actually make-believe fox holes dug by Indian children to play "Indians at war."

Bear Hunter, it is claimed, was shot, then whipped, kicked and tortured by the soldiers. One of the soldiers purportedly took his rifle, stepped to a burning campfire and heated his bayonet until it was a glowing red. He then ran the burning hot metal through the chief's ears.

Although several histories state that Bannock Indians were encamped with the Shoshoni at Battle Creek, no evidence exists that such was the case, and certainly no Bannock chieftains were present. Of the other chiefs, Sanpitch and Pocatello — if they had been present at all — were reported by Connor as still at large after the battle. Most likely they had left the camp days before the event.

Of Connor's 303 men in the expedition, only about 200 engaged the enemy. Seventy-nine were left behind on the road, suffering from severe frostbite. Others who didn't participate included those guarding the train and those with the howitzers, which Connor was never able to bring into the battle. A total of twenty-six Volunteers died either on the field, or later from their wounds. At least forty-five more men were wounded, mostly in the upper torso, bearing witness to the closeness of the fighting. One soldier, who had been a nine-month volunteer in the East and had taken part in the first Bull Run fight, thought the Bear River battle was "infinitely more interesting and warm" than the affair in Virginia.[32]

Connor once again, as at Buena Vista, apparently showed great personal bravery. He was reported to be continually in the thickest part of the fight, seldom out of range of Indian rifles, showing no fear of exposing himself. He and the other officers remained mounted throughout the fray, resulting in a high proportion of casualties. He took a bullet through his hat, but remained uninjured.

It was evening before Connor could take his men back to the south side of the river, where they loaded the dead into wagons and then spent a cold and miserable night tending the wounded and frostbitten. Only one officer and twenty-five men could be found who were fit for duty. One soldier, Corporal Hiram S. Tuttle, never forgot those hours:

"The night of January 29th, 1863 I never shal far get (how can I) there we camped on the Bank of Bear River with our dead dieing wounded and frozen 2 feet of snow on the ground nothing for fire but green Willows which would burn about as well as the snow oh! the groans of the frozen it seems to ring in my ears yet the poor fellows some lost their toes some a portion of their feet I worked all night bringing water from the river to wett cloths to draw frost from their frozen limbs I had not sleep any for two nights befor it was a dreadful night to me but managed to get through the night while some never saw the morning."[33]

The Indians too suffered that night. After the soldiers left, Sagwitch, and some others who had escaped, returned to the terrible scene of death and destruction. All the teepees except Sagwitch's had been destroyed. Inside it he found his dead wife with his infant daughter at her side, still alive. Sagwitch had the baby put into her craddleboard and hung from a nearby tree in hope that some settler would find the girl and raise her.

That night every means of transportation available in nearby Franklin was obtained to rush the wounded soldiers to Camp Douglas. Porter Rockwell is credited with spurring the citizens of

Franklin to provide transportation, sheets and other things needed by the agonized men. Doctor Reid started with his charges in eighteen sleighs the next morning when a moderation of the weather eased their suffering somewhat. Private Lee of Company K, a ball in his leg, was one of those transported in this manner. When he would awake from time to time, he wondered which he would do first — freeze or bleed to death.

Surgeon Jonathan M. Williamson of the cavalry and a Dr. Walcott Steel of Dayton, Nevada, met the party at Ogden, along with "Parson" Anderson. Mrs. McLean, alarmed at reports of her husband's death, rode day and night to reach him and render him her "kind offices," sitting in the ambulance "like an angel of goodness."[34] The correspondent of the Sacramento *Daily Union* expressed the wish that the other brave fellows could have the same ministering spirits around them.

The wounded stayed the night at Ogden, where the bishop showed them every attention and provided for all their needs. Two of the Twelve Apostles, John Taylor and George A. Smith, happened to be in Ogden at the time, and were seen visiting and encouraging both the soldiers and surgeons.

At Farmington, twenty miles from Salt Lake City, another Mormon, "Brother Grover," told the surgeons that everything in his house was at their disposal, "money or no money," and his family and hired help provided a hot meal for the party of wounded soldiers. Governor Harding was there and asked the *Union* correspondent to thank the people of the northern settlements, in his name, for their attention to the troops. At Farmington, a shift was made from the sleighs to eighteen wagons and the wounded went on, arriving at Camp Douglas the night of February 2. The wounds of Lieutenant Darwin Chase necessitated leaving him behind in Farmington, where he died on the fourth.

Colonel George S. Evans, the new commander of the Second Cavalry, who had been left in charge at Douglas, made every provision possible for the care of the wounded, considering the incomplete state of the post. After receiving an express from Connor, he had equipped the theater and the chaplain's big meetinghouse tent as hospitals, heating them as best they could be. Mrs. Reid and other wives offered their help in caring for the men.

The balance of the command was detained by snows on the pass between Wellsville and Brigham City, and didn't arrive until the evening of February 4. They entered camp driving about 100 of the 175 Indian horses captured, the rest being ridden by Hoyt's weary infantrymen, now known as the "light cavalry." Conner and Porter Rockwell rode together in a buggy, leading the procession.

Connor's report of the battle states that no assistance was offered him by Mormons on his march to the battlefield, that no one was disposed to divulge any information regarding the Indians and that he was charged enormous prices for every article furnished to the command. Such, of course, was not the case on his victorious return journey. Aside from the sleighs, teams and food provided, the bishop at Wellsville assisted the command in getting over the snow-drifted pass to Brigham City. One correspondent noted some "heartless scoundrelism" along the road home but, in general, he gave high praise for the help offered by the Mormon people.[35]

Connor, while expressing pride in the whole command, specifically cited Majors McGarry and Gallagher, along with the company officers and Surgeon Reid, for their skill and bravery. His report included, however, another swipe at the Mormons by giving credence to rumors that the Indians at Battle Creek had received their rifles and ammunition from the inhabitants of the territory, in exchange for the property of massacred emigrants.[36]

On February 5, fifteen of the dead Californians were buried with full honors in the new military cemetery south of the camp. In spite of it being a cold, raw day, many persons from Salt Lake attended to pay their respects. One historian reported that, until this time, scarcely any of the local populace had set foot within the encampment, but "now there was quite a score of carriages from the city, many equestrians and a large concourse of people on foot, and had it been generally known, thousands from the city would have paid reverent tribute to the slain, for it was duly appreciated that they had fallen in the service of Utah."[37] The coffins lay in a row in the quartermaster's storeroom until one p.m. when they were taken to the cemetery, accompanied by the whole command in procession. There, Chaplain Anderson read the burial service and three volleys were fired over the graves in tribute. After the burial, the band struck up a gay tune to which the Volunteers marched back to camp to resume the duties of the living.

The next day Lieutenant Chase was buried in an impressive Masonic and military ceremony, led by a group of about twenty Masons from the area, including Marshall Gibbs, Chief Justice Kinney and Secretary Frank Fuller. Chase had been a Royal Arch Mason and was also said to have been one of the most promising Mormon elders in his youth. He is supposed to have been ordained into the Quorum of Seventies on the cornerstone of the temple in Far West. Living in San Francisco at the time of his enlistment, he had by then drifted from the beliefs of the church.

Three more Volunteers, who died after the return to Camp Douglas, were buried on Saturday the seventh, and two more on Sunday — all with the same military honors. Another trooper, wounded in the neck, held on until November. Lieutenant David J. Berry of cavalry Company A died at Camp Union, near Sacramento, California, on May 9, 1865, of "inflammation of the bowels, liver and lungs" — all Bear River complications. He thus became the last fatality.

All that was left to do after the burials was to dispose of the spoils of battle. Connor had everything sold at auction, after certain animals that had been recovered were returned to their former owners.

The Bear River engagement was one of the most successful ever conducted against the Indian peoples in the nation's westward expansion and, although it was far more fierce and bloody than those at Sand Creek and Wounded Knee, it has received little, if any, notoriety. Observers all seem to agree that the defeat by Connor completely broke the spirit and power of the Shoshoni people in the region, and allowed uninterrupted expansion of Mormon settlements, as well as development of mines, railroads and other commercial interests in the area, without their interference. The defeat also led directly to several significant treaties with the Shoshoni and Bannocks. Even the Mormons, whose policy toward the "Lamanites" was a peaceful one, were ecstatic over the results of the battle, and were impressed with the bravery of the Volunteers, both in the battle itself and in the frigid march of 140 miles. The people of Logan stated at the time that they looked upon the coming of Colonel Connor to relieve them of their Indian problem as "a providence of the Almighty."[38]

Our Corporal Tuttle, who spent such a miserable night after the battle, wrote two years after the event from his home in California, expressing well how the soldiers themselves must have felt about their work at Bear River: "I am the only one here that was there and no one to say a word about it, yet still it is as fresh to my memory as on that morning when I beheld my comrades fall in deadly strife, and by losing their lives gave freedom to the thousands of travelers who seek new homes amid the western wilderness."[39]

Connor executed the battle perfectly regarding the use of surprise and his choice of the hour and season. He seems to have underestimated the strength of the Indian position, but after the initial shock of this discovery, he did a superb job of directing the fight. For years thereafter, observant army commanders attempted to strike at the Indians during winter or early spring, when they could be surprised in a fixed location. While it is only probable that the Bear River battle served as the tactical model for Sand Creek and Wounded Knee, it is certain that it established Colonel Connor as the foremost Indian fighter of the time. A month after the battle, the *Rocky Mountain News*, commenting on recent depredations in northwestern Colorado, posed the question: "Would it not be better to employ a few more men like Colonel Connor, and wipe the treacherous vagabonds from the face of the earth? . . . It requires no prophet to foresee that our increasing perplexities with the different tribes will eventually lead to their extermination."[40]

Indeed, Connor's newly-won fame would, in several years, cause him to be selected to lead another major expedition against the hostiles for these very Coloradans, but the outcome in that case would not be so felicitous.

Monument to the men who died at the Battle of Bear River, Fort Douglas Cemetery. (Courtesy Utah State Historical Society)

March Madness 6

"O God of life and glory,
Hear Thou a people's prayer:
Bless, bless our prophet Brigham,
And let him thy fullness share . . .

"He draws from Christ, the Fountain
of everlasting truth,
The wise and prudent counsels
Which he gives to age and youth."

— From a hymn composed by
Eliza R. Snow[1]

I

While most Mormon settlers in Cache Valley were grateful to the California soldiers for their fight on the Bear River, it had done nothing to relieve deeper-seated animosities between Mormon and Gentile in the ideological struggle over the future of Utah Territory. Hearts would continue to harden, and leaders on both sides would become more and more strident, resulting in an open and hateful confrontation in the spring of 1863.

It had been a difficult session for the Utah legislature. After Governor Harding had insulted Mormon lawmakers with his address at their opening session, he had vetoed fourteen of the twenty bills they had sent him. They, in turn, had taken revenge by refusing to appropriate monies to run the federal district courts.

Justice Charles Waite, however, had no intention of letting the

Mormon legislature hamstring him. Near the end of January, in a letter to Attorney-General Bates, the judge recommended that Congress either amend the Organic Act, or pass a criminal code applicable to the territories that would provide federal funds to run the Utah district courts — at least for cases involving high crimes. Waite, whose Second Judicial District encompassed Mountain Meadows, cited the 1857 massacre as one such crime which demanded justice. "The murder of over a hundred persons in cold blood, without any provocation, and for purposes of plunder only," Waite said, "is a circumstance that may well attract attention even in the midst of a desolating war."[2]

A few months earlier, Waite had drafted legislation containing other, more drastic changes to the Organic Act. It would have severely restricted the functions of the Mormon-controlled probate courts, required jury selection by the U.S. Marshal, and allowed the governor to appoint militia officers. His proposal had been endorsed by Harding and Justice Drake and sent off to Congress for consideration.[3]

Waite was not the only government official writing to his superiors that winter regarding matters in Zion. Still smarting over the legislature's refusal to print his address, Governor Harding told Secretary of State Seward in early February that his "secret service" had determined that Brigham Young was procuring and manufacturing arms, ammunition, heavy ordnance, and "a new weapon, partly battle-ax, partly a lance, for what purpose may readily be imagined."[4]

Just a few days before, Brigham Young had violated the law against polygamy by being "sealed" to a pretty new bride, after a long courtship in which he had managed to make himself look exceedingly ridiculous. The "elderly young woman,"[5] twenty-eight year old Harriet Amelia Folsom, would ultimately become the aging prophet's best-known wife, and the one who would command his undivided attention.

Inspired, no doubt, by this most recent marriage of the prophet, Governor Harding told Seward that Young was adding more "unprotected and demented victims" to his harem every week. Although Brigham admitted that he could scarcely remember all his wives' names, "when he sees . . . some young girl first blooming into womanhood, he informs her, or generally her parents, that in order to make her salvation sure in this and the world to come, he feels it to be his duty to have her sealed unto him."[6]

The apprehensive Harding must still have had the fate of previous carpetbaggers on his mind when, only a few weeks later, he wrote General Wright to urge retention of Connor's command. He told Wright that he was sure the Mormons would incite the recently defeated Indians to take revenge on the Gentiles should the troops leave. And, if Connor were to leave, he said "the federal officers might as well also leave because they would have no more authority."[7] In his reply, Wright assured Harding that these were also his views, and that rather than removing Connor, plans had been made to reinforce him in early spring.

In a letter remarkably similar in date and content to those which Harding had written, Colonel Connor also told Wright of the many recent violations of the Morrill Bill by Mormons, whom he labeled the "lowest class of foreigners and aliens" and "disloyal to a man." As concrete evidence of disloyalty, the Utah commander forwarded a price list for commodities he had recently received from one of the bishops on Brigham's trade committee. Connor thought there were only two ways to make the Mormons obey the law: either divide Utah Territory into four parts and add these to adjoining territories, or declare martial law and reinforce him to a level of 3,000 men with additional cannon.[8]

Although he had learned of the proposed Organic Act amendments a month earlier, it would be March before the "Lion of the Lord" made a calculated move to rid himself of unsavory federal officers. On the third of the month, a mass meeting was held in the tabernacle for the "investigation" of certain acts of Harding, Waite and Drake. To indict the officials in the minds of the assembled people for having formulated the amendments, Albert Carrington read extracts from several letters bearing on the subject which had been received from Utah's congressional delegate. It didn't matter that, by this time, the bill had been referred to the Committee on the Judiciary where it was dying a slow death.[9]

The prophet Brigham then arose to deliver one of his famous "give 'em hell" speeches. First, he expressed pleasure that the North and South were bent on destroying themselves in the war, since they had shed Joseph Smith's blood. Next, according to Colonel Connor's report, Young tore into Governor Harding, labeling him a "nigger worshiper" and "black-hearted abolitionist." Then, the Mormon leader was said to have conducted this frenzied interrogation of his audience:

"'Do you acknowledge this man Harding as your Governor?' (Voices) 'No; you are our Governor.' 'Yes,' he said, 'I am your Governor. Will you allow such a man to remain in the Territory? (Voices) 'No; put him out.' 'Yes,' replied Brigham, 'put him out; Harding and Drake and Waite must leave the Territory. If they will not resign, and if the President will not remove them, the people must attend to it. I will let him know who is Governor.'"

As for the two judges, Brigham is supposed to have called them "perfect fools and tools for the Governor," saying that if they had their way the marshal would choose juries of "cut-throats, blacklegs, soldiers and desperadoes of California."[10]

The versions of Brigham's speech recorded in the *Deseret News* and in Mormon Church records are somewhat milder than that reported by Connor, but similar in context. Young himself later admitted he had "used some expressions rougher than is usual for me in public speaking."[11]

The meeting produced a petition asking the President to remove Harding and the two justices from office on the grounds that they were working to create mischief and strife between the troops at Camp Douglas and the people of the territory. Lincoln was asked to replace them with men who would "regard the rights of all . . . leaving alone the affairs of others.[12]

Just one day after the gathering in the tabernacle, a committee of three Mormon leaders — apostle John Taylor, Orson Pratt, Sr., and Jeter Clinton — called on Harding and Drake to present the petition and ask for their resignations. Waite, who was out of town, was sent a letter containing the same request. All three of the spurned officials flatly refused to comply with the Mormon demand. Waite's reply was mild and polite but — if their versions are to be believed — Harding and Drake both soundly rebuked the committee.

Drake pointed out that as a citizen he had a right to petition the government to amend the laws, and that Taylor, a "foreigner," was particularly impudent in making accusations. Comparing the delegation to horse thieves and murderers, Drake told them to go back to their master Brigham and tell him that he had not come there by

Brigham's permission, and he would not leave by his orders. "I have given no cause of offense to anyone," the judge said, "I have not entered a Mormon house since I came here, your wives and daughters have not been disturbed by me, and I have not even looked upon your concubines or lewd women."[13]

Governor Harding was now openly scorned in the Mormon newspaper. He was chided for his frequent references to having known Joseph Smith and having preserved the proof sheet of the title page of the *Book of Mormon*. Reminiscent of the editorial treatment previously given to other officials, his sanity was even questioned.[14]

Such pretense and posturing would continue on both sides throughout the month. A counter-petition was forwarded to President Lincoln, signed by all the officers at Camp Douglas and many other Gentiles, recommending retention of Harding and the others. Brigham's next move was the relocation of all the ordnance of the territorial militia from the arsenal to his Beehive House, and the establishment of a large guard in and around that place every night. It was reported that his people were at work making cartridges and casting cannon balls, and that a telescope had been placed on the roof of one of his houses so that every move at Camp Douglas could be carefully observed.

On Sunday, March 8, Young spoke again in the tabernacle, denigrating the administration in Washington and affirming that he would see his militia "in hell first" before he would provide any soldiers to help fight the Rebels, so long as Connor's soldiers were garrisoned in his vicinity. Heber Kimball came next to the podium to deliver a similarly defiant speech.[15] Stenhouse, who was privy to happenings on the Mormon side, described the atmosphere that existed during the month:

"The Tabernacle resounded with fierce denunciations every Sunday. Mischief-makers poured into the ears of the Prophet every story that could increase his prejudice against Colonel Connor; and the latter heard quite as much to incense him against Brigham. A collision for a long time seemed inevitable. The Prophet was then in his glory; the nation was engaged in war; the prophecies of the modern Seer were being fulfilled; and the republic was going to pieces — he had nothing to fear."[16]

Colonel Connor had been telegraphing reports of the current

trouble to General Wright from the very beginning, affirming that he had no plans to bother Brigham, and speculating that the Mormon leader feared arrest for uttering treasonable language.[17] On the afternoon of March 9, an alarmed Connor reported that Brigham had just raised the United States flag above his house and called his people to arms. Within just thirty minutes, over a thousand militiamen had been seen to rush to their leader's aid. Guns, lead and powder were brought from their hiding places; scaffolding was hurriedly erected inside the walls of Beehive House; two cannons were wheeled into place, and other houses were occupied that commanded the route from Camp Douglas. William Ajax, a member of the battalion from the 6th and 7th wards, was one of those who responded, and was quickly put to work building scaffolding at Heber Kimball's house. He would later recall standing guard for many days with weapons loaded and at the ready.[18]

The perplexed Connor wasn't sure if Brigham was trying to frighten the Californians or was himself frightened, but he was cynical enough to comment to Wright that this was the very first time Brigham had flown the national ensign since the Californians had arrived in Utah.[19]

Events would later prove that Brigham Young sincerely believed he was about to be arrested — not for uttering treasonable language but for his most recent violation of the anti-polygamy law. Justice Waite was supposed to have just issued an arrest warrant and, after Brigham had been seized, court would be held at Camp Douglas, or wherever else the Gentiles pleased. Previous rumors had been confirmed to Brigham's apparent satisfaction that very day when, at the conclusion of a meeting of Colonel Connor and Judge Waite, a Mormon spy loitering nearby thought he overheard Connor say "These men must be surprised." The eavesdropper immediately rushed to Brigham, and the flag was hoisted to signal the muster of the militia.[20]

In actual fact, Connor and Waite had formulated no such plans for Brigham's arrest. The conversation overheard by Brigham's spy concerned a Mormon elder — a neighbor of Waite — who had recently married the three widows of a wealthy merchant. According to Stenhouse, Waite thought the marriage would be an excellent opportunity to test the new law, and Connor agreed to arrest the man if a way could be found to obtain the arrest order — the problem being that Waite would have to issue such an order in Judge Kinney's district, with Kinney present.

After his fright that day, Brigham Young decided to take the wind out of his enemy's sails by causing himself to be arrested. Chief Justice Kinney was contacted and he dutifully issued a writ, based on a complaint by "one of the brethren,"[21] for violation of the law against polygamy. The writ was served by Marshal Gibbs that evening and Brigham went before the chief justice, only to be released on bond of $2,000 until the next term of the grand jury later that month.

The tension continued. Connor arrested, then released a certain Colonel Ross of the Nauvoo Legion, who had met with Brigham Young several times and who was briefly suspected of being a Southern emissary. On the afternoon of the twelfth, the hoisting of the signal flag caused another muster of armed men at Brigham's residence. Connor informed Wright that the Mormons had sworn they would cut off any Utah-bound reinforcements and then attack him. Wright would staunchly support Connor throughout the crisis, but he felt obliged now to remind the Utah commander to be prudent and cautious and hold his troops well in hand until the expected day of retribution. Connor was ordered to communicate any important developments directly to army headquarters, and Wright himself took pains to assure General Halleck in Washington that caution would be used.[22]

The beleaguered colonel was finally able to submit a written report to General Wright on the fifteenth. He pleaded, as before, either for reinforcement of his command or for its complete removal until enough troops could be spared to come back and forever stop the "outrageous, unnatural and treasonable institutions." While his men were in no immediate danger, the feisty Irishman said he feared that if the present preparations were to continue, he might be compelled to "strike at the heads of the Church," and he couldn't just sit and wait to be attacked, since he was greatly outnumbered and outgunned.

While making overt demonstrations, so the world at large might note their plight, the Mormon leadership was, at the same time, working vigorously behind the scenes to properly frighten those who might be affected by an interruption of commerce or communication through Utah Territory. One reference to such activity can be found in a March 13 letter written by David O. Calder of the Mormon tithing office. Calder told his correspondent, G. Q. Cannon, that "outside friends" of the Mormons had telegraphed those interested in the mail and telegraph lines, saying they must work for the removal of the troops and the federal officials, or else the mail and telegraph lines would be destroyed. "Their moneyed interest," Calder said, "has given them great energy on our behalf. . . . We fully expect the Colonel, Governor, and Judges will be recalled."[24]

One of the "outside friends" was J. H. Wade, president of the Pacific Telegraph Company. From his headquarters in Cleveland, on the twentieth, he wired a contact in Washington that the collision about to take place in Salt Lake City had been brought on by misrepresentations as to Mormon loyalty. Wade asked if the government couldn't be induced to suspend proceedings until he and a colleague could come to the capital and explain what they had learned from their acquaintance with the Mormons in the past two years.[25]

Another particular friend of the Mormons was Overland Mail czar Ben Holladay. As a boy of fourteen, he had been the personal courier for Brigadier-General Alexander Doniphan of the Missouri militia during the time when the Mormons were being driven from that state. Doniphan is said to have refused to carry out an order to execute Joseph Smith, and to have secretly informed Brigham Young of attacks being planned by frontier mobs. By carrying Doniphan's messages to Young, Holladay won the future leader's everlasting gratitude. His financial success was assured when he came to Salt Lake City and entered business after receiving favored status from Brigham. Holladay made the Mormon capital his headquarters and he generally took care not to offend the Saints.[26]

By now, General Halleck had jumped headlong into the Utah problem. In a March 19 telegram the general-in-chief reminded Connor that all arms and munitions which might be intended for use against the United States were subject to seizure. Halleck also told the colonel to be prudent and cautious, but that if he decided to act, to do so with firmness and decision. Simultaneously, he ordered General Wright to reinforce the Volunteers as soon as possible and, to accomplish this, Wright was given authority to raise additional troops in California or Nevada.[27] Wright, of course, had been planning all along to send Connor's three detached infantry companies to Utah as soon as the roads were clear of snow and forage was available beyond the Sierra. And, as the crisis had worsened, he had also informed Halleck of his intention to send one or two additional companies of cavalry.[28] Now, given the authority to levy new troops, more substantial steps would be taken.

In the final three days of the month, more fuel was added to the continuing conflict by the culmination of legal proceedings against the Morrisite men. Some of the ninety or more who had been indicted for taking part in the battle at Kingston Fort had long since fled Utah, but the cases of those who had chosen to remain, or who had been imprisoned, had just been disposed of in Justice Kinney's Third District Court. Of the ten who were accused of killing the two posse members, seven were convicted of murder in the second degree, and received sentences ranging from ten to fifteen years in prison. Sixty-six lesser offenders had each been fined $100 for resisting arrest.

After the sentencing, petitions were immediately drawn up for the unconditional pardon of the Morrisite men. On the night of March 29, while they were being circulated for signatures, still another insane scramble to arms occurred when news arrived at Camp Douglas that Connor had been appointed a brigadier-general for his Bear River victory. A noisy celebration began at post headquarters, complete with loud music and frequent "administering of the oath." This was harmless enough but, when Connor's appreciative subordinates decided to honor him with an eleven-gun salute at about 10 p.m., it proved to be the wrong move.

As mentioned, the agreed-upon daytime signal for the militia to assemble and protect the person of Brigham Young was the hoisting of a flag above his Beehive residence. At night, the signal was to be the firing of a cannon from the hillside to the east. By now, the Mormon leaders thought their posturing had so intimidated the commander of the Volunteers that if he were to come, it would be by making a dash in the dead of night on the prophet's bedroom to seize and hustle him off to the United States before assistance could be organized. Stenhouse, who was involved in it, later vividly described the antsy Mormon militia's reaction to the ceremonial salute:

"As hastily as garments could be thrown on, and arms could be seized, the brethren were seen hurrying from their homes towards the Prophet's residence. The struggle was apparently at hand. The signal cannon had been distinctly heard, and, as there was a gentle current of air from the east, those who lived west of the Prophet could hear the very music to which the Volunteers were supposed to be marching into the heart of the city!"[29]

This, like the other alarms, came to nothing. A few days later the Mormon newspaper even took pains to compliment the new brigadier on his promotion — in a backhanded sort of way. At this point, Connor's opponents still apparently held a certain respect for him, if not for his civilian cohorts. The author of the piece called him "a brave soldier, who will yet honor the appointment," and whose backbone would carry him where the country could yet appreciate him if he kept clear of "politicians and wire-workers."[30]

On the evening of March 30 Governor Harding was handed the petitions for pardon of the Morrisite men. They had been signed by over 600 of Connor's men, many Gentile businessmen and all of the federal officials except Judge Kinney. Many Morrisite women had visited Harding during the previous few days to plead in behalf of their men. The governor said he had also received threats, including one from Bishop Woolley, who had told him that he couldn't answer for his safety if he were to indulge the criminals.

Harding further claimed that a few Mormons had made furtive visits after dark to his quarters to show their sympathy, but that only one — the infamous Bill Hickman — had dared sign the petitions. If Harding is to be believed, Hickman rode fourteen miles that night of March 30 to sign them in defiance of Brigham.[31] Harding had first met Hickman late in 1862 at Gilbert's store in Salt Lake City. Since the man's reputation as a supposed Danite was well known, Harding was apprehensive at first, but soon came to trust Hickman and found him a likeable sort in spite of his coarseness. Hickman even visited Harding several times that winter and took dinner with him. Harding declined a reciprocal invitation from Hickman to visit his ranch, where the governor might see for himself "the kind of stock" who were the mothers of Bill's children.

The day after this nocturnal visit, the governor issued two documents, unconditionally pardoning all of the Morrisites. Ironically,

The notorious Bill Hickman, who served as one of Gen. Connor's guides. (Courtesy Utah State Historical Society)

they were signed by Secretary of State Frank Fuller, who, as acting governor the previous year, had authorized the formation of Robert Burton's posse to arrest the Morrisite leaders.

II

With Brigham Young's beehive fully astir, Connor didn't need the new Indian problems that began to plague him with the onset of spring — this time to the south and west of Salt Lake City. On March 22, a band of Goshiutes, under their war chief White Horse, swooped down and took possession of the stage station at Eight Mile, just west of Deep Creek, killing the two station keepers. When the eastbound stage pulled into the station a short time afterward, it too was attacked. The driver, "Happy Harry" Harper, was killed and the passenger beside him severely wounded by a bullet in the head. Three others were riding inside the coach, one of whom was Judge C. N. Mott, newly-elected delegate to Congress from Nevada. Mott crawled out under fire, grabbed the lines from the dead driver and drove the stage to safety at the Deep Creek station.

Howard R. Egan, the Mormon trailblazer and militiaman, was at Deep Creek when the stage arrived. He would later comment that, in spite of having lost "about a teaspoonful of his brains," the wounded passenger lived to be returned to his family in the East.

Egan was one of a party of men who rode to Eight Mile the next day to see what had become of the station keepers. While the Indians had disappeared, their handiwork remained for all to see. The station cook was found lying stripped and scalped, his body slashed all over. His tongue had been cut out and his face first daubed with blood and then covered over with flour "to make him a white man again." The naked body of the station hay stacker and hustler was found in the brush some distance from the station. His body remained uncut, and Egan supposed it to be because the Indians had killed him before they got to him.[32]

When news of the attack reached Camp Douglas, troops at Fort Ruby were ordered to hurry one hundred miles eastward to the scene by stagecoach, and Major Gallagher, who was in Salt Lake City recovering from his Bear River wounds, departed immediately to resume command at Ruby. Although he was reluctant to do so in view of the current Mormon fright, Connor also dispatched a full company of cavalry under Captain Sam Smith, and a separate detachment under Lieutenant Quinn, toward Ruby Valley on the twenty-fifth.

Gallagher arrived at his post and began dispersing infantrymen to Overland stations in the vicinity, but it would be a month before the cavalry would arrive, recruit their horses and take the field in earnest against the Goshiutes. The major reported finding a large band of friendly Indians camped near the post upon his return, who claimed to be at war with the hostiles attacking the road. He was upset that a reliable interpreter wasn't available so he could learn more from these Indians. The only person he could find to communicate with the band was "an unsavory character named Hawes."[33] Little did the major know that "Hawes" was renegade Mormon trader Alpheus Haws who, with other members of his family, had for years manipulated the Indian bands of the region to attack and plunder emigrants.

Trouble now came from another direction. Second-Lieutenant Anthony Ethier had been sent out from Camp Douglas in late March with twenty-five cavalrymen to search the area south of Great Salt Lake, where Indians had recently driven off a herd of cattle. After traversing more than 250 miles of the rocky, desolate terrain of Skull Valley and the Cedar Mountains, Ethier arrived empty-handed a few days later with his troop at Rush Valley. Here he received an order from the newly-appointed General Connor to return to Camp Douglas immediately, prompted undoubtedly by the Mormon crisis of March 29.

As the soldiers were passing old Camp Crittenden on the afternoon of April 1, a band of Indians was seen coming out of Trough Canyon. With his horses jaded and footsore, the lieutenant quickly appropriated an Overland Mail coach from the station agent and stuffed himself and thirteen of his men into it to pursue. Another eight of his men followed on the best horses.

The Indians proved to be about 100 of Little Soldier's band of Shoshoni, known more commonly as "Weber Utes." Ethier overtook them in the vicinity of Cedar Fort, a small settlement on the west side of Cedar Valley. Here two braves began riding the war circle, while the other Indians remained hidden from view. Ethier consulted some of the white inhabitants regarding the disposition of the unseen braves, then formed his men into a battle line and advanced, only to be forced back when suddenly fired upon from an unexpected direction.

The dismounted men advanced again into another withering fire from the well-hidden Shoshoni. As Ethier was withdrawing a second time he learned that his horses were about to be captured. Although there were Mormon men loitering within 100 yards of both the horses and the fighting, they had made no attempt to prevent the loss of the animals. After the Californians repulsed this latest threat they prepared to depart, the lieutenant offering to leave a guard of twelve men in the town. The Mormon citizens at first refused, then after consulting amongst themselves, asked Ethier if eight troopers might stay. Ethier was about to post the guard and depart when he saw a certain Mr. Savage — whom he recognized as a Mormon freighter — ride out to the hills and speak to the Indians, now in plain sight. Suspecting treachery, the lieutenant took his entire troop back to the Crittenden telegraph office in order to communicate with Camp Douglas.

General Connor dispatched Captain George Price in the middle of that night with fifty-one additional cavalrymen. They joined Ethier at Cedar Fort the next morning, April 2, and for the next several days, conducted an unsuccessful search for Little Soldier's band. Then, while the Volunteers were camped on the evening of April 4 at Spanish Fork, several Indians were sighted in the nearby hills. A scouting party was immediately sent out and soon returned to report that the red men had entered Spanish Fork Canyon. It was only an hour until sunset, but Price had "Boots and Saddles" and "To Horse" immediately sounded, taking the men away from supper. In less than five minutes — such was their eagerness — the entire detachment, except for a small guard, was in the saddle and en route to the canyon, four miles from the camp.

When Price arrived at the canyon he could see the enemy posted on both sides of its mouth. He split his force into three detachments and advanced upstream, the Indians giving way before their fire. After an eager pursuit of about a mile, Price realized how dark it had become and, to avoid being trapped in the rugged canyon by an enemy of unknown strength, he recalled his men and started back to camp. Now it was the Indians' turn. They hovered in the rear, sniping, as the troopers retreated in the darkness, their horses at a walk. Several lively skirmishes ensued when Price's men rushed back on their pursuers several times in futile attempts to trap them. The Californians reached their camp safely and, after a fruitless scout of the canyon the next morning, returned to Camp Douglas. Price had lost no men, and with unusual frankness, admitted he had no idea how many Weber Utes had been killed.[34]

Reports of these engagements, along with a statement by Overland Mail agent William Wallace verifying complicity, served only to reinforce Connor's belief that it was the Mormons, as usual, who had encouraged, if not instigated the recent raids in order to get his men out of Salt Lake City. Ethier was sure he had been given falsified information about the position and numbers of the Indians at Cedar Fort. Furthermore, he claimed to have learned from Mr. Savage's wife that, after his pow-wow on the hill with the Indians, the freighter had gone immediately to Salt Lake City to report to Brigham Young.[35]

If there remained any doubt in General Connor's mind about a Mormon-Indian conspiracy, it was soon removed by an incident at Pleasant Grove, some thirty miles south of Salt Lake City. On April 11, 1863, Lieutenant Francis Honeyman and five artillerymen left Camp Douglas driving an ambulance in which was concealed a disassembled howitzer. Honeyman and his men were the advance element of an operation designed to punish Little Soldier, and were to be joined later by the main force of the expedition under Colonel George Evans. When Honeyman's small party arrived in Pleasant Grove next morning, its animals were placed in the corral of a Mormon settler, and Honeyman and his men put their feet up in a house across the road to await the arrival of Evans and his men.

At about six p.m., Little Soldier and some one hundred Weber Utes "came rushing down upon the town, and dismounting on the outskirts deployed into the town,"[36] skulking behind adobe fences and haystacks until they completely surrounded the building occupied by the soldiers. When the Indians opened fire, Honeyman and his five men quickly assembled the howitzer, took it outside and tried to fire, but were forced back with the weapon into the house.

Firing from the protection of a fence, the Indians riddled the house with bullets — with little effect — and, after a short time, they turned their attention to the government horses and mules in

Patrick A. Gallagher, Major, Third Infantry California Volunteers. (Courtesy Utah State Historical Society)

the corral. When Honeyman saw that he was about to lose the animals, he and his men opened fire with the howitzer through the window, preferring to kill the livestock rather than let the Indians take it.

The first shot of grape killed five of the mules in the corral, along with three Indians. While a second round did no damage to either mules or Indians, the walls of the adobe house began to split, causing Honeyman to promptly order an end to the howitzer fire. Many Pleasant Grove residents watched this entire entertainment from vantage points on housetops and haystacks, without offering the troopers any assistance. Finally, about eight that evening, Honeyman's attackers withdrew, making off with his provisions, blankets and seven animals.

William H. Seegmiller was a Mormon teamster whose Salt Lake-bound train was camped at Pleasant Grove that evening. Before attacking Honeyman, Little Soldier and his well-armed warriors, faces painted black, had come into the freighters' camp to learn where to find the soldiers and whether or not they were "Americats." Little Soldier told Seegmiller he was seeking revenge for the soldiers' killing of an Indian the previous day near Spanish Fork.

During the night, Honeyman sent several men to report to Colonel Evans, who by this time had reached the Point of the Mountain at the south end of Salt Lake valley. Evans and his ninety-six cavalrymen, with Porter Rockwell accompanying them, hurried on to arrive at Pleasant Grove at three in the morning. Teamster Seegmiller noticed with pious disgust that Rockwell seemed tipsy from the effects of too much whiskey as the guide mingled in the soldiers' camp. Seegmiller's attitude, however, would change the next day when, as he was visiting Brigham Young in Salt Lake City, Rockwell came in all decked out in a black broadcloth suit and black silk hat to report the events in Pleasant Grove. "I concluded then," Seegmiller later said, "that Rockwell lived a double life in the interest of his friends and God's cause on earth. I will ever remember him with esteem."[37]

Captain Price arrived at eleven a.m. on the thirteenth with Company M and replacement animals for Honeyman. The large force now at Evans's disposal searched the Provo Canyon area before finally finding signs of the Indians leading toward Spanish

Fork canyon. Evans camped on the evening of the fourteenth at Provo and, to give the impression that he intended to spend the night there, he ordered forage for delivery in the morning.

At midnight, the troops were awakened and marched to arrive at the mouth of the canyon just at daylight. Here, many of the troopers were dismounted and their horses picketed and left, along with the provision wagon and ambulance, in the care of Lieutenant James Finnerty and twenty men. With a heavy rain beginning to fall in the early light, Evans sent Price with forty men across the river to the left (north) side of the canyon, to deploy as flankers and skirmishers. The colonel, with Lieutenants Ethier, Peel and Honeyman, the howitzer and fifty men then pushed off up the center of the canyon.

It took but a short time to find Little Soldier. After moving up the canyon about a mile, struggling across the many spurs that ran down into the Spanish Fork, Evans's men began receiving fire from Indians everywhere in their front. Lieutenant Honeyman, having climbed high on a spur with the howitzer, immediately began dropping shell amongst the enemy while the center of Evans's force moved steadily up the canyon to arrive at the brink of the deep side ravine hiding the Indian main force.

Evans recalled in his report that when his men opened with their revolvers on the Weber Utes at close quarters, and when "it came to meeting the cool but piercing eye of the white men in deadly conflict, face to face, the red-skins quailed, and they began to give way." The fight then became a running one, the Indians taking advantage of every outlet from the main canyon as they retreated. At about eleven o'clock, after chasing his enemy fourteen miles up the canyon and "scattering him like quails," Evans ordered "Recall" and "Assembly" sounded.[38]

The colonel reported that about thirty warriors and their chief had been killed, and many more were wounded. His men recaptured four animals and some of the equipment stolen from Lieutenant Honeyman, as well as eighteen ponies and assorted plunder belonging to the Indians. The cost to the whites was two wounded and one killed — Lieutenant F. A. Peel, regimental quartermaster of the Second.

In another instance, in late April, when Southern Utes made several minor attacks on the stage line to the east of Salt Lake City,

Connor told General Wright that "hordes" of Indians were congregating in the vicinity of the Mormon settlements south of the city — incited, supplied and armed by Brigham — and were ready to strike the Overland and emigrant routes. Connor's "spies"[39] had even told him that Mormons disguised as Indians were to join in the attacks. Connor complained of his inability to strike the natives so long as the Mormons informed them of his every movement. In absolute frustration, the new brigadier once again urged either reinforcement or removal of his small, scattered command.

With Indian problems heaped on Mormon problems, heaped on imagined problems, to reinforce Connor now became an urgent priority for his superiors. In late March, General Wright had started to send Captain Brown's cavalry company from Fort Churchill to Ruby Valley to augment the infantry there, but had been forced to redirect them almost immediately to respond to Indian troubles in the Owen's Lake region.

Earlier, with the authority General Halleck had given him to raise troops in California or Nevada, Wright had asked acting Governor Orion Clemens of Nevada Territory for two companies of cavalry and two of infantry. After recruiting had begun, still more were requested. And as Connor's pleas for additional men became ever more desperate, other means were sought to support him, including an attempt to get cavalry from Colorado.

On April 15, Halleck even suggested the possibility of raising some companies in Utah, or from passing emigrant trains. Connor was quick to tell his seniors that such plans were impractical, since the Mormons could never be induced to enlist, and because all of the emigrants had gold fever. As an alternative, Connor asked permission to enlist a company from amongst the Morrisites for a twelve month period, with the understanding that they would be used to garrison a post he would like to establish on Bear River near the Soda Springs. Off duty, the Morrisite soldiers would be allowed to farm and build homes. Connor said if the "poor but industrious" Morrisites couldn't be enlisted on the stated terms they would still be willing to do the necessary post duties, provided he could issue them arms and rations and, in either case, their services would allow a company of his infantry to be used elsewhere. Any thought of using Morrisites as soldiers soon ended, however, upon learning they would be required to enlist for three years or the duration of the war.[40] Thus, as events would prove, it would finally be late summer before additional troops would arrive to augment the Californians.

III

Although by April overt military demonstrations and midnight alarms had ceased, the war of words between Mormon and Gentile continued unabated. This proved to be the month the grand jury of the Third Judicial District joined in the fray.

The mass petition to President Lincoln for the removal of the federal officials had also, somewhat parenthetically, claimed that Camp Douglas was situated within the limits of Salt Lake City. Now, in another attempt to be rid of the camp, the jury declared it to be a "nuisance" because of the alleged reduced flow and fouling of Red Butte Creek.[41] The jury also recommended that Judge Kinney censure the governor for his pardon of the Morrisites. The outraged jurymen compared Harding to a "pestiferous cesspool . . . breeding disease and death" for having turned convicted "criminals" loose upon the community.[42]

Soon after receiving the recommendation, and without acting on it, Kinney discharged the jury. The judge, now a candidate to be Utah's delegate to Congress, complimented the members on a good job and on the superior vigilance shown in Utah in arresting and convicting criminals. As his final act, Kinney approved a motion by a juror that, inasmuch as the grand jury had been discharged without finding an indictment against him, Brigham Young should be discharged from his bond.[43]

T. B. H. Stenhouse was not surprised that the jury, "composed of apostles, bishops, and elders," many of whom were polygamists themselves, found no evidence to satisfy them that Young had married Amelia Folsom, when, in fact, there was no act of Brigham's social life better known than that marriage. According to the Mormon publisher, it had provided confidential amusement and gossip for months. Brigham was said to have sent his competition for her hand off on missions, and offered them commercial privilege and other inducements in order to win the woman. "His carriage lingered by her mother's door for hours nearly every day," Stenhouse said. "He got barbered and perfumed every morning, and replaced his homespun garments with broadcloth. . . .

Col. Robert T. Burton, commander of the Mormon militia which suppressed the Morrisites at Kingston Fort. (Courtesy Utah State Historical Society)

that no one of that Grand Jury knew that Brigham Young had married Amelia Folsom, is very strange."[44]

Young made another attempt to rid himself of Camp Douglas a few weeks later when he ordered Mayor Abraham Smoot to abate the nuisance by moving Connor and his men out of the city limits. After Connor heard of the order he told Stenhouse, "I know sir, that Brigham Young could use up this handful of men; but there are sixty thousand men in California who would avenge our blood."[45] Stenhouse agreed, and thought that had Brigham's order been obeyed perhaps the entire country might have responded and that the Mormon church might have ceased to exist. To Mayor Smoot apparently belongs the credit for stalling long enough to allow Brigham to reconsider his order.

Thus ended the great crisis of March 1863. Even though both sides had managed to look foolish, cool heads were able ultimately to prevail. As for the Morrisites, after the pardons they became the objects of renewed bitterness and persecution. Even more of them found it expedient to take refuge at Camp Douglas for protection and to obtain a living. The Goshiutes would continue to plague the Overland to the west of Salt Lake City but, by the attack in Spanish Fork Canyon, troubles with the tribes to the south would for a time be solved.

President Lincoln waited until June before taking any action on the problem of Utah officials. With other, more earth-shaking matters to attend to, he was obviously ambivalent regarding the Mormon question. On June 6, he related one of his many epigrams to Stenhouse, who was then in Washington:

"Stenhouse, when I was a boy on the farm in Illinois there was a great deal of timber on the farms which we had to clear away. Occasionally we would come to a log which had fallen down. It was too hard to split, too wet to burn and too heavy to move, so we plowed around it. That's what I intend to do with the Mormons. You go back and tell Brigham Young that if he will let me alone I will let him alone."[46]

Lincoln's decision gave both sides a little something to cheer about. To please the Mormons, Governor Harding would be replaced by James Duane Doty, the seemingly inoffensive superintendent of Indian affairs. To please the Gentiles, Secretary Frank Fuller and Chief Justice Kinney would be superseded by Amos

Reed and John Titus, respectively. Doty, age sixty-four, had spent his youth in the frontier settlements of Michigan, had been a lawyer, a member of the Michigan legislature and a congressman from both that state and Wisconsin. Titus was a Pennsylvanian and Reed was son of John Reed of Colesville, New York, who in the summer of 1830 had defended Joseph Smith at his trial there.

Although Justice Waite was retained, he would soon resign in disgust and move to practice law in Idaho City, after holding a term of court at which there was not a single case on the docket. Old Judge Drake remained staunchly at his post, but was said to be merely going through the motions of holding court.[47]

Stephen Harding left Salt Lake City on June 11, banished to Valparaíso to be U.S. Consul. In later years he received a mixed assessment from his contemporaries. While historian H. H. Bancroft called him an energetic and able lawyer, and a man of personal courage, others implied that he was a womanizer.[48]

With Harding gone from the territory, there would be no overt crises for another year. Brigham Young, writing to George Q. Cannon in England later that month, sounded almost content:

"Since Harding's departure . . . without the least demonstration from any party, and only one individual to bid him good-bye, the transient persons here continue very quiet, and apparently without hope of being able to create any disturbance during the present administration. They certainly will be unable to, if President Lincoln stands by his statement made to Brother Stenhouse on the 6th instant., viz: 'I will let them alone if they will let me alone.' We have ever been anxious to let them alone further than preaching to them the gospel and doing them good when they would permit us, and if they will cease interfering with us unjustly and unlawfully . . . they will have no pretext nor chance for collision during this rule."[49]

Original site of Morristown, or Soda Springs, Idaho. Bear River and Alexander Reservoir are in the background. (Author's photo)

The Regenerators 7

"They say they'll send an army,
To set the Mormons right,
Regenerate all Utah,
And show us Christian light;
Release our wives and daughters,
And put us men to flight;
For all are talking of Utah."[1]

— From *The Beehive Songster*

I

Sometime during his first turbulent winter in Zion, Patrick Connor must have come to the conclusion that, since he was unlikely ever to receive enough troops to control the Mormon leaders, he must attempt to bring the common people of Utah into the mainstream of 19th Century American life. Beginning in the spring of 1863, he set out to peacefully "regenerate" Utah — as his Mormon opponents would characterize it — by providing protection to those outside the church, establishing an opposition press, and by trying to attract a large non-Mormon population to the territory.

"The secret of the power of these leaders," he would later say, "lies in this one word — isolation. So long as they were able to keep their people from association with the outside world they were safe. . . . [only a] few years will elapse before Utah will be redeemed from her infamy and degradation and contribute a loyal and healthy support to our common country."[2]

The Morrisite refugees provided an opportunity for the first step. Connor decided to use them as the nucleus of an anti-Mormon settlement, and a refuge for all who desired to leave the Mormon Church and had no means to emigrate farther. This scheme dovetailed nicely with his desire to establish another military post at the Soda Springs in Idaho Territory. He thought a garrison there, on the trail to Oregon, California and the Montana mines, and near a "summer resort" of the hostile Shoshoni, would be most effective.[3]

After obtaining General Wright's approval, Connor gave the glad tidings to the Morrisites. Not only were they allowed to apply for transportation for themselves and their families, but Connor had them tell all others who wanted to leave Utah that the train he was about to send out would have room enough for all. This news spread rapidly, and ultimately so many Morrisites and others took advantage of the opportunity to leave that arrangements were made for a second party to accompany an empty military train being sent to Carson City, Nevada. Those who were most destitute were given rations and other necessities.

On May 5, 1863, both trains moved together out of Camp Douglas, one headed north, the other south, like "two wings of a great eagle," as described by one Morrisite who was still hopeful for the future of the religion.[4] The 150 souls bound for Carson City would arrive safely within several weeks to disperse throughout Nevada and elsewhere. The company destined for Soda Springs, where Connor proposed to establish a garrison, comprised 53 families, seven single men and four widows — 160 civilians in all — and was escorted by Captain David Black and his Company H of the Third Infantry.

General Connor, accompanied by his staff and Indian Superintendent Doty, with Company H of the cavalry as escort, left Camp Douglas the next day and overtook Black's contingent on the road north of Salt Lake City. At Brigham City the expedition split, the infantry and the Morrisites following the usual trail along the Bear River through Cache and Marsh Valleys, while Connor and his cavalry crossed at the lower ferry, ascended the plateau between the Malad and Bear Rivers and then moved directly toward the Snake River.

Connor was still looking for Sagwitch, Pocatello and Sanpitch, believing one or more of the chiefs had committed recent minor depredations against emigrants and settlers. After leaving Brigham

City, he made two night marches in hope of surprising an Indian camp, but none was found. His expedition arrived May 13 at the Snake River ferry, east of old Fort Hall, where the Blackfoot River empties into the Snake. Here were found several large emigrant trains bound northward to the mines, and nearby was a camp of over 250 Shoshoni who professed friendship toward the whites.

That night a conference was held with the leading chiefs in the presence of the entire band. Addressing them through an interpreter, Connor spoke bluntly. While he promised summary punishment of Indians who took the lives and property of emigrants and settlers, he gave assurances that whites who trespassed on Indian rights also would be punished to the full extent of his power. After smoking with the chiefs, the Indian men and women danced for the whites and the general ordered a small quantity of food distributed.

Bill Hickman, serving the expedition as a guide, gave a pithy assessment of this pow-wow on the Snake:

"The General got to Snake River, found a good many Indians, and had a talk with them and they promised to be good: and so they will — when they are dead."[5]

Ever restless and inquisitive, Connor decided to look for a way to shorten the distance traveled by those bound from the East to the Montana mines. Before leaving the ferry, he detached Lieutenant Cyrus D. Clark and twenty-five men to find a pass whereby a wagon road might be cut north from Soda Springs to cross the Snake some sixty miles farther upstream. Clark and his men followed the river to Eagle Rock, a point about eight miles north of present-day Idaho Falls. Here they found a place suitable to Connor's plans and then, with Hickman as guide, traveled seventy miles southward across the mountains to Soda Springs. Connor reckoned the new route would save seventy miles from Soda Springs to Bannack, while still providing good water and grass. Within the next month, the ferry was running at Eagle Rock with ten soldiers guarding it for the rest of the emigration season.[6]

The general and the main body of cavalry traveled southeast to arrive at Soda Springs on the seventeenth. While waiting for the infantry and settlers, more detachments were sent out to explore. One expedition went south to find a more direct route from Soda Springs to Cache Valley and, as a result, a new, shorter wagon road would be made by soldiers in early November, along the west bank of the Bear.[7] Connor hoped that, when connected with the new road north from Soda Springs explored by Lieutenant Clark, the total distance from Salt Lake City to Bannack would be reduced to under 350 miles. That fall, Captain James L. Fisk, an army quartermaster, traveled from Bannack to Salt Lake City on an "express," which consisted of a covered wagon running once a week. At Connor's new ferry he saw 150 wagons, bound from Denver to the eastern slope mines, waiting to cross. The express carrying Fisk traveled over Connor's new road, which the captain assessed as still being exceedingly rough.[8]

On May 20, Company H and the Morrisites reached their destination at the great bend of the Bear River. Here a two-hundred acre town site was selected on the north bank, four miles east of where Soda Springs Valley opens into Old Crater Valley. Nearby were the famous Steamboat and Beer springs, and the reddish-brown mineral outcroppings so well known to pioneers traveling the Oregon Trail, described by such early explorers as Captain Bonneville and Fremont. Also close by was the wagonbox grave in which George Goodhart two years previously had buried an entire family of emigrants, after finding them massacred by Indians. It was a beautiful spot, abounding with fish and game and with a plenteous supply of timber for fuel and the building of homes.

The expeditions Connor had sent out had satisfied him as to the fertility and cultivability of the region around Soda Springs — his only doubt being the short growing season and the altitude. Ominously, the morning after the Morrisites arrived they awoke to find themselves covered with a layer of snow.

Soda Springs, or Morristown as it would sometimes be called, was surveyed and platted in a triangular shape, between Soda Creek and the Bear River, with its streets parallel to these streams. Lieutenant Francis M. Shoemaker was designated as the land trustee, with the right of patent for deeding a 25 by 130 foot parcel to those heads of household who would build houses or improvements. A one square mile military reservation was laid out adjoining the town to the east, its southern boundary following the course of the Bear River. The post, Camp Connor, was officially established by Captain Black's Special Orders No. 1 on May 23, 1863.[9]

The general remained only six days at Soda Springs. On the 23rd, just before leaving for Camp Douglas, he assembled the soldiers and civilians in the meadow near the river, and from a large flat rock he addressed them, for some reason feeling obliged to remind the Morrisites of the need for loyalty to their country.[10]

On the return trip an unsuccessful scout was sent into Bear Lake Valley to search for Sagwitch and, from Franklin, a side trip was made to the Bear River battlefield. Here, from among the many grisly relics still scattered about, Surgeon Reid took possession of what he believed to be the skulls of Chiefs Lehi and Bear Hunter. Connor arrived back at Camp Douglas on May 31 to proudly report his extensive explorations to General Wright,claiming they had been conducted over country about which previously "only the most vague and crude ideas were held."[11]

Captain Black and the men of Company H would garrison the lonely Soda Springs post until their enlistments expired nearly a year and a half later. From the beginning, the soldiers were bound to the Morrisites by the commonality and isolation of their situation, and by the fact that the civilians were for the most part dependent on the government for rations and seed until able to provide for themselves. The rest of that summer and fall was spent in building the military post and a log house for each family. The hard work was made easier by an occasional open-air dance held on tarpaulins laid over meadow grasses near the river. One such dance took place on July 20, after Lieutenant Shoemaker had joined a certain Neils Anderson and fifteen-year-old Mary Christopherson in marriage. It was Mary whose jaw had been shot away during the fight at Kingston Fort and who, for the rest of her life, would cover her lower face with a handkerchief whenever she met a stranger. This marriage, perhaps the first in Idaho Territory, would produce eight children, including the first white child to be born in Soda Springs.[12]

A soldier correspondent, writing in late February, has given us a vivid picture of what it was like at Camp Connor during its first winter. In spite of snow and ice, and usual temperatures of 10 to 35 degrees below zero, Black's infantry company was said to be the "coziest little huddle of Soldier Boys" the writer had seen. The men were living in two "comfortable" quarters built of pine, each

80 by 15 feet in size and partitioned for ten-man messes. Each mess had a fireplace, chimney, window and a door, and was furnished with bunks, tables and benches, and "every convenience that a soldier can device [*sic*] in habitations of so rude a nature, and so roughly constructed."

Fronting these quarters was a small guardhouse, and behind it facing the parade ground were the officer's quarters — a long building, 50 by 12 feet, partitioned into three apartments and having an "L" attached to the east end, which was used as a common kitchen and dining room. One hundred yards behind the officer's quarters were more log buildings, used as quarters for the three soldier's wives who served as company laundresses. As for the rest of the tiny camp:

"On the same row and to the left of the laundress' quarters, the celebrated philological, phrenological and spontaneous barber holds forth. He has erected a large and commodious saloon, in which your phiz can be relieved of its coating, be it luxuriant as friend Randolph's, or of a more moderate growth, resembling our friend Bobby Burns', from 'Dubling' . . . His chairs are constructed in a manner to insure comfort, ease and luxury to his customers — being a pine bench, minus the back. His razors are noted for their keenness and acuteness of touch. His water is of a corresponding temperature of that indicated by Fahrenheit on a certain cold morning . . .

"To the left of the garrison, and distant therefrom about one hundred yards, stands a very prominent edifice, in which is the sole medium through which the followers of Uncle Sam located in the wilds of Idaho, pass from the monotonous routine of camp life, to the Sunday divertisements, amusements, etc., natural to their disposition and inclinations. Within the walls of this building the gay lasses of Morristown — (oh, shocking! how could I be guilty of the expression,) I meant Soda City — swing their crinoline with a grace and recherche that would befittingly become a bon ton of the Fifth Avenue; here one may witness a gal-axy that is surprisingly dazzling; here you may feast your eyes upon the merriment of the light fantastic toe, so gaily tripped by the ladies of Idaho, and the little soldier boys who are highly honored, and on whom the bewitching eyes and captivating smiles are so beneficently bestowed and so graciously conferrred by their fair donors, and . . . I do most candidly assure you that these deuced little witches are the most aggravating possessors of all that ensnares man that one could meet for many a day . . ."[13]

The building where the Morrisite "witches" displayed their dancing skills was a two-story adobe affair, the lower story housing a post supply and store, and the upper story a hall for social gatherings, council and court meetings.[14] It also housed the local chapter of the Good Templars temperance lodge, which enrolled forty-five soldiers, laundresses and Morrisite girls that first winter.

II

A time of peacemaking with the Indians of the region would soon begin but, before all bands could be brought to the council circle, still more blood would be shed. After the Bear River battle and the skirmishes with Little Soldier, the Goshiutes were the major remaining problem in the Department of Utah. To quell them, the brutal Captain Sam Smith was to be General Connor's instrument of retribution. Once he began, Smith would operate ruthlessly and without pause from Fort Ruby, using his Company K and a detachment under Lieutenant Quinn.

Smith's first expedition was delayed by the need to rest and shoe his animals but, by May 5, he and Quinn had begun the killing. Acting on information obtained by Major Gallagher from friendly Indians in Ruby Valley, and with four of these natives as hostage-guides, Smith located a band of 150 supposed hostiles about forty miles south of Schell Creek. Here the Goshiutes had camped on a hillside in the shelter of a butte.[15]

After dark, Smith divided his forces and surrounded the camp. At daybreak, a pistol shot signaled the beginning of a slaughter that quickly ended twenty-four Indian lives. The following day, five more were killed as they rode over a ridge, returning to the camp from a hunting expedition. On May 6, Smith and his men surprised another band camped near Cedar Swamp, fifty miles south of Spring Valley Station. Swampy ground was said to have impeded the cavalry somewhat, but nonetheless the soldiers were able to dispose quickly of 23 of the Goshiutes. By the tenth, the cavalrymen were back at Fort Ruby after covering 250 miles and killing, in all, 53 Goshiutes. The sole cavalry casualty had been an arrow wound in the back of Private John L. Cree.[16]

By this time, infantry Company E had been distributed along the mail route between Salt Lake City and Austin to guard the stations with small detachments and ride the stages when deemed necessary. On May 19, a coach carrying one of these military escorts was ambushed by Goshiutes between Canyon and Willow Springs stations, and the driver, W. R. Simpson, killed. The return fire of the four soldier guards was useless against the well-hidden Indians, but the whites escaped further harm when Howard Egan — who somehow always managed to be in the vicinity when these troubles occurred — took up the reins and drove to the next station. A second stage was attacked near Schell Creek a week later, without harm to its occupants.

Yet another coach was attacked only twenty-five miles west of Salt Lake City on June 10 — this time by Southern Utes. Mormon driver Wood Reynolds and a companion — the only persons aboard — were killed, scalped and mutilated, and the mail was cut to pieces and scattered. This incident prompted Connor to issue a flurry of messages to his commanders along the line. One instructed them to arrest any white men suspected of instigating the Indian attacks, and declared a limited martial law in the district as authority for such arrests. Another called for the use of soldier drivers, if necessary, to keep the mails moving.[17]

On the twentieth Captain Smith and his cavalry surprised and killed ten Indians in a camp near Government Springs. Although an Overland Mail Company horse was found in their possession, it is not likely that these were the natives responsible for the stage coach attacks[18]

Later that month, the wife of an Overland Mail Company blacksmith from Ruby Valley, who was at the time visiting the small Mormon settlement at Salt Creek (Nephi), wrote her husband that Indians had entered town with scalps of the men they had killed, along with plunder "belonging to the stage," and that the bishop had treated the savages to tobacco and ordered the people to feed them. The Mormon behavior, the woman said, "made me so mad that I pitched into them and told them what I thought of them, and then I felt better."[19]

These latest attacks prompted General Connor to renew his plea to Wright for doubling his "much scattered" forces. It was rumored, he said, that 1,600 Utes were in the southern settlements, ready to attack the Californians and destroy the mail line. He was "surrounded by enemies, white and red," and only had sixty men available for duty at Camp Douglas.[20]

Canyon Station, Nevada, would be attacked twice that summer. On the morning of June 23 Corporals William Hervey and Ira Abbott of Company E left the station as a guard for the daily water cart. After they left, the other two men of the station guard — Privates Jacob Burgher and Jacob Elliott — took it upon themselves to go off hunting, leaving the station unguarded in disobedience to standing orders. When the returning water party got within 500 yards of the station, twenty Indians hiding in the sagebrush opened fire. Corporal Hervey was killed by the first volley. Abbott, though wounded by a ball through his neck, jumped from the wagon, seized Hervey's weapons and returned fire, as did the driver of the cart. After reaching the station and finding the rest of the guard gone, an express was sent to Deep Creek for help. Eight cavalrymen arrived, a search was made, and the bodies of Elliott and Burgher were soon found, both riddled with ball holes and horribly mutilated. The three corpses were taken to Deep Creek and buried.[21]

The second attack on the station occurred on July 8. This time it was burned to the ground after four soldiers and one civilian were surprised and killed, unable to fire a shot in return. The Indians apparently had waited to strike until the white men had been called to breakfast in their dugout. All were down in the hole without their guns except the hostler, William Riley, who was currying a horse just outside the stable. As the Indians opened fire, Riley was shot through the ankle and, although he tried to escape down the canyon, he was quickly caught and killed.

Most of the men at breakfast were killed as they tried to leave the dugout to get their arms which were stacked in the south end of the barn. Not one of them was able to reach his gun. One tried an escape down the canyon and — although he got farther than Riley had —he too was caught and killed. Since this unfortunate soldier was bald-headed, but had a good growth of whiskers on his chin, the Indians chose to "scalp" his beard. All the dead whites were stripped of their clothes and left where they had fallen.[22]

In response to this raid, Captain Smith and two companies left for Deep Creek again with rations for sixty days. For orders, he had "carte blanche so far as this tribe is concerned." Smith would now be pursuing Goshiutes constantly until peace was achieved, not returning to Camp Douglas with his company until November 1.[23] While the captain would find no more fights, infantry Company E would eventually avenge its dead soldiers. In early August, a detachment under Lieutenant Josiah Hosmer surprised a Goshiute camp forty miles east of Ruby Valley and killed five Indians.[24]

General Connor was also cooperating this summer of 1863 — in a half-hearted manner — with his District of Oregon counterpart, Brigadier-General Benjamin Alvord. The Oregon commander informed him of the planned yearly expedition by Colonel R. F. Maury, First Oregon Cavalry, from Fort Lapwai to the Fort Hall area. A new post, Fort Boise, would be established by Major Lugenbeel of the U.S. Ninth Infantry and troops from Fort Walla Walla, to provide protection for Boise Valley miners and Oregon Trail emigrants. Most emigrants were expected to travel north of the Snake River, across the Camas Prairie. Maury was to visit Lugenbeel, then clear away any Indians he found on the prairie, a traditional food-gathering area of the Shoshoni. Connor was asked to provide protection as far west as the Salmon Falls for those traveling south of the river.[25]

III

On July 2, while Union and Confederate forces were locked in a death grip at far-off Gettysburg, peace was finally achieved with the first of the Great Basin Indian tribes. Some one thousand Eastern Shoshoni in ten different bands loyal to Chief Washakie gathered to conclude a treaty at Fort Bridger with Governor Doty, the acting Indian superintendent. A month earlier at Bridger, General Connor had himself talked to six hundred of these same Indians and had received 150 stolen horses as a gesture of peace. Simultaneously, he had increased pressure for capitulation in the region by augmenting the Bridger garrison with Captain Price's company of cavalry, and by dispatching expeditions from there in search of Pocatello and Sanpitch.[26]

The provisions of the Fort Bridger Treaty called for "perpetual peace," and guaranteed safe passage along the trail. White settlements could be established and the Pacific railroad constructed without Indian interference. For the Eastern Shoshoni, their terri-

Little Soldier, "Weber Ute" chieftain (Courtesy Utah State Historical Society)

tory was very roughly defined, and an annuity in goods was to be paid to them in the amount of $10,000 for twenty years.[27]

The next step toward peace with the tribes was taken on Connor's initiative. After consulting with Doty, he located Little Soldier's Weber Utes, provided them with presents and induced the chief to come to Camp Douglas on June 27 to parley. An understanding was reached in which Little Soldier agreed to give up all government livestock in his possession. He, in return, received thirteen ponies captured by soldiers in the April fight in Spanish Fork Canyon. These dealings with Little Soldier led to peace overtures from several Southern Ute chiefs. Thus, messengers were sent out by Connor naming July 14 at the Spanish Fork Reservation in Utah Valley as the time and place for more treaty making.[28]

The general left Camp Douglas on the tenth, in company with his staff, Governor Doty, and an escort of twenty cavalrymen, for the sixty mile trip to the reservation. His party took the stage road and spent the night at Porter Rockwell's Hot Springs Brewery Hotel, located near Point of the Mountain. This inn, which catered to Overland stage passengers and a large Mormon and Gentile clientele, had been run by Rockwell since 1858 as the sort of place where a man could get a beer, stop overnight or just pass the time of day.

Chaplain Anderson, who had come along as staff, seemed exceedingly impressed with Rockwell, whom he called a "'bird' — a whole-souled, smart, active Mormon." The chaplain was later able to supply his readers with some insights which he had no doubt gained in Rockwell's taproom:

"Tradition says that he was in other days the chief of the Danites. . . . Whether Porter is the veritable Blue Beard and bloodstained hero of the thousand and one tales one hears deponent can't say. If so, that part of the business is, in his expressive language, 'played out.' He is now the most affable of men, generous, attentive and kind to all — a most hospitable host — a good liver, and — my eyes! — a first rate drinker, fond of his whiskey, which he says is made of 'wheat,' and is always ready to do the 'squar thing' whether he's 'round' or not."

The next morning the hung-over peacemakers left Rockwell's for the trip through the settlements of American Fork, Lehi, Spanish Fork and Payson. Anderson took note of the uniform similarity of these towns—all were situated at the foot of the mountains with fresh streams running through; no liquor was to be had; children abounded but money was short, requiring the use of barter. Of the people, he remarked that "their whole aim in life seems to be to glorify Zion, live comfortably and frugally, get *another* wife, and raise an immense number of pretty, tow-headed children. In the last they are eminently successful. . . ."[29] All of the houses were made of adobe, since the scarcity of wood prevented its use or the burning of bricks. Besides, Anderson said, all available wood was being used to make bedsteads and cradles.

Connor's party halted that evening at Springville and, the next morning, he met the chiefs and their warriors at the farmhouse on the reservation a few miles south. The bands present were those of chiefs Antero, Tabby, Kanosh (of Mountain Meadows renown), Ute-Pete, Au-ke-wah-kus and Black Hawk. The general addressed the Utes briefly with his boilerplate speech, after which Doty spoke and distributed presents of tobacco, beef and flour. Then the chiefs, one after another, delivered conciliatory speeches, all pledging peace. With this, the pow-wow closed and the Indians returned to their camp, reportedly well-pleased with the results.

Connor seemed satisfied that the Utes were tired of war and would abide by the treaty. As for the Shoshoni to the north, Connor told General Wright that they were once more united under their peace chief Washakie, and were living "in quiet contentment" near Fort Bridger under the guardianship of the Indian department. Wright also was told that even Pocatello was tired of war and had twice sent emissaries to request a conference. One was therefore to be held July 30 at Brigham City to deal with both the Shoshoni chief and the Bannocks with whom his band ranged.

The brigadier thus was able to report peace with the Indians in every direction, except for the hundred or so Goshiute braves still actively hostile on the stage line between Deep Creek and Ruby Valley. These few still were being actively pursued by Captain Smith, and Connor had little doubt that on hearing of the treaty just completed, the Goshiutes — those who might escape Smith — would sue for peace.

Now that Indian problems were nearly solved, Wright received a lengthy and fervent plea to bring the Californians home, and let the Nevada cavalry companies — which were then being raised — guard the stage and telegraph lines. Connor reminded Wright that his presence was a constant irritation to the Mormons, regardless of how prudent or circumspect he and his men might try to be. He repeated again his contention that to "take hold of the Mormon question with a strong hand . . . and enforce the laws of the land" would require prompt and significant reinforcement, but Connor said he knew such was not the present intention of the government.[30]

Wright would not bring the Californians home. He claimed they were still needed for Overland protection and "the general safety of the country."[31] Instead, he flirted briefly with a half-way measure to reduce tensions in Utah. On July 31, he instructed Connor to prepare to abandon Camp Douglas and reoccupy Camp Crittenden, if the old camp could be purchased under reasonable terms. If such could be arranged, Connor was to begin manning it with his missing infantry companies, which were by now on the way from California.

Governor Doty vehemently opposed the change of location, and told Wright so in an impassioned letter dated August 9. Doty still harbored fears for his safety and that of other federal officials. If a collision with the Mormons were to occur, the officers would require "instant protection and assistance." Doty also argued that Connor's troops were needed to continue asserting American, rather than Mormon authority over the Indians, and it was his purpose to "make them continue to feel and acknowledge it."[32] The governor urged Wright not only to continue to man Camp Douglas and Fort Ruby at their present levels, but to increase the forces at Camp Connor and Fort Bridger and establish a new post in the Uintah Valley where the Utes were to be gathered.

General Wright bowed to this political pressure, assuring Doty he had already decided against the relocation. On August 19 he told Connor negotiations to repurchase Crittenden might continue if he desired, but he should stay at Douglas if he thought best. The next day, in an unrelated action, a change was made in District of Utah boundaries, removing that part of Nevada west of Fort Ruby and adding the new post at Soda Springs.[33]

Thus ended a sincere attempt by P. Edward Connor to get out of Utah.

Treaty-making continued, as planned, on July 30 when Doty and Connor met with about one thousand Northwestern Shoshoni at Brigham City. Pocatello was there, as were chiefs Tormontso, Torsor-vetz and Sanpitch, the latter having missed the gatherings at Fort Bridger and Springville. The few members of the bands of Bear Hunter and Sagwitch who had survived the Bear River battle were likewise present. Sagwitch himself, severely wounded by one of Connor's men while on the way to the council, could not attend, but nonetheless joined in the agreement, which was similar to those previously negotiated.[34]

The results of Connor's fights and subsequent treaty making were immediately obvious on the emigrant trail that year. On August 23 from his camp on the Portneuf River, Colonel Maury wrote Connor that the entire emigration had thus far gone through without trouble. Maury said he had found over 700 frightened Indians living near Fort Hall, including some Bannocks who urgently desired peace. Both he and General Alvord would later credit the absence of trouble that year to the treaties made thus far.[35]

When the first installment of the long-awaited reinforcements finally arrived in Salt Lake City on September 17, they were gaily escorted through the streets by the Camp Douglas brass band playing "sweet and patriotic notes."[36] The 400 new men consisted of infantry Companies A, C and D; Company L of the Second California Cavalry, and a detachment of cavalry recruits. Lieutenant Colonel J. B. Moore, who had marched the troops as far as Fort Ruby, remained there in command of Companies B and E of the Third. Not surprisingly, the sight of all these additional soldiers renewed fears for Brigham Young's safety, and resulted in a short-lived muster of 500 Mormon militia at the tabernacle.[37]

The new troops were reported to be in fine order, and proud mention was made of their unanimous vote for the Union ticket in the August election. The inevitable comparisons were made with the voting that had just taken place in Utah. The Mormon campaigns were evaluated as having been extremely dull, there having been no electioneering, no fights and no whiskey. And, there had been only one candidate for delegate for Congress — Judge Kinney. One observer, who thought Kinney's unanimous election had saved a lot of trouble and printers ink, said he had heard Brigham Young was to author a forthcoming work entitled "Politics Made Easy," or "The People Played Out."[38]

Both Connor and Governor Doty left Salt Lake about the same

time in late September, planning to meet shortly in Soda Springs to deal with the Bannocks. But first General Connor, accompanied by twenty-five cavalrymen and with Bill Hickman as guide, was off for a long trek into the Goose Creek Mountains of southern Idaho. Most likely the trip was being made to confirm reports of precious minerals in the region.

Governor Doty went to Ruby Valley to meet Governor Nye of Nevada and, on October 1, they made a treaty there with the two principal bands of Western Shoshoni — the Tosowitch, or White Knives, and the Unkoahs. This agreement stipulated that the mail and telegraph, and the forthcoming railroad would remain free of Indian interference. It allowed whites to explore for minerals, erect mills, and cut timber. For this, an annuity of $5,000 was to be paid.[39]

The Goshiutes, who had made peace overtures as early as August 20, were finally brought to terms on October 12. With Connor and Doty absent, Chaplain Anderson and Secretary Reed were sent to conduct negotiations at Grantsville, in the Tooele Valley. The pair made the trip in an ambulance drawn by mules, accompanied only by a driver. In short order they made a satisfactory treaty which allowed for trouble-free white settlement and uninterrupted lines of communication in return for an annuity of $1,000.[40]

On October 14, the Soda Springs treaty was made by Connor and Doty with the remaining one thousand or so "mixed bands of Bannocks and Shoshones." The principal Indian leaders to approve the agreement were Bannock chief "Le Grand Coquin" (The Great Rogue),[41] and two sub-chiefs, Tahgee and Matigund — the band of the latter being the one normally found in the vicinity of the lower Snake River ferry. Tindoah and several other chiefs had sent word that they would be parties to the treaty, but had been compelled by the lateness of the season to leave for their buffalo hunting grounds.

By this agreement, the Bannocks promised not to molest travelers along the Oregon and California trails, or along the new roads between Salt Lake City and the Boise and Montana mines, and to abide by the provisions of the treaty made in July at Fort Bridger by the Shoshoni. For its part, the government was to pay $5,000 per year in annuity goods to compensate for damages done to pasture lands and hunting grounds. Unfortunately this amount was to come from the $10,000 previously promised Chief Washakie and his Eastern Shoshoni at Fort Bridger; and this fact would later result in some dissatisfaction.

Both the general and governor seemed pleased with their peacemaking efforts of that year. Doty estimated that 8,650 Shoshoni, "Goships"[42] and Bannocks were parties to the agreements, and at a price he considered a bargain — a mere $20,000 annually to the Shoshoni and Bannocks and $1,000 to the Goshiutes. All of the agreements made that year were confirmed by the Senate, with minor amendments, and returned for the Indians' consent. All but the Bannocks eventually agreed to the changes and, even in their case, the treaty remained a de facto agreement until replaced by another in 1868.

Having made these treaties, General Connor did his best to see they were honored. The following year, upon hearing that the annuities were overdue, he and Doty wrote a joint letter to the Office of Indian Affairs warning that the government should "take great care to comply with its obligations to the Indians" and look for alternate means, if necessary, to fulfill the agreements.[43]

IV

In the fall, with Indian troubles for the most part settled, the work of redeeming the people of Utah could begin in earnest. Mining and prospecting were in the blood of Patrick Connor and his soldiers. It is hardly surprising, therefore, that he should choose these as the principal means of instituting change in Utah — particularly since, by developing the territory's resources, he perhaps could bring good fortune to himself and those loyal to him.

Gold had been on the Volunteers' minds right from the start. Within a month of their arrival, soldier correspondents were reporting explorations and supposed discoveries. One story had it that Methodist Bishop Matthew Simpson, while visiting Brigham Young in 1862, was told by the prophet that a person could stand in his doorway and see all the gold a man could wish for.[44] But, in spite of the Volunteers' expectations, the real mineral wealth of Utah would prove to be silver and copper, not gold.

The Mormons had exploited very few of the minerals available in the Great Basin. A little coal had been used, and a poor quality of lead and iron produced, but no effort sanctioned by the church had been made to seek out precious metals. This inactivity was due mainly to Brigham Young's desire to maintain the Saints as remote from outside influences as possible.

Serious attempts by the Volunteers to seek out Utah's mineral resources didn't begin until late that summer of 1863. They would start in Bingham Canyon, a gorge on the east slope of the Oquirrh Mountains just thirty miles south of Salt Lake City. Here, a woodcutter and sawyer named George B. Ogilvie — an employee of Mormon Bishop Archibald Gardner — picked up a piece of silver-bearing ore and sent it to General Connor, who had it assayed. Subsequently, the general visited the canyon with a group of officers and their wives on a "pic-nic party," and the wife of Regimental Surgeon Reid, while rambling on the mountainside, found another loose piece of ore.

The Californians located the vein, and named the mine the "Jordan." Connor drew up a set of regulations and by-laws, and a meeting of interested parties was held September 17 at Bishop Gardner's Jordan ward house in the settlement nearest the point of discovery. The by-laws were approved, Gardner was elected recorder and the West Mountain Quartz Mining District was organized. The district took in the Oquirrh range between 40 and 41 degrees north latitude and between the Jordan River and longitude 114 west.

Three claims were recorded on that same date by Gardner in the name of the West Mountain Mining Company. One notice shows Ogilvie claiming the discoverer's shares with the other shareholders being General Connor, Bishop Gardner, Dr. Reid, Henry Bexted and Samuel Egbert; another notice lists Mrs. Reid with the discoverer's shares, and includes Dr. Reid, Private Arthur Heitz and Mrs. Connor; a third notice — apparently a compromise — contains the greatest number of names, and lists the discoverer's shares for Ogilvie. Included on the latter claim are such unlikely names as "Avenging Angel" Bill Hickman and Colonel R. C. Drum, General Wright's assistant adjutant general in San Francisco. The three claims, taken together, contain all the names of those supposed by various sources to have been the first to find ore.[45]

In late October Connor informed General Wright of his plan to use mining as a means of battling Brigham. He would invite into the territory a large number of Gentiles, using valuable minerals as the lure. Then, intercourse with *normal* people would show the common Mormon that the government was not his enemy, as the leaders had said. This, Connor said, was the only sure, peaceful means of settling the Mormon question at an early date "without the increased expenditure of a dollar by Government, or . . . without the loss of a single soldier in conflict."[46]

Connor already had issued instructions to his post and detachment commanders, directing them to support and encourage their men to go prospecting when it wouldn't interfere with military duties. He was exceedingly enthusiastic about what had been achieved thus far. Gold, silver, lead and copper had been discovered in almost every direction: strikes had been made at Egan Canyon and Ruby Valley to the west and within twenty-five to fifty miles east and west of Salt Lake City; near Camp Connor to the north were large deposits of salt, sulphur and extensive beds of coal; the Goose Creek Mountains to the northwest were believed to contain rich mines of precious metals.

Mining fever ran unchecked that fall. The strike near Egan Canyon station mentioned by Connor occurred on September 10, when Thomas Beighle, a soldier of Company E, found gold. By December at least fourteen ledges of silver and gold-bearing quartz were said to have been located, some assaying as high as $2,000 per ton in gold and silver. Some big-thinkers had already ordered three quartz mills for delivery in the spring, while others had begun to lay out a city. The discoveries to the east of Salt Lake City resulted in formation of the Wasatch Mountain Mining District, which encompassed the Wasatch Range from the Weber River to latitude forty north.[47]

Colonel Pollock, the commander of Camp Douglas, is listed on November 17, along with Ogilvie, the two Reids, Lieutenant Finnerty and several others, as an owner of the Vedette Silver and Copper Mining Company. The extent of mining fever can readily be seen in Pollock's proposal to macadamize his parade ground and roads leading to the camp using only mineral samples that were to be found on the mantels of the camp's living quarters.[48]

Lieutenant-Colonel Moore, the Fort Ruby commander, was one officer who disapproved of allowing soldiers to prospect. On October 3 he protested to Connor's adjutant. Moore couldn't imagine that the general had meant for a large exploring party to be sent from Ruby, or for large parties of soldiers to "gobble up all the mining and water privileges" to the exclusion of civilians.

Moore groused about the excitement Connor's directive had caused amongst his men. To comply, he said, twenty-percent of them would be granted seven days' leave to go prospecting. But there was another irritation. Lieutenant Steven Jocelyn had just arrived at Ruby with a communication from Connor directing Moore to furnish facilities for accomplishment of an undisclosed mission. Moore, who had not been cut in, asked to be relieved of his command, saying it was mortifying that Connor had sent a lieutenant on a mission near his post that couldn't be entrusted to its commander.[49]

What Jocelyn's mission was, and why Moore was excluded are not known. Chances are it had to do with prospecting, since Jocelyn was formerly a miner from the region of Sonora, California. Moore had not been near Connor enough to become one of his cronies and confidants, he was also a poor leader. At Ruby he was hated by his men because of frequent floggings and orders to "pack sand" for slight infractions.[50]

Brigham Young didn't care for the mining either and, as early as October 6, he sensed Connor's plan. Speaking at the fall conference of his church, he wondered who was paying for all this prospecting activity by soldiers. "Were they really sent here," he asked, "to protect the mail and telegraph lines, or to discover . . . rich diggings . . . with a view to flood the country with just such a population as they desire, to destroy, if possible, the identity of the 'Mormon' community, and every truth and virtue that remains?"[51]

V

Another major tool to be used in the redemption of Utah Territory was brought into play on November 20, 1863, with the appearance of the weekly *Union Vedette*, a newspaper purportedly "published by the officers and enlisted men of the California Volunteers." In fact, General Connor had, at great personal expense, imported the press, paper and ink required to start the enterprise. For the next four years, the *Vedette* would allow expression of the Gentile and military viewpoint and serve as an outlet for Connor's ideas, criticisms and frustrations — its banner unabashedly proclaiming: "A champion brave, alert and strong — to aid the right, oppose the wrong."

As has been noted, the only paper published for the 80,000 people in the territory when the Volunteers arrived was the *Deseret News,* a weekly, church-controlled organ established in June 1850. Most of the *News* was usually taken up by sermons or writings of church leaders. It also contained a plethora of agricultural and horticultural information, news of various Mormon missions and so forth, but very little of what could be called the Gentile viewpoint of the world or of territorial affairs.

The single previous non-Mormon journalistic effort in Utah had been a weekly, *Kirk Anderson's Valley Tan,* published beginning in November 1858 by the former editor of the *Missouri Republican.* After the outspoken Anderson became intimidated and frightened, he fled the territory in secret in May 1859 and thereafter the paper was published at Camp Floyd, under the shortened name *Valley Tan.* Both it and a Mormon-sponsored rebuttal, the *Mountaineer,* died when the army began leaving in 1860.

The first editor of Connor's paper was Captain Charles H. Hempstead, a professional gambler's son who had risen to become a prominent California attorney and politician. A noted orator and skilled writer, the captain had served as private secretary to Governor Bigler, and as secretary of state for California in the early 1850s. He also had been superintendent of the San Francisco mint for a short time before volunteering for military service in late 1862.[52] Private Van B. DeLashmutt whom we met on the march from California — was the *Vedette's* first printer, having worked at age fifteen as printer's devil for the *Oregon Statesman* at Salem.

General Connor's idea in starting the paper was to separate the "sheep from the goats," that is, the inherently good, common Mormon people from the evil Mormon leaders. Hempstead's salutary in the first issue expressed regret that relations between the "mass of the people" and the military hadn't been amicable, and stated the paper's aim was to correct the "misrepresentation" that had brought the condition about. Hempstead said he felt sure that "the teachings which border on treason"[53] hadn't found a lasting place in hearts and minds of most Utahans.

The *Vedette* would become a daily on January 4, 1864 — the first ever published in the territory. For most of its life it was a lively and humorous little paper, especially when compared to the somber *Deseret News*. It carried extensive news of the war, foreign affairs, Utah legislative happenings and — most important to its soldier readers — news of California. And, although the publisher was an Irishman, it routinely ran some of the many Irish jokes of the day in which a tippling "Paddy" was usually the foil.

A good number of the local Gentile merchants, and even a few businesses run by Mormons, routinely advertised in its pages. To further help finance the paper, some book and job printing was done in the *Vedette* office. Perhaps the earliest work was the second edition of "A Vocabulary of the Snake or Shoshone Dialect," by interpreter Joseph A. Gebow, bearing a date of January 1, 1864. Later, on October 20, 1864, the printing office turned out the first issue of *Peep o'Day*, a literary and scientific magazine edited by E. L. T. Harrison and Edward Tullidge and backed financially by the Walker Brothers, Colonel Kahn and John Chislett. This first magazine published west of the Missouri ended after only six issues about a month later, due to bad business judgments, the high price of paper and the inability of the *Vedette* paper stocks to continue to support it.[54]

The *Vedette* sold well to soldiers, and it was particularly welcome reading at remote posts like Forts Bridger and Ruby and at Camp Connor. But, while Brigham Young was said to have read it daily, it was never widely read by Mormons, and therefore failed to sway the "masses." It was, however, quoted widely in California and the East, and did much to call attention to conditions in Utah. To a lesser extent, it promoted General Connor's mining interests and no doubt served to attract a number of Gentiles to the region. The first issue, in fact, contained a circular regarding the mineral wealth to be found in the territory. Connor promised the "industrious and enterprising who may come hither" that every proper facility would be extended to them and they would be given full protection while mining and prospecting, provided that private rights were not infringed upon.

VI

Companies A and B of the First Nevada Cavalry, 180 men strong, arrived from Fort Churchill on November 21, long after the Indian troubles of the year had been settled, and after the confrontation with Brigham Young had abated — but just in time to add to General Connor's food and forage worries for the winter.

The commanders of both new companies were products of the same school of hard knocks as Connor. Captain Elias B. Zabriskie of Company A had fought at Buena Vista as a young man, and had recently been district attorney of the Third Nevada Territorial District Court. Noyes Baldwin, captain of Company B, was a former "forty-niner" and contractor and builder in California, who had come to Nevada with the rush, and who most recently had run a hotel in Silver City. Zabriskie's company, recruited in Silver City, had been the first to fill its roster after recruiting began the previous April, but it had been difficult getting men to enlist in this mining region where a laborer could make three to four dollars per day, and where Confederate sympathies still persisted.

General Connor's troops, new and old alike, were busy finishing their permanent quarters and were getting in their own firewood from nearby hills when the first snowstorm hit in early December. There had been prior trouble over contracts for wood, hay, oats, beef and flour when Connor had insisted that they all be given to Gentiles. The steep rise in prices which ensued prevented the contractors from filling their agreements at the prices allowed by the government.[55]

According to Mormon apostle Wilford Woodruff, with winter hard upon them and no flour forthcoming, Connor's representatives appealed to Bishop John Sharp for help "to save themselves from starvation." Woodruff also claimed the Mormons ultimately were offered $12.00 per hundred for the flour, whereas earlier the contractors had been able to offer only $6.50. The bishop was said to have told Connor's commissary that, if he were to help them, he would have to treat them as he did those in his ward, and at his insistence, the officer was required to show what he had on hand in stores. Finding that the soldiers had but a few days' breadstuff, the bishop, with Brigham's help, would "undertake to feed the Army" in spite of the expected scarcity of grain before another harvest.[56]

It is hard to imagine the proud Connor begging for help, or suffering this type of indignity, but a later communication from Brigham Young to George Cannon in England indicates that he may have capitulated. Calling the Volunteers a mean "lot of diggers," Brigham said that after ransacking the countryside for gold and finding none, they now were unable to provide themselves with bread. And, in spite of Connor's rejection of Bishop Sharp's bid to furnish flour, Brigham had directed the bishop to keep the volunteers in breadstuff, but the extra amount being supplied was causing the price of wheat and flour to rise.[57]

That some price-fixing was beginning to take place seems certain. When Captain Fisk passed through Salt Lake City in November, he heard Bishop Woolley in the tabernacle "incite his flock to sneer at the 'blue skins,'" — meaning Connor's soldiers — and tell them not to sell any article of produce and, in less than a year, a bushel of wheat would be worth "more than a bushel of greenbacks." Fisk thought the Mormon capital "should have been long ago leveled with its salt beds for its lechery and its open insolence towards the general government."[58]

Despite the continued grumblings and the squabbling over prices, there would be a certain measure of peace that second winter the Volunteers were to spend in Zion. Brigham Young seemed content, for the time being, to let the Lord work his will to thwart Connor's "evil designs" to attract outsiders and regenerate Utah. The Mormon prophet assured George Q. Cannon in England that, even though the "humbug in relation to the mines" continued, no gold had as yet turned up, and he had faith that the Lord would "continue to hide the treasures in the earth."[59]

Those Troublesome "Sojer Boys" 8

"Employment of the troops, [consists of] erecting shelter from the weather, building good quarters for officers and men, drilling, scouting, protection of the overland mail and telegraph, killing Indians, and marrying apostate Mormon women. . . . The habits of the soldiers are excellent, moral and temperate. . . ."

— Annual report for 1864 of Chief Medical Officer Reid, District of Utah[1]

I

After all hopes that the Volunteers might return to California had been quashed by General Wright, work began in earnest to build a more comfortable and functional Camp Douglas. The task was finally finished in late December 1863 with the completion of barracks for the newly-arrived Nevada companies.

The buildings Connor's men erected were nearly all made of logs cut from the surrounding canyons. They were whitewashed on the outside, had plastered interior walls, and were built with large, open verandas in front. The post was centered around a 440 by 440 foot parade ground and its flagstaff. At the upper end was a headquarters building, with four sets of officers' quarters placed on each side. The latter, described as "small huts," were 40 by 26 feet and contained a double set of quarters, each with four rooms. Twelve similar quarters for married non-commissioned officers were built on a line parallel with, and 75 yards in the rear of the officers' quarters. Along the two sides of the parade ground were eleven enlisted men's barracks, each 85 by 28 feet in size. At the lower end of the parade rectangle sat a stone guardhouse, flanked on one side by a stone arsenal and on the other by a magazine.[2]

A fairly spacious hospital was erected 100 yards in the rear of the married soldiers' quarters. Behind it was a garden several acres in size, and close by on either side sat quarters for the post commander and surgeon. Beginning in February 1864, General Connor would reside in a "commodious and very pretty adobe dwelling" about 200 yards from the parade ground to the north, adjacent to his headquarters building.[3] A variety of other structures was required to complete the camp: quarters for the laundresses, a sutler's store with a residence in the rear, an ordnance store house; an icehouse capable of holding 300 tons of ice, and — clustered together below one set of barracks — quartermaster storehouses, stables, barns, a coal house, wood and hay yards and workshops.

Much to the dissatisfaction of the Mormons below in the city, Red Butte Creek was diverted at the point where it issues from the canyon east of the camp. Near that point was a reservoir from which ice was obtained. Ditches were run from the creek to provide a constant stream through camp for irrigation and for flushing the deep ravines at the rear of each set of barracks, into which the drains of the camp emptied. Around the parade ground, and at other places where the water ran, young locust and mulberry trees were planted. Water for culinary purposes was taken from a spring just above the cemetery and was hauled in carts and placed in barrels at individual kitchens.

The cemetery, in which so much Utah history lies buried, lay to the southeast and across one of the ravines, about 500 yards from the parade ground. It had been laid out when the first death in the command occurred in December 1862 and was dedicated at the first of the Bear River anniversary celebrations held at Camp Douglas and various posts as long as there were Volunteers to hold them.

During 1863, plans had been made to erect a monument to the men killed in the fight, based on an idea originating with Principal Musician James Cantell of the Third. Since the companies had contributed $1,631 — more than enough for the monument — some of the money was used to build a wall around the cemetery, install an iron gate and plant young locust trees. The monument itself, completed May 1864 and still standing today, is a three foot high sen-

Officer's Quarters, Camp Douglas, Utah Territory, ca. 1865.

tinel on a seventeen foot base made of red sandstone from the hills east of the post.

That first Bear River anniversary celebration on January 29, 1864 was an elaborate one. It began with a dress parade and an eleven-gun salute. Soldier and civilian guests alike then marched to the cemetery to hear Captain Hempstead's dedicatory oration and the reading of General Connor's special order releasing all the men in the guardhouse, except deserters. In the evening, elaborate balls were held for enlisted men and officers. The highlight of the evening for the officers was actress Mrs. Selden Irwin's recitation of a Bear River "Anniversary Lay" composed especially for the occasion. It was reported that, before gaiety was restored by a midnight supper and more dancing, "many a stout heart was moved to tears as the sufferings and heroism of our brave troops one year ago, were rehearsed by the fair reader."[4]

Several businesses sprang up on or around the post, among them a jewelry and watch repair, a "daguerrean gallery," a shaving, shampooing and hair-cutting "saloon," and a livery stable, which also ran an express into Salt Lake City twice daily. A post restaurant and catering service also soon came into existence.

The hub of the camp — for the lonely enlisted soldiers at least — was the theater and dance hall, forty by seventy feet in size, which was built by a private company at a cost of $2,000 in soldier subscriptions. It was apparently located well to the west of the main camp. One of its first uses was the Christmas eve ball held in 1863, at which the public was invited to partake of some "fine bear meat" for five dollars a head.[5]

Performances usually began at eight p.m., three nights a week. Some of the first talent to appear was of the home-grown soldier variety, doing melodrama, burlesque and minstrelsy in a troop known as the "Union Varieties." "George Pardy 'the inimitable,' Miss Raffaelle the 'graceful and accomplished' and other imported stars of the rarest lustre" were reported to have delighted the "sojer boys" the first few weeks of the theater's life, and even the "shakey saints" were said to be enjoying the shows.[6] Later on, these acts were replaced by others of similar sophistication — that "laughable farce of 'Bombasto Furiouso,'" for example, and a certain Mr. Nethercott of San Francisco with his "pleasant exhibition of fencing with cutlass, small and broad sword."

Most popular was the civilian group known variously as the "Metropolitan Minstrels" or the "National Minstrel Troupe," which featured Billy Shepard, the "inimitable negro delineator and jig dancer." Shepard, according to a *Vedette* reviewer, was "an excellent imitator of the old fashioned plantation darkey."[7] This well-traveled correspondent claimed to have seen the "Essence of Old Virginia" danced by the Christy, Buckley, Wood and Peel troupes in New York, but never had he seen it done in better style than by Shepard. This same loosely organized group of performers left Salt Lake on occasion to tour the Mormon settlements, calling themselves the "Utah Minstrels."

The theater also did service as a schoolhouse. Since there was strong sentiment not to use the local schools, a private one was established on the post in April 1864 by Colonel Pollock with Zenas Cushman of Company F as teacher. Later, Cushman would also offer classes for the soldiers.[8]

Life in camp — be it Douglas, Bridger, Ruby or Connor — could best be described as routine and dull, with its drills, company inspections, guard mounts, and, of course, fatigue duties. The thirteen dollars per month of the private soldier didn't allow much diversion from this routine. One dollar a month went to have white shirts, collars and other laundry done, and the men paid for being shaved by the company barber once or twice a week. Just getting into Salt Lake City cost seventy-five cents, and the price of a dance and dinner on the base was six dollars.

Several factors exacerbated the inadequacy of the pay. First, the paymaster's visits were irregular and infrequent and — more often than not — dances and parties were postponed because he failed to appear when expected. When he did come, the troops were paid for three or four months at a time and this undoubtedly caused "feast or famine" situations. The second problem was that the "greenbacks" paid to the soldiers were not accepted at par either in Utah or California, where they were spent by many of the men's families.

Other than the theater, little recreation was available at Camp Douglas. A regimental library of some 900 volumes had been solicited by Chaplain Anderson while still in Stockton and transported with the troops to Utah. It was located in the Chaplain's tent, from which volumes were distributed locally as well as to outlying posts.

Clubs and organizations, a popular, low-cost diversion of the day, existed in profusion in and about Camp Douglas. An Odd Fellows lodge came into existence in January 1865, and at least two temperance societies — the Dashaway Association and the Good Templars — were organized by soldiers soon after arrival in Utah. The Camp Douglas Templars, in fact, had 263 members at one time, united in the fight against "King alcohol and his army."[9]

A Camp Douglas gymnastic club and the Union Base Ball Club were both organized in 1864. The baseball club was begun for the purpose of "enjoying all the benefits in the way of health and strength, to which the game indicated is so eminently conducive."[10] Two hours per day were to have been devoted to this "healthy and manly sport," beginning at the enervating hour of five a.m., but nothing more was heard of the club after its debut.

One organization, a chapter of which appeared at Camp Connor, has, alas, not survived the test of time. This was the "One Thousand and One" (O.T.O.), which was said to date back to the days of Noah, and had its grand lodge in Denver. During that first cold winter in Soda Springs, one of the Denver founders helped the bored soldiers of Company H organize a chapter of the society. The principles upon which it was based were "morality, truth, charity, jollity and mirth." Every member, prior to initiation, had to be solemnly impressed with the "absolute necessity of aiding and devising schemes whereby fun can be derived," and had to possess "an unprecedented degree of fortitude . . . to overcome all obstacles, obstructions and impediments which may meet him on his dangerous road." The biggest obstacle for a candidate to overcome was most likely the initiation itself, whose rigors required a prior examination by the hospital steward.

The men at Soda Springs knew how to enjoy themselves, and the first frolic held by the O.T.O. was no exception. Their hall was elaborately decorated for the occasion with wagon covers, American flags and variegated blankets of red, white and blue. With the floor polished as smooth as holy stone could make it, the affair began at eight p.m. when the members entered in full O.T.O. regalia to the strains of the association's overture. Salutations were made to the royal arch, after which members separated to join their partners and, under the direction of the worthy marshal (Private Jack Rainey), the ball began with an introductory march.

Playing the quadrilles, schottishs, reels, polkas and lancers for this affair was an "orchestra" of two violins and a flute, led by one C. P. Hadley, a "truly celebrated violinist, lately imported from Denver," who most likely was the same fellow who had given the soldiers the inspiration for the O.T.O. The dancing went on until midnight when everyone piled into sleighs to be driven to the "Hotel of Klemgard" for a late supper — one of the sleighs overturning on the way in a snowdrift. After eating, it was back to the hall for dancing until "after the drummer had patted Reveille."[11]

A more serious group to form amongst the Californians was the Fenian Brotherhood. With so many Irish serving as soldiers, it was predictable that many under Connor's command would join this significant movement of the era, which would become the inspiration for the Irish Republican Army of today. In 1864 the movement's founder, James Stephens, came to the United States to organize societies in the Union armies and it was from this visit that very active chapters were formed at Camp Douglas and Fort Ruby.

II

The isolation of the people at Camp Douglas and the Gentile businessmen of Salt Lake caused them to become a world unto themselves. Excluded from the Saints' homes and activities, soldiers and civilians alike took great delight in "Mormon-watching." Every aspect of Mormon life seems to have fascinated the outsiders: the lack of dissension in the church; the Mormon fondness for dancing and their vigorous method of doing it; the barter system in which "Valley Tan" homemade goods or produce were used; the haggling by women in homemade clothes while shopping; Mormon superstitions and their belief in dreams, sayings and visions — all were fair game for comment.

If Mormon-watching was the favorite Gentile diversion, the favorite place to do it was the Salt Lake theater. With Brigham Young as the driving force, a fine playhouse had been completed and opened to the public in March 1862. Being thrifty folk, the Mormons had made nails for the project from the iron they had salvaged after burning General Johnston's wagons in 1857. About 1,500 persons could be seated, and perhaps another 500 accommodated for parties and dancing.[12] Most of the players, stagehands, and orchestra were Mormon members of the "Deseret Dramatic Association" of which Brigham Young was the first president. Some of his daughters — dubbed the "Big Ten" — were active players and dancers. The theater season usually opened in early October and performances were held every Wednesday and Saturday evening. The *Vedette* routinely advertised the playbill and its boorish drama critic just as routinely tore each production to pieces.

At Young's theater, Mormon-watching Gentiles could frequently see firsthand such unusual happenings as a man using a turkey for the price of admission and getting two chickens in change. Women often brought young babies with them and there was a great deal of conversing and socializing. Some patrons enjoyed pails of soup between acts and, on one occasion, a proud matron passed around her new false teeth, the first in the territory. The one custom that probably didn't amuse the Gentile theatergoers was that of concluding each performance by singing "God Bless Brigham Young." It's a safe bet that most of them didn't even hum along.[13]

One observer gave scant notice to the play, but managed to tell his readers all they wanted to hear about polygamy. Brigham, he said, sometimes could be found in his private box with his latest wife, but more often was seen in a conspicuous seat in the parquette from which he could view his multitude of wives, who sat in that part of the theater irreverently known as "Brigham's corral." The wives were said to all lack expression or soul, some sad and dejected looking, and not one possessing anything like an animated or intellectual expression. Seen sitting near Brigham was a noted bishop with four of his wives. The bishop — his hat still on in the presence of the "insignificant part of creation" — took the inside seat, leaving the four ladies outside "as body-guard, probably in case of danger."

The correspondent admitted that most Mormon women were perfectly content with their lot, and that "to be the fourth, sixth, or tenth wife of a bishop or an elder, seems to be the highest ambition of a large portion of the young women." He had even heard one say that she "would not have a man for a husband that she did not consider worthy of more wives than herself!"[14]

The Seldon M. Irwins were the first outsiders engaged to play to Utah audiences. They were in Salt Lake for the season of 1863–64 and again beginning in September 1865. They were the especial favorites of the officers at Camp Douglas. Sometimes required to play up to seven different parts, these two hardy troupers gave their audiences such then unforgettable pieces as "The Corsican Brothers" and "A Day in Seville."

But it was the noted actress, Julia Dean Hayne, who became the queen of the Salt Lake City Theater during her eleven-month engagement beginning in the summer of 1865.[15] Her first performance, on August 11, provided ammunition with which the snobbish *Vedette* reviewer could cut down the unsophisticated Mormon audience. His article, entitled "She Had it Bad," read as follows:

"At least a dozen different remarks, rich and ludicrous, were made by many of the Mormons and the Mormonesses while witnessing Mrs. Julia Dean Hayne in the character of Camille. . . . Unused to the simulations of the stage, and — with not a few — for the first time in a theater, the unlettered immigrants from the pauper precincts of the old world, were no more endowed with thinking power than to absolutely believe that the said artiste's *coughing* as the "consumptive Camille" was *constitutionally* and *strictly* real! Said one old Welsh woman within hearing, 'Praise the Lord! It's too bad the President (meaning Brigham) would allow the dear good lady to play tonight with such a shocking cough!' And another, with an old-fashioned hair-pin holding together a hoary head of hair resembling tow, forced her way from the rear, on to the stage, inquiring of the property man to let her see 'that poor sick lady' that she might give her a few sups of herb decoction which she held in a bottle, that she 'knew would ease the poor creature's throat!' 'What a pity the poor thing's so short of breath,' said one, and 'Dear me but she's got it bad!' said another consumption sympathizer!"[16]

III

Social ostracism led to the formation, in November 1864, of the Gentile organization known as the Young Men's Literary Association, or Y.M.L.A. Captain Hempstead was elected its first president. Some of the active members included Judge Titus, Governor Doty, Captain D. B. Stover, and merchants Frank B. Gilbert, Elias

Ranschoff, Samuel Kahn, and Fred Auerbach. The group rented Daft's Hall, the second story of Daft's store on Main Street, for its literary and social meetings and dances.[17]

Captain Hempstead had just been on a trip to Denver with General Connor, and it was surely the two of them who convinced the Reverend Norman McLeod to leave a comfortable home and a growing congregation in that city and come to Utah. The Congregationalist minister arrived January 18, 1865, under sponsorship of the Y.M.L.A., having also been named by Connor as chaplain of the military district. On the twenty-second he preached his first sermons at Daft's Hall and Camp Douglas. Two weeks later, McLeod opened a Sunday school for some thirty children and about a dozen young men.[18]

Later in the month, McLeod founded the First Christian Society and organized the First Church of Jesus Christ (Congregational). During the year he and the Y.M.L.A. drummed up subscriptions and built Independence Hall on Third South Street in the city. The hall was an adobe structure that seated two hundred or more. The title of the property was vested in the name of the trustees of McLeod's church, including General Connor, Judge Titus, Captain Hempstead, and many others. McLeod began preaching and lecturing there beginning in November. That same month, with Hempstead and Mormon dissidents Sharp Walker and Frank Gilbert as trustees, a "select school" was opened at the hall, with a Miss Louise Seymour as teacher.[19]

While no Catholic churches would be established in Utah until after the Volunteers' departure, possibly the first mass in the territory was celebrated in the Camp Douglas Theater on September 2, 1864 by Father John Raverdy. The priest had been sent into the hinterlands from the Diocese of Santa Fe, and stopped for two days as Connor's guest on his way from Denver to Virginia City, Montana Territory. The mass was attended by the few Catholics in the city, as well as in the camp. Raverdy also baptized six children, one of whom was undoubtedly Connor's year-old daughter, Kate.[20]

Katherine Francis Conner — born in Salt Lake on September 7, 1863 — quickly became the "baby of the regiment." Known as "Brownberry" for the suntan she got from failing to wear her yellow sunbonnets, Kate would later remember that, of all the "gallant officers," Captain Price was her favorite. She shadowed "papa Price"

Captain Charles Hempstead. (Courtesy Fort Douglas Museum)

everywhere, even following him into the dining room when her parents were entertaining, to ask him for part of his dinner.[21]

The personal lives of the Connors seem to have been fairly happy, in spite of their isolation. They were frequent and generous hosts to their officers and Gentile guests and, in one case — a July 4, 1864 party — to such an unlikely personage as Colonel Robert Burton of the Nauvoo Legion.

An incident occurred in Salt Lake City, also in July 1864, which not only gives us a good deal of insight into Connor's temper, his feisty nature and his occasional conflict with a few of his officers, but also gives us a peep at the unmentioned goings-on at Camp Douglas.

On the afternoon of Saturday, July 2, downtown Salt Lake City was abuzz with rumors that General Connor and Captain Izatus Potts of his command had themselves a "rough and tumble" in the public street. Ths proved to be almost, but not quite, correct. It seems that, in March, Potts had been tried by court-martial at Camp Douglas on a charge of having used language unbecoming an officer and a gentleman. The charge apparently had been brought by several of his fellow officers who regarded some of Potts' remarks about the moral condition at Camp Douglas as an imputation against their wives. The charge had been preferred in spite of Potts' explanation that his words had no reference to the officers' wives, but simply to certain "ladies" who had "swarmed" to Douglas, some of whom he had seen when on duty "in various improper places at the latest hour of the evening, and at the earliest hour in the morning."

As a result of the court-martial, army Pacific headquarters suspended Potts from duty for three months without pay. In June he was restored to duty but then, unexpectedly, on July first he was told the War Department had dismissed him from the service effective May 26. The culmination of Potts's story went unreported by the *Vedette*, but appeared as follows in the Mormon press:

"On Saturday the Captain came to town, and, it appears, 'smiled' too much over his 'deliverance,' and while in the ecstasies of his new position he saw the General with some other gentlemen in . . . the Salt Lake House, and there addressed him in relation to his discharge, former service, etc. Gen. Connor, under the circumstances, treated the Captain in a very gentlemanly manner;

and after ineffectually trying to get rid of him, the General withdrew and went into Gilbert's store, where, shortly afterwards, the Captain followed. He put his hand roughly on the General's shoulder, which was quickly resented, and in a moment more the Captain's throat and the General's hand were in close proximity; and following that, with lightning velocity, the General is said to have tapped Gilbert's floor with the Captain's poll, to the entire satiety of the latter. In the scuffle, the General received a slight scratch on the cheek, but with that exception, he came off with all the glory."[22]

In spite of Mormon attempts to closet their women, the soldiers were able to fraternize a good deal with the natives. A good many of the fair sex had come to Camp Douglas and undoubtedly a bit of soldier hanky-panky went on, but the larger percentage of these ladies would end up as honest women. One prominent visitor to Camp Douglas, Samuel Bowles, reported that, by the end of 1864, about twenty-five women — all former Mormons — had gone to California with their discharged soldier husbands. Six months later, he said, some fifty or more women still were in the camp for "protection," or had been "seduced away" from unhappy homes and "fractional husbands," and he thought nearly all these women would find husbands among the soldiers. Bowles also told of a man asking permission to bring his daughters up from the city to save them from polygamy, "into which the bishops and elders of the church were urging them." Many of the women that were "coaxed off" to Camp Douglas were second and third wives of plural marriages.[23]

Another observer said of these Mormon women that they "are ever ready to elope with a Gentile who has the courage and can get away with them. . . . Very naturally, they prefer a whole Gentile to one tenth of a Mormon. The most effectual way of breaking up the whole system would be to send an army of 10,000 unmarried men there, and, protect every man who married and brought a Mormon woman to camp. We might, in this way, get rid of the nuisance without bloodshed, or incurring the odium of religious persecution."[24]

Most of the marriages were performed by Connor's adjutants, the supreme court justices or the commanding officers at the posts, with the general's backing. In one instance, he dispatched some

Nevada cavalrymen to Farmington to take back a child that had been taken forcefully from her mother and new soldier husband.[25] General Connor was careful, however, to give no real cause for Mormon complaint regarding his men. If he would send the cavalry to recover the child of a soldier's new Mormon wife, he also would frequently turn alleged offenders over to Mormon civil authorities for trial, and would punish scrupulously those whom courts-martial had found guilty of crimes against the Utah populace.

IV

Further unsuccessful attempts were made in late 1863 and early 1864 to have the California and Nevada Volunteers ousted from Salt Lake City. Utah's new delegate to Congress, Mr. Kinney, first offered a resolution asking that the Committee on Military Affairs inquire into the causes that had led to the stationing of a large army amongst the loyal people of Utah. This having failed, Kinney appealed to General Halleck, making the familiar argument that Camp Douglas was situated within the corporate limits of the city, "much to the inconvenience of the people." Kinney argued that since it was well known Connor and his men wanted to get into the fight on the Potomac, they should be sent there.[26]

General Connor was, of course, incensed. Asked to comment on Kinney's letter, the Irishman took the opportunity to recite for Halleck all his recent troubles with the Mormons: army contractors were unable to obtain the forage and commodities he needed because of the exorbitant prices being charged, or because the Mormon authorities refused to allow them to be sold; a cavalry detachment sent south for the protection of miners had not been sold forage or given shelter; miners wintering in Franklin had been threatened, abused, and told that they couldn't prospect near Brigham City.[27]

The incident in Franklin is most likely what prompted Connor to publish a second circular, on March 1, 1864, regarding miners. It was similar in content to that which had been issued the previous fall, with one striking exception — it now promised that persons using violence against anyone in pursuit of his lawful occupation would be tried as a public enemy and "punished to the utmost extent of martial law."[28]

Unable to buy much forage, and lacking adequate grazing near Camp Douglas, General Connor had to search for means to prevent his cavalry from becoming dismounted. A logical choice was the old military reservation in Rush Valley. This reserve, southwest of Salt Lake City, had been established in 1855 by Colonel Steptoe and used for winter grazing of animals being taken from Fort Leavenworth to Benicia. In March or April 1864, acting on orders from General Wright, Connor expanded the reservation to about 5,000 acres and, in a related action, purchased the old Camp Crittenden (Floyd) property from the owner for $1,100.

Lieutenant-Colonel Jones and Captain Smith were sent to select a site for a new cavalry camp. The result was establishment that spring of "Camp Relief," just east of Rush Lake near the site of Steptoe's former camp. The two or three acre lake was fed by Clover Creek from the south, and located about two miles south of a remarkable natural earth dam separating the Rush and Toelle valleys. Around it was an abundance of lush grass. Six troops of cavalry horses, all in bad condition, were sent there immediately to graze, and plans were made to harvest hay in the fall. In June a more permanent "Camp Conness" was established nearby on Clover Creek, and Camp Relief, such as it had been, was abandoned.[29]

Part of the cavalry was dispersed in May, with the mission of protecting miners. More important, however, they were being sent out to expand the exploration for precious metals. Berry's Company A was ordered south for three months to Tintic Valley and thence to the Meadow Valley Mining District, one hundred miles west of Cedar City, near present-day Pioche. Here the "Panaker" silver ledges had just been discovered during the winter. Captain Noyes Baldwin and Company B of the Nevada cavalry were dispatched to the Uintah Valley, where they were to establish a supply depot and then proceed to Fort Bridger by the first of August.[30]

Captain Smith and his company were sent with rations for sixty days to scour the Snake River country east of City of Rocks in search of five lodges of hostile Shoshoni who had not joined in the treaties of the previous year, and who lately had committed depredations on emigrants. Catherine Waite, the wife of the former associate justice, and another woman "fleeing from Mormon persecution" accompanied Smith. On May 24, after setting up a base camp fifteen miles east of City of Rocks on the northwest branch of Raft River, Smith provided the two women with an escort to Fort Boise.[31]

All three company commanders were told to devote most of their attention to discovery of precious metals — placer gold in particular — and, if any was found, to inform headquarters immediately.

Captain George Price and Company M were brought back from Fort Bridger and were sent to explore a route for an all-season military road from Salt Lake City to Fort Mojave, Arizona Territory, or to some other point farther up the Colorado River where steamers might bring supplies. Such a road, Connor thought, would both ease his logistic problems and help speed the development and "regeneration" of Utah. Price's task, made more difficult by his poorly-conditioned livestock, would take three months to complete. At its conclusion the captain reported that the road from Salt Lake to the mouth of El Dorado Canyon, seventy-four miles above Fort Mojave, was superior in every respect to the Carson City-Salt Lake route, and that steamboats could navigate easily up river to the canyon.

Although General Connor later would report the shipment of some supplies by Price's route, nothing substantial ever resulted from the expedition, probably because of serious difficulties in navigating the treacherous Colorado that Price failed to recognize. Brigham Young also would attempt to open a route such as Connor had in mind. In October — prompted perhaps by Connor's experiment — he decided to colonize the Virgin and Muddy river valleys. By January 1865 Brigham's plans to build a warehouse at El Dorado canyon were well underway and, at his urging, the Utah Produce Company was organized to ship goods using the route. This effort, like Connor's, would come to naught.[32]

The cavalry companies remaining in Rush Valley after the dispersal — particularly Captain Brown's Company L — got busy prospecting for silver in the mountains east of the new camp. Discoveries by these troopers led to a meeting June eleventh to write bylaws for the Rush Valley Mining District. The new district embraced the west slope of the Oquirrh Mountains and was set off from the original West Mountain district established the previous fall. Some of those involved in establishing the new district were

Captain M. J. Lewis, First Lieutenant Henry R. Miller, Captain S. E. Jocelyn, Corporal E. C. Chase, and Privates Arthur Heitz and James W. Gibson.[33]

The *Vedette* began promoting the area as possibly one of the richest districts in Utah. Extensive ledges of silver-bearing galena were said to crop out everywhere and assays indicated $50 to $195 per ton in silver and $39 in gold. The paper chided Brigham Young for his recent remarks that soldiers and the ungodly never would find the riches of the territory — that when God wanted the gold to be discovered for adornment of the temple, He would disclose it to the prophet. Captain Hempstead disclaimed any ability to prophesy on his own part, but said that "within a twelve month, both gold and silver shall . . . have been found and extracted by gentile and Saint's hands throughout these mountains in quantities to make Saints stare."[34]

The newspaper also took note of a mining notice found stuck over a claim in Rush Valley, which had been signed by some well known ladies — "all of them fully able to control *minors.*" The claim read:

"We, the undersigned, 'strong minded' women, do hereby declare and make manifest our intention and right, to take up 'feet' or anything else in our own names, and to work the same, independent of 'any other man.' Therefore we claim and take up on this 'women's ledge,' two hundred feet each, and two other hundred feet for discovery, with all its dips, spurs, angles, variations, and every other right the law, custom, or guns of this district give to lodes, veins, leads, etc., so taken up, claimed, and possessed."[35]

This remarkable document had been signed by Mrs. Connor, Mrs. Pollock, Mrs. Nevitt and a number of other wives from Camp Douglas.

Prospecting continued during the year in other areas as well. At least two locations in addition to the original "Jordan" were discovered in Bingham Canyon — the "Galena" in January and the "Empire" in February. That summer, one of Connor's men also discovered silver-bearing ore in Little Cottonwood Canyon, which led to organization of the Mountain Lake Mining District. But discoveries to the east of Salt Lake were not destined to be developed until four years later when other men would open mines of remarkable richness, such as the fabulous "Emma."

V

A matter of particular irritation to Brigham Young in this spring of 1864 was the support General Connor was giving to the "Josephite" faction of Mormonism. This group had formed around Emma Smith, first wife of Mormonism's founder, who had chosen to remain with her children in Illinois when Brigham Young won control of the church and led the "Brighamite" exodus to Utah. Emma remarried a certain Lewis C. Bidamon and, with his help, formed a "Reorganized" Church of Jesus Christ of Latter-day Saints, based on her claims that her eldest son, Joseph Smith III, was the rightful successor to his father. The young Smith had been ordained president of the new church in 1860.

Twenty-eight-year-old Edmund C. Briggs was one of those instrumental in convincing Joseph to head the Reorganization. On August 7, 1863, Briggs and companion Alexander McCord arrived in Salt Lake City and, a few days later, visited Brigham Young and twenty-five of his counselors to obtain permission to proselytize. Needless to say, the meeting was unfriendly. Brigham could see no place in Utah for an apostate group, and he promised Briggs and McCord that he would oppose them with all his power — that no home or meetinghouse would welcome Josephite missionaries. Many Mormons still felt affection toward Joseph Smith's children but, like Brigham, they believed Emma had corrupted them — that she was a "wicked, wicked, wicked woman and always was."[36]

Briggs and McCord fell back on the Gentile community. They called first on Governor Doty, who told them he would see that their rights were protected. Other help was given by officers at Camp Douglas and by Secretary Amos Reed and Judge Waite. Briggs was also the Connors' guest on several occasions. The general offered him help and protection and gave him full access to the *Vedette*, which was about to make its debut. Briggs thought Connor was "very much a gentleman," and Johanna a "worthy lady."[37]

General Connor was pleased to help the Josephites in any way he could, since his argument with the Mormon Church mostly concerned disloyalty to the Union and the tenet of polygamy. The young Joseph Smith III proudly pointed out that his people were both loyal and law-abiding and, unlike Brigham Young's "modern polygamic believers," they worshipped "God and not Adam," and did not "believe it to be lawful for any man to have a plurality of wives."[38]

With Connor's help Briggs and McCord preached their message. Joseph Smith III, in fact, would say later that Connor had warned Young that the Josephites must not be molested or mistreated in any way, and that Young would be held personally responsible for their safety. At first the missionaries met in Judge Waite's home, but soon they were speaking at Independence Hall and wherever Gentiles or Mormons would allow them to enter. In spite of any warning Connor might have given, by the spring of 1864, the missionaries were being subjected to much physical and verbal abuse. Their living quarters were pelted with rocks and filth, the men were stoned after a number of meetings and, in one instance, shots were fired at them.[39]

While the Josephites would succeed in establishing only a few local congregations in Utah, they did win a number of converts who chose to migrate eastward out of the territory. That spring, as he would for the next several years, General Connor provided a military escort as far as Green River for a large train.[40]

VI

Patrick Connor's support of the Josephites was undoubtedly a major factor in causing the next crisis he would face in Utah. Unlike the March 1863 imbroglio, however, this time he would not be blessed with a sympathetic superior officer. On July 1, 1864, Brigadier General Wright—out of favor with radical California politicians—was relieved of command by Major General Irvin McDowell.

The camaraderie Connor had experienced with Wright was no more. The new commander—sometimes rude and aloof—was a bad listener, known to defer too much to the wishes of his superiors. He often failed to control his temper, and his personal demeanor did not arouse any warmth or enthusiasm in his subordinates. This general neither smoked nor drank nor swapped stories but, instead, remained stiffly formal in his dealings with one and all. McDowell had spent his entire career in staff jobs until he had been given command of an army of 35,000 at the battle of First Bull Run. Since his defeat in that fight he had been dogged with failure. Finding himself exiled to California surely hadn't improved his personality.

Quick to communicate his philosophies to the new commander, in his first letter Connor recounted his past victories over Mormon and Indian foes, including the steps being taken to encourage mining. Except for continued violations of the anti-polygamy law, he declared, affairs in Utah could be said "to be wearing a cheerful aspect beyond any former period."[41]

Just one week after this rosy report, Connor informed McDowell that Brigham Young had initiated a movement to force a change in the territory's currency from national treasury notes to gold coin, and that a convention was to be held in early August to set prices under the new policy. Commodity prices, already high, were now to rise even more. Connor thought Brigham's motive was to weaken the federal government by depreciating the value of its currency.

A new Mormon newspaper, the *Daily Telegraph*, had just been started on July 5, with T. B. H. Stenhouse as its editor, as an apparent counter to the *Vedette*. While the *Deseret News* had tended to remain above the fray and ignore the *Vedette*, the new sheet, with no visible church ties, would be free to rebut it. Stenhouse, a former postmaster and newspaper correspondent, was a polygamist himself and, at the time, was still a firm believer in Mormonism.

Connor informed McDowell of the new paper and its support for the gold movement and asked for instructions. The ink had hardly dried on his letter when Connor acted without further reference to McDowell. Seemingly on impulse, on July 9 he issued an order designating Captain Hempstead as provost marshal and Captain Brown with cavalry Company L as provost guard in Salt Lake City. A few days earlier, Connor's quartermaster had rented a church-owned adobe building situated directly opposite the south gate of Temple Square, for use as a military storehouse. On Sunday the tenth, Brown's cavalry took possession of the building, just as afternoon worshippers were assembling in the tabernacle across the street.

Once again, farcical posturing ensued. Bishop Sharp attempted to void the lease or restrict the building's use to the purpose for which it had been rented. Brigham rushed back prematurely from a trip to Provo and immediately ordered the southern entrance to

Temple Square sealed up. As in the previous year, he summoned citizen soldiers to duty, and soon Connor's provost guard could hear them marching day and night to fife and drum inside the closed walls of the temple grounds.

While establishment of a provost guard was normal in cities near military posts — and one had been established recently by General McDowell's order in Virginia City — Connor's motives involved more than just a desire to police his soldiers while they were visiting in the city. He had done it, he told McDowell, to check the "machinations of those bold, bad men"[42] who were trying to injure the government by the gold currency movement.

By July 13 General Connor had become genuinely alarmed. He reported one thousand hostile Mormons to be under arms, encouraged by news from the East, and threatening to drive the provost guard from the city. He complained that his command was much scattered but, if conflict came, he felt he could hold his position until reinforcements could arrive from neighboring territories.

Some idea of the anxiety Brigham had caused at Camp Douglas can be garnered from the reminiscences of Corporal Tuttle — from whom we last heard as he was freezing on the banks of the Bear River. He would remember that he was sent with a twelve-pound gun one evening to join Company L in the city. The Mormons had six hundred men on guard that night and, as he was leaving camp, Colonel Pollock told him not to let them get the cannon. "Coln they will never get that gun until they get me,"[43] Tuttle replied, causing Pollock to remind Tuttle not to let the Mormons get him either. After arriving safely in the city, the corporal drilled four men of Brown's Company L nearly all that night in the manual of load and fire.

On July 15 Connor reported that things were quieting down and that danger of conflict had passed, in spite of continuing nightly drills inside Brigham's yard with artillery and infantry. On that same date, McDowell offered his first bit of advice to Connor:

"The Major General Commanding . . . approves of your determination to avoid a conflict with the Mormons. Do so by all means. Is there not some other cause than the mere presence of the guard in the city? Examine closely. Remove the guard and troops rather than their presence should cost a war."[44]

Four days later, Connor was instructed by telegram to withdraw the guard, since the necessity for posting it in the city was "not apparent," and since it might cause "much dissatisfaction." McDowell said he didn't deem it "expedient" to interfere by military force to regulate the currency of the District of Utah.[45]

Connor then wrote a long letter to amplify his telegrams and to explain the background for his actions. McDowell was assured that the provost guard was being used merely as a pretext by Brigham for arousing his people, and that only by firmness had Connor prevented a collision. Connor could continue to accomplish his mission, if sustained in his actions by McDowell, and as long as the military forces in the territory were sufficiently numerous to hold Young in check.[46]

Major McGarry arrived from California on the morning of the twenty-third, hand-carrying a sarcastic and critical letter that McDowell had written on the sixteenth. While the cautious McDowell said he had confidence in Connor, he thought the Utah Commander should ask himself "are we at this time . . . in a condition to undertake to carry on a war against the Mormons?" He wondered if perhaps if all the "bad government and worse morals" in Utah couldn't be overlooked — for at least the present — in order to avoid weakening the government, "now taxed to its utmost and struggling for its very existence."

McDowell reminded Connor that no men were available to reinforce him. He must therefore "avoid contact" with the Mormons, attend to his duty of protecting the mail line and not "endeavor to correct the evil conduct, manifest as it is, of the inhabitants."[47] McDowell said he couldn't give specific instructions from such a distance on how to accomplish this, so he would leave the details to Connor. As a precaution, he had provided Connor with a telegraphic cipher for future communications.

Connor telegraphed McDowell that night, telling him of McGarry's arrival, that all was quiet, and that his wishes would be complied with. But, still unwilling to give up, in another letter the next day Connor said that, if given another three or four companies from Fort Churchill, he would take responsibility for both the protection of the overland mail and a peaceable solution of the Mormon question.

This latest communication dripped with polite sarcasm and intimations of the shame that would come from giving up the good fight. Speaking to McDowell's assistant adjutant general, Connor said he was aware of how difficult it must be, "even after the fullest exposition in writing," for someone at a distance to comprehend fully the state of affairs existing in Utah. Surely by now, however, McDowell understood that, in case of a foreign war, "the overland mail would stand in far more danger from the Mormons than from the Indians" and that it was necessary to impress on Brigham that there was both the intention and power to hold him in check. McDowell could be assured that Connor wouldn't initiate any hostilities as long as peace was possible "without dishonor."[48]

McDowell retreated. He informed Connor that he might keep a "small police guard, less than a company," in the city to keep the troops from committing disorders, but that it was to "have nothing to do with the Mormon question."[49] McDowell said he would send a company of Nevada infantry to Fort Ruby so the companies there could be brought to Camp Douglas, and would arrange to give the remaining Nevada cavalry companies to Connor when he could.

General McDowell didn't tell his superiors anything about the Utah crisis until August 18, when he recapped the whole story and forwarded some of the correspondence. "General Connor," he said, "bears the reputation of being a good soldier, and his last letter [of July 24th] shows he deserves the reputation."[50] But this would not be McDowell's last word regarding Connor's handling of the provost guard crisis.

All the fuss, after all, had not affected the intentions of either side. The guard would remain in the city for nearly two years and the church leaders would proceed with several "gold-basis" price conventions in August, as planned. Scales of regulated prices were set and only gold would be accepted. Brigham Young would justify these actions by claiming a need to insure that adequate subsistence stocks would remain for Mormon use. The thwarted Patrick Connor took the only option that seemed available, and began importing flour from the East, the first train of forty wagons arriving at Camp Douglas within a few weeks.[51]

Kate Connor, only daughter of Major General P. E. Connor, taken about age three. (Courtesy Utah State Historical Society)

Trouble on the Plains 9

"Some men fight when they have to; Some men fight when one comes to them; Now and then a man goes out after a fight. General Connor was one of the latter class."[1]

— C. C. Goodwin, 1913

I

General Connor had been a frequent visitor to the newly-discovered mines in Rush Valley, giving impetus to the exploitation starting to take place there. The Rush Valley Smelting Company was formed in June 1864 by the officers at Camp Douglas and, before another month had passed, a new town was being touted by a "company of enterprising gentlemen" who had surveyed a site about two miles from the mines, at the head of the valley and adjoining the military reservation. This grandiose new burg — called Stockton after Connor's California hometown — was being designed for up to 10,000 residents, and would have sixty blocks of twenty lots each. At the time of the initial report, a first building was nearly completed and was to be opened shortly as a hotel, restaurant and saloon.[2]

A seven-mile long ditch had been dug, through which the creek from East Canyon was now said to be coursing into an immense natural reservoir to the northwest. From the mouth of the reservoir, the stream flowed into a race for quartz mills and sawmills then being constructed. Before emptying into Rush Valley Lake, the creek flowed through yet another smaller reservoir just above the new smelting furnaces being erected in the suburbs south of town. Two furnaces had been finished by mid-August and, according to reports, were satisfactorily tested in the presence of Connor, Judge McCurdy, Colonel Pollock and others.[3] One of these smelters, the "Pioneer," was largely the enterprise of Connor and Lieutenant James Finnerty. The other belonged to the Rush Valley Smelting Company, and was most likely owned by other soldiers.

Most of those who had promoted Rush Valley and labored there during the summer had done so in anticipation of their imminent discharge. In October, the three year period of service for most of the Californians would expire and, to lure men into reenlisting as "Veteran Volunteers," the siren song of regimental recruiting officers had begun as early as the previous February.

The enticements to reenlist in 1864 were not unlike those of today. Not only were good food, clothing and medical attention available, but a soldier could save his money, and at the end have a "nice little fortune, plus the invaluable education of a soldier and a certificate of honorable service in the great war for the preservation of American liberty and Independence, which will be to him and his children a prize more valuable than money and more imperishable than gold and silver."[4]

Anticipating expected losses, in early October General McDowell suggested that Connor and Governor Doty cooperate in recruiting four companies of infantry in Utah. He surmised that since troops in Utah were there simply for the protection of overland communications — and had "no special reference to the Mormons" — church authorities would not oppose raising the companies. Of course, McDowell said, the men who were to command the companies had to be of "unquestionable loyalty to the U.S." Apparently Doty thought such persons might be difficult to find, since he refused to raise the troops, for reasons — as Connor explained to McDowell — "which commended themselves to his judgment, and which he would be pleased to give if the department commander so desires."[5]

Mustering out began on October 4 and continued throughout the month. Considerably more than half of the Californians chose to leave, including such valued officers as Major Gallagher, Captains Black, Hosmer, Smith and Finnerty. The discharged soldiers went in all directions. Some opted to try their luck in the Bannack, Boise or Rush Valley mines. Many in Black's company married Morrisite girls and returned to Soda Springs. A few like Luke Osterhout — who opened a saloon — chose to remain in Salt Lake.

Those returning to California who wished to do so were authorized to ride in an empty government wagon train to Camp Union at Sacramento. On October 27, as the departing train passed the provost guard building off Temple Square, the guard raised a new flag to honor the veterans, evoking a chorus of resounding cheers from soldiers and former soldiers alike. Captain Hempstead made an emotional speech, after which the train moved slowly on, carrying the men to their new lives. Spurred by the departure of this contingent, the *Daily Telegraph* put aside dissension long enough to remark favorably that "some of them were Good Templars and decent men — altogether, we wished them a goodbye, and as they glided away in the distance, we were not so certain but we might yet see worse men than many of the California Volunteers."[6]

By the first of November the process was completed and Connor was left with slightly over 800 men under his command at the various posts. Major McGarry had returned again to California with his headquarters staff, and Companies L and M, under Captains Brown and Price, were the only remaining California cavalry in Utah. Companies C and F of the Nevada cavalry were on duty at Camp Douglas, as was the Nevada cavalry commander, Lieutenant-Colonel Milo George. Fort Bridger was commanded by Major John M. O'Neil and was garrisoned by Companies A and B of the Nevada cavalry. The Third Infantry had now been reduced to a mere battalion of four companies under the command of Lieutenant-Colonel Moore, who would himself resign within a few weeks, apparently still chafing under Connor's brand of leadership.[7]

II

No Indian troubles had occurred in the District of Utah during 1864, save one Cheyenne raid on a mail station near the crossing of the Green River in late July. Such, unfortunately, was not the case in western Nebraska, northeastern Colorado and western Kansas. In these areas, beginning in April, the press of white "civilization" against Indian intractability had brought about fierce raids — principally by Cheyennes — against mail stations, ranches, freighters and emigrants. Stock had been run off, trains plundered and freighters killed and scalped. The burning of stations had interrupted the mail and telegraph for extensive periods of time.

By August, the entire route from some distance east of Fort Kearny all the way to Denver was paralyzed. Settlements in the valley of the Little Blue and areas around the Arkansas River and Fort Larned were struck, men killed, and women and children carried off. Food supplies became critical and many whites fled to the Colorado capital for safety. On the tenth, Governor John Evans wrote the commissioner of Indian affairs, asking him to obtain reenforcement of troops in Colorado and authority to raise a militia. Evans also wired Secretary Stanton stating that a force of 10,000 would be needed to defend and put down hostilities and, unless they could be sent at once, Colorado would be cut off and destroyed. On the twelfth, a proclamation by Evans appeared in the *Rocky Mountain News* authorizing all citizens to pursue, kill and destroy the hostiles and take their property as recompense.[8]

Authority to raise a mounted regiment of 100-day militia was quickly granted and, just as quickly, the Third Colorado was formed, under command of Colonel George L. Shoup. The commander of the District of Colorado, under whose aegis the militia was organized, was Colonel J. M. Chivington who, earlier in the war, had foregone duties as a military chaplain for a commission in which he could fight. While the ambitious Chivington had done a creditable job leading Colorado troops in an attack on Confederates at La Glorieta Pass east of Santa Fe, his intransigence in dealing with the Indian situation had intensified, rather than abated, that problem. He, like Evans, had developed a fierce hatred of red men and was opposed to making peace until they had been thoroughly cowed.

On August 23 Chivington declared martial law in the territory, as Indian raids continued unchecked. During the first two weeks of September, Major-General Samuel R. Curtis, commander of the Department of Kansas at Fort Leavenworth, led an expedition of over 600 troops and Pawnees from Fort Kearny southward into Kansas. Despite continuing depredations, Curtis found no Indians and, before his expedition could be completed, he was recalled to counter a new Confederate threat to Missouri and Kansas from General Sterling Price.

At the instigation of Major Wynkoop, commanding at Fort Lyon, Governor Evans and Chivington held talks with Black Kettle and other Southern Cheyenne and Arapaho chiefs in Denver in late September. Little was accomplished, since both sides refused to accept any responsibility for the present predicament. Neither Evans nor Chivington was ready yet for peace, and both suspected that the chiefs had come to parley only because of the onset of winter. General Curtis also had wired his refusal to come to terms as yet. As the conference ended, Chivington gave the chiefs the impression that when they were ready to lay down their arms, they could go to Major Wynkoop at Fort Lyon to do so. These particular bands therefore moved — some to Fort Lyon and some to Sand Creek, about forty miles northeast of the fort — and began receiving rations. Indian attacks in the region continued.

By October, Ben Holladay had become frantic, claiming to have lost almost half a million dollars thus far during the year. On the fifteenth he wired Secretary Stanton, threatening to stop the mails unless something was done to prevent the depredations. He urged the immediate assignment of General Connor to the job of punishing the marauders, pointing out the "wholesome dread" the Indians now had of his name. With winter approaching, Holladay thought it was the "right time for the work"[9] and that Connor was the man to do it.

The Overland Mail czar was a man by Indians possessed during this period. It was also at his request that, about a week after his appeal to Stanton, General Connor captured the infamous Pocatello, chief of the Bannock Creek Shoshoni. In August, Holladay had begun tri-weekly services from Salt Lake to the Montana mines, Boise and Walla Walla, after winning the contract away from Oliver and Company. Based on the report of one of his assistant superintendents, Holladay complained that Pocatello had been threatening, intimidating and taking food from the keepers of his new stations south of the Snake.

Connor, who thought he had a treaty with Pocatello, was angered by the alleged infractions and quickly ordered his arrest without bothering to consult Indian Superintendent O. H. Irish. A detachment of Nevada cavalry caught the chief within a few days near Brigham City and he was thrown in the Camp Douglas guardhouse. He was interrogated at length by Connor, Governor Doty, Colonel Irish, Holladay and others. Irish even threatened to delay distribution of annuity goods until the matter was settled, but Pocatello repeatedly denied any wrongdoing. General Connor then told his prisoner that he would be questioned further and, if the charges were not sustained, he would be released and compensated for his detention. If, however, the charges proved to be true, he would send the chief back to the country where he had murdered so many whites and "hang him between Heaven and earth — a warning to all bad Indians."[10]

Irish, alarmed at Connor's threat, made several unsuccessful appeals for the general to allow Pocatello to be tried by civil authorities. To this, Connor replied that more than twenty of his soldiers were buried within sight, "killed by this murderer and his band,"[11] and that he would take sole responsibility for punishing him if guilty. Pocatello had, of course, killed his share of whites in his day, but none had been Connor's soldiers. Irish, his feathers ruffled by rejection of his request, quickly fired off a letter to Commissioner of Indian Affairs William Dole to report the incident.

By November 4 Holladay had decided the charges were "not of the serious character he at first apprehended,"[12] and asked that the matter be dropped. Connor turned Pocatello over to Irish and the Indian was released — and, apparently none too soon. Based on Irish's letter, the matter had been referred to President Lincoln by Dole. Lincoln was said to have directed Stanton, on November 26, to telegraph Connor that he was not to execute the chief. There is no evidence, however, that the telegram was ever sent.

Meanwhile, Ben Holladay's appeal to Secretary Stanton to assign Connor to solve the problems to the east had been answered by General Halleck. Halleck authorized General Connor to extend his protection of the overland route as far east as Fort Kearny, without regard for the lines of Curtis' department. It was an ambiguous order, and Connor tried unsuccessfully the next several days to get command of all troops between Salt Lake City and Kearny. But Halleck, it seems, didn't want to transfer troops or change command arrangements. Connor promptly informed General McDowell of these orders and, believing it to be what Halleck desired, he asked McDowell for permission to send the two California cavalry companies eastward.[13]

Just a few days before receiving Halleck's instructions, General Connor had forwarded a letter to the War Department, via McDowell, requesting a sixty-day leave of absence to take care of private business in New York City. Connor had never taken any leave in his nine years of military service, but he said he now felt his policies had caused such improved conditions in Utah that he could reconcile his duty with such a prolonged absence.[14] He had been spending his every spare hour in Rush Valley and was just then wooing a certain Mr. Warren Leland, owner of the Metropolitan Hotel in New York City, to obtain capital for development of the region.

Leland recently had been given a tour of Stockton, in company with a certain Mr. Crocker and Mr. Nevett, the sutler at Camp Douglas. By now, Stockton — the "Emporium of regenerated Utah" — had thirty buildings, mostly single-story and of adobe, and was said to be quite a lively town compared to the surrounding "saintly" settlements. Major Gallagher had taken up residence there and was trying to farm, mine and run a grocery and dry goods store. His business on "Connor Avenue" was in the town's only two-story building, the upper floor of which was meant to be a Freemason's Hall.[15]

Accounts of Leland's visit readily show the new metropolis was not teetotal. After a demonstration of Connor's smelter, the New Yorker was observed all too frequently entering the "dry" goods store where he established "most cordial and intimate relations with its portly proprietor." Nevett, the "good natured and ever welcome Sutler," was also said to be "continually asking a fellow to take astronomical observations through a peculiar telescope, several of which he carried in a little square box."[16]

After being entertained at a lavish ball in his honor, Leland toured Idaho Territory and Oregon and returned to New York, apparently convinced of the feasibility of Connor's project. That year the Knickerbocker and Argenta Mining and Smelting Company was organized in New York to operate in Rush Valley, and the corporation would expend about $100,000 on mines and material before abandoning the enterprise in 1865.[17]

Connor put aside any thought of taking leave after receiving Halleck's order, and entered wholeheartedly into plans for an Indian campaign. He wired Colonel Chivington, asking if a fight could be had during the winter and how many troops the colonel could spare. A startled Chivington, protective of his authority, asked

General Curtis if department lines had been changed, or if Connor had the authority to give him orders, stating that the mail line was "perfectly protected to Julesburg."[18]

If Chivington didn't want Connor interfering, Governor Evans of Colorado did. In response to a wire Connor had sent him, Evans said he thought the Indians could be chastened that winter, and he urged Connor to bring all the troops he could so that he might "pursue, kill and destroy them."[19]

Still having received no direction from McDowell, on October 30 Connor told him that he would soon start Companies L and M of his California cavalry for Denver and he himself would travel there by stage to gather information, "examine the field,"[20] and make preparations for the campaign he thought would be practicable. If an expedition was not possible, he would put the troops into winter quarters. Accordingly, the general, accompanied by Ben Holladay and Captain Hempstead, left Salt Lake City by stagecoach on November 5 for Denver.

Earlier, in the summer of 1862, Indian raids had caused Holladay to abandon the North Platte route to Salt Lake City and move to a somewhat shorter and safer one. The new road — the Cherokee Trail — ran up the South Platte to the mouth of the Cache la Poudre and followed it to Virginia Dale. From there it traversed the Laramie Plains and, after crossing the North Platte at the mouth of Sage Creek, ran west through Bridger Pass to the Green River and Fort Bridger, where it joined the old route. To provide a military post close to this new lower road, Fort Halleck had been established that fall at the north base of Elk Mountain, where the Cherokee Trail rounded the Medicine Bow range.

During his trip, on the cold, snowy night of November 9, 1864, during a brief rest stop while crossing the continental divide, the general confided to Captain Hempstead some of his youthful dreams of seeing the Rocky Mountains. Tales of the adventures of hunters and trappers had inspired him to enlist as a private in the dragoons, and he felt acute disappointment when he found that his regiment would not be serving in the Rockies. Even after the Mexican War, Connor said, he still had wanted to go there, but instead traveled to California. Now, finally, Captain Hempstead wrote, the "old time private" had achieved his dream.[21]

General Connor stopped at Camp Collins on the thirteenth, and arrived in Denver the following day to meet with Governor Evans and Colonel Chivington. Knowing that Connor was coming, Chivington by now had made his own plans for the Indians, and they didn't involve any outside interference. On the day Connor left Salt Lake, Chivington had replaced Major Wyncoop at Fort Lyon with Major Scott J. Anthony — like himself an avowed Indian hater. Anthony subsequently had given Black Kettle assurances that if his people remained in their camp at Sand Creek, they would be under the protection of Fort Lyon. Upon Connor's arrival, Chivington issued orders for the Third Colorado, then camped at Bijou Basin, to proceed to Fort Lyon, from which place they would march on Sand Creek.[22]

Of his interaction with Connor, Chivington later would say his impression was that Connor had been sent to see if the existing commanders were prosecuting the campaign against the Indians efficiently. He recalled that Connor spoke to him just as he was leaving to overtake his Colorado troops, about November 19, and said:

"'I think from the temper of the men that you have and all I can learn that you will give these Indians a most terrible threshing if you catch them, and if it was in the mountains, and you had them in a cañon and your troops at one end of it and the Bear river at the other, as I had the Pi-Utes, you could catch them; but I am afraid on these plains you won't do it.'

"I said: 'Possibly I may not, but I think I shall . . .'

"And as I was about to ride off he said:

"'If you do catch them wire me just as soon as you can get to a telegraph office, for I shall want to know it, and I start by the next coach for Salt Lake.'

"I promised him I would do so, when he looked back at me and said: 'Colonel, where are these Indians?'

"I said: General, that is the trick that wins in this game. . . . There are but two persons who know their exact location, and they are myself and Colonel George L. Shoup."[23]

Connor seems to have had no hint of Chivington's deception of the Cheyennes, nor of their present peaceful status. Reporting from Denver on November 21 directly to General Halleck, he related that the several district commanders involved had refused him the use of troops for an expedition against the Indian band that he had been told was "now in winter quarters on the Republican Fork and the Arkansas River." He recommended that no campaign be undertaken until one could be sent that would result in their "signal chastisement."[24]

Thwarted, the Utah commander took time to examine the mines at Central and Black Hawk Cities near Denver, then returned to Salt Lake, arriving on November 30. He already had halted Companies L and M at Fort Bridger and told them to go into winter quarters after they had struggled to reach that place through a howling snowstorm. The day before Connor arrived home, Chivington and 700 of his Coloradans descended on the Cheyennes of Black Kettle and White Antelope at Sand Creek to wreak a bloody massacre.

A few months later, when intimations surfaced that Connor had somehow been involved in Chivington's handiwork, the *Vedette* would insist that the Colorado troops were already eighty miles from Denver before Connor ever reached there.[25]

Connor returned to Utah just in time to receive a blistering from General McDowell. In endorsing Connor's leave request, McDowell told General Halleck that the present quiet in Utah had not been achieved due to Connor's efforts, as claimed in the request. Rather, only by Connor's having acquiesced to McDowell's instructions had a war with the Mormons been averted the past summer.

McDowell also complained that Connor had overstepped the bounds of Halleck's instructions by leaving his district and trying to take troops with him, and then by attempting to get command of troops in Colorado so that he might carry out a systematic campaign. The protection Connor had been asked to provide, McDowell said, was to have been only by such forces as he might have been able to detach, and that, since Price's rebel army had been driven off by General Curtis, no further reason existed for Connor to involve himself in affairs outside Utah.[26]

III

It was not long before Colonel Chivington's handiwork came back on Colorado. On January 6 a thousand or more Sioux, Arapaho and Cheyennes, in confederation with the survivors of Sand Creek, overwhelmed Julesburg, 150 miles northeast of Denver.

The attack began when a detachment of soldiers was lured out of nearby Fort Rankin and fifteen of its men killed before they could fight their way back to the post. This was followed by an attack on the mail station, just after the westbound coach had arrived and as the passengers were sitting down to breakfast. Seeing the Indian horde coming, the whites fled to the fort. The stagecoach and station were destroyed and sacked, the squaws carrying off large quantities of flour, sugar and shelled corn. An army paymaster, who had been a passenger on the coach, abandoned his money box in the station. It was broken open and some of the money hacked up and strewed about, but thereafter was ignored — the Indians disappointed to find only bundles of "green paper."

A mule train was attacked the same day, and one man killed. Two former soldiers traveling east in a wagon also were overtaken and struck down. This unfortunate pair had scalps and other "relics" from well-known warriors killed at Sand Creek in their valises, "about which they had talked a great deal on the road."[27] When the Indians broke into the valises and discovered the contents, they were said to be so enraged that they hacked the soldiers' bodies to pieces.

The Julesburg attack caused a renewal of great excitement in Denver and marked the start of a concentrated, two-week Indian rampage in the South Platte Valley to the west of Julesburg. Beginning January 14, four stage stations and nine ranches along seventy-five miles of the road were attacked and, in some cases, burned and plundered. Wagon trains were captured, and the telegraph destroyed. All of the cattle between Julesburg and Wisconsin Ranch — 1,500 head — were driven off in a five-day period. The Indian camps on the north side of the Platte remained safe while warriors crossed the river on the ice to conduct their raids, and the only soldiers available, at Valley Station and Fort Rankin, proved inadequate to drive them away.

General Connor had been hard at work behind the scenes, bypassing the unsupportive McDowell, to obtain the job of quelling the plains Indians. In his report to Halleck of November 21 he had made several recommendations regarding protection of the mail route, alleging that he could guard the road as far east as the Big Blue with only two additional regiments. Connor's plan would place, at each stage station between Nevada's Virginia City and Kiowa Station on the Little Blue, a detachment of five cavalrymen to accompany each coach. Every one or two hundred miles, he would also establish a permanent company or headquarters so that, in emergencies, as much cavalry as was required could be concentrated in a hurry.

That Connor had also been lobbying several important civilians seems apparent. On January 11, 1865, at the urging of Ben Holladay and Senator Samuel C. Pomeroy of Kansas, General Halleck called General Grant's attention to Connor's report, as well as to one submitted by General Curtis. Curtis was by now, however, out of favor with the civilians for his failure to provide adequate protection against the red men.

More light is shed on Connor's efforts in a letter written the next day by Secretary of the Interior J. P. Usher to Secretary Stanton, stating the necessity for removal of the Indians in the Platte and Republican river valleys so that Union Pacific Railroad surveyors could work safely and without being interrupted by attacks as they had been. The secretary said representations had been made to him that, if Connor were to be given authority eastward to the Little Blue along the Union Pacific route, the general could ensure the protection of railroad working parties as well as emigrants against hostile Indians. Usher urged that Connor be given the job.

Construction of the Union Pacific had begun at Omaha in late 1863 and had been proceeding slowly due to a lack of money and manpower, but now, with the war nearly over, work would soon begin in earnest.

Connor's ambition had driven him to focus all the influence he could bring to bear in order to get himself named to the proposed new job. Soon after Usher's letter, Stanton was hit with yet another on the subject, this time from Governor Doty of Utah, mail company representatives Rumfield and Reynolds, Western Union manager G. W. Carleton and others asking that a department be created under Connor, to include Nebraska, Colorado, Utah and Montana. Without it, they said, they felt unable to maintain communication with the East.[28]

A concerned and impatient Governor John Evans wrote General Curtis on January 20 to ask if his Coloradans wouldn't soon be relieved of the "terrible isolation"[29] caused by Chivington's attack. He told Curtis that the Colorado delegate to Congress and Mr. Otis of the mail company had visited with General Grant regarding the problems on the plains, and that the secretary of war was still waiting for Grant to arrive and act on the recommendations, including Connor's, which had been laid before him.

There were two new players in the West who would be affected by any command changes decided upon. The first of these, Major-General John Pope, had just assumed command of the Military Division of the Missouri. The other — subordinate to Pope — was Major-General Grenville Dodge, who had been in command of the Department of Missouri for just about a month.

For a time, before being sent to the relative obscurity of his new assignment, the dark and handsome Pope had been highly regarded. He had been called by Lincoln in June 1862 to take command of the newly-formed Army of Virginia and energize the campaigns of the Eastern theater. Pope announced to his new command that he had come from the West where he was accustomed to seeing the backsides of the enemy, and from an army whose policy it had been to attack and not entrench. Pompous pronouncements such as this had not been enough to prevent Pope from nearly losing the war at Second Bull Run.

Major-General Grenville Dodge had spent his early years as a highly-respected railroad surveyor in the Midwest. At the outbreak of the Civil War, he was living in Council Bluffs, engaged in various mercantile enterprises and in promoting railroad construction. He had entered the war as commander of the Fourth Iowa Infantry and proved himself capable both at the battle of Pea Ridge and later while commanding the Sixteenth Corps of the Army of Tennessee in Georgia. Dodge had become a trusted favorite of Grant by taking possession of and rebuilding the Mobile and Ohio Railroad, thus giving Grant the transportation he needed to support the Chattanooga campaign

Shortly after Dodge took command of the Department of Missouri, he also assumed duties as the de facto chief engineer of the Union Pacific Railroad, although it would be January 1866 before he would be officially so designated. At the time Connor would first meet him, he was receiving $5,000 per year as a "consulting engineer" in addition to his military pay.[30]

On February 1 General Halleck transmitted the recommmendations of Connor and Curtis to General Pope at his headquarters in St. Louis. Grant had returned them to the War Department without giving any instructions, and Halleck therefore assumed that Grant thought there were enough troops on the plains. Halleck himself waffled in taking any action. He thought the extent of the hostilities might have been exaggerated or perhaps even gotten up by Holladay to cover up failures to deliver the mails. Halleck's solution to the problem was to tell Pope to send the papers to Dodge who was to "give the whole matter his immediate care and attention."[31]

No one could convince those along the Platte that hostilities were exaggerated. Julesburg was struck again by a large Indian band on February 2, and now Cheyennes and their confederates were also on the telegraph line to the northwest, destroying wire, cutting and burning poles and attacking stations. For much of the month, troops at Fort Laramie were required to run telegraphic communications by express rider over the broken part of the line.[32] When mail, passengers and freight got through to Denver at all, it was in large, escorted trains. On the sixth, Governor Evans called for six companies of volunteer militia to open the road to Julesburg. Colonel Thomas Moonlight, Chivington's successor as commander of the Colorado district, imposed martial law two days later and closed down all businesses until 360 men were furnished to comply with Evans' appeal.

Somehow, even the soldiers on the line had heard of Connor's proposition to defend it. On February 3, from Sweetwater Telegraph Station, young Hervey Johnson wrote to his sister, Sybil, telling her how the Indian question could be settled:

"The only way to 'cure them out' will be to send out here about fifteen thousand men to go into their villages, and plunder, burn and kill, without regard to age or sex. *They* make no distinctions in their depredations and that is the way to play the game with them. I think very probably there will be something of that kind done in the spring, especially if General Connor takes the management of the concern . . . his troops are all old miners perfect Indian hunters. Not long ago, some of the authorities at Washington asked him if it would be safe for emigrants to cross the plains. He told them if they would give him his way, that they would be perfectly safe in less than sixty days. . . . The plan that is carried on at the fort now would soon play out if Connor was allowed to run the machine. Every day there, one may see old squaws carrying off sacks of flour, bacon beans . . . etc. while their sons are out committing depredations along the road. Such things are not allowed at . . . Camp Douglas and other military posts west of the mountains."[33]

On February 6, with the Indian attacks still continuing, Generals Grant and Halleck were a bit more convinced of the need for action. Halleck told Pope that Connor's plan had been "favorably considered by Grant"[34] and inasmuch as the mail company wanted it so badly, Pope should state his views.

Pope went along with the tide, although he had expressed earlier a preference for another officer. In a somewhat windy communication, he told Halleck he had talked with persons "interested commercially" in Colorado and concluded that it would be desirable to accommodate them, "both to give them confidence in the plans and purposes of the Government and to preclude them from any captious complaints afterward."[35] He suggested that a new Department of the Plains be created at once, with its headquarters in Denver, to give Connor command of the whole region. Pope also assured Halleck that, with the addition of two infantry regiments he had been promised, he could place enough men at once into the new department to ensure safety.

Thus the eager and ambitious Irishman had succeeded in winning for himself an expanded responsibility. While it would be over a month before the Department of the Plains was officially created, within just a few days the District of Utah, except for Fort Ruby and the troops in Nevada, was taken from McDowell's Pacific command and included in Dodge's Department of Missouri. Connor was told to proceed to Denver and await his orders.

IV

During this third winter in Utah — the last of the Civil War — matters between the unwanted Volunteer soldiery and their Mormon hosts had changed for the worst. The provost guard crisis and ensuing price conventions had brought about an economic isolation as complete and far-reaching as the social one. General Connor's refusal to buy through the bishops at regulated prices inevitably caused some suffering in the command. Government animals were near starvation at Camp Douglas and Fort Bridger, and a scarcity of wood was causing his men to grumble.

Perhaps partially as a result of Connor's frustrations, in January the *Vedette* became suddenly rabid in its anti-Mormon invective. Captain Hempstead had turned over the editorship to Howard Livingston on December 21, but about this time the Reverend Norman McLeod arrived in Utah, and one must suspect that much of the new bitterness came from his pen. Loyalty, polygamy, "celestial marriage," the belief in blood atonement for the remission of sins, the Mountain Meadows massacre, the question of Utah statehood, the legislature, the practice of tithing which was said to be impoverishing the average citizen to enrich church leaders — all these became fair game for editorials.

Both Stenhouse's "Dead Sea" *Telegraph* and the "church organ" were routinely denigrated, but it was Brigham himself who took most of the insult. He was variously dubbed the "Pasha of the Desert," a "comedian" or the "man of tithing and of many wives." One-line jokes about him were used as column fillers. It was reputed, for example, that "the prettiest girls in Utah marry Young," and that "Brigham was a pig to have so many spare ribs." The Mormon leader was well aware of these changes in Connor's paper. In a January letter to his son, Brigham Jr., and Daniel Wells, he mentioned its unusual bitterness, but thought it would soon exhaust itself for want of fuel.[36]

Another change that surely attracted Brigham's notice, and undoubtedly galled him, was the defection of "destroying angel" Bill Hickman to the Gentile camp. Aside from using him as a guide, General Connor had given Hickman a job investigating the theft of some army mules from the Rush Valley reserve during this winter of 1864-65.[37] According to Hickman, he found and returned the mules, then informed the Salt Lake City police captain of the whereabouts of the "gang of notorious Salt Lake robbers" who had been responsible. Hickman received no reward — instead, he himself was indicted by the grand jury for larceny.

After raising bail of $5,000, he was released and Captain Hempstead was assigned to act as his defense counsel. In a hearing before the probate court, the captain argued that Hickman was in the service of the United States and demanded that he be surrendered for a military trial. The court, however, ruled that Hickman must be tried by civil authorities, inasmuch as there was no war in Utah. Hempstead appealed this and, oddly enough, a few days later Hickman was discharged and the case dropped.[38]

Hickman later said that the judge, police and church were all after him because of his work for Connor. He took credit himself for his sudden release, claiming that after being in court for five days he told the prosecutor that he would "give him just one hour to enter a nolle prosequi in his case" or he would "use up his thieving one-horse court with all its thieving officers."[39]

A strange but mutual respect existed between General Connor and the former Danite. Hickman apparently had broken with Brigham Young about the time of the Morrisite pardon in March 1863. He later said Young had sent for him and told him: "That Gen. Connor is nothing but an Irish ditcher, and don't belong in this country and you are the man to get him out of it." Hickman said he merely laughed and didn't respond to Brigham's request. Six months later, Young purportedly tried to solicit Hickman's talents again, saying that Connor was a bad man and ought to be "used up." He supposedly offered a larger sum of money and suggested that Hickman could do it easily and lay the blame on the Indians, since he traveled with Connor as a guide. Hickman claimed this prompted him, for the first time in his life, to speak up to Young in refusal, saying that Connor was an honorable man, and the best officer in Utah.[40] According to another source, in later years Connor revealed that Hickman had come to him after this second solicitation and told him that "Brigham had promised him a thousand dollars if he would send a ball through my brain and lay the murder to the Indians."[41]

What Connor really thought of the polygamous ruffian can't be said, but Hickman certainly admired the general. Of him, he said that, in all his activities, he "took his own course quietly along, regarding them [the Mormon leaders] as a big dog would the barking of fists, or a locomotive the buzzing of flies."[42]

V

Much has been made by certain historians of a brief period of good feeling that took place at war's end in Utah, just prior to General Connor's departure for his new duties on the plains, but there is no evidence that it resulted in any real change of heart on the part of either faction.

On February 21, after receiving the news of the fall of Charleston, a large, impromptu procession of Gentiles was formed at Camp Douglas and paraded loudly through the city. When passing Brigham's Lion House, the Camp Douglas band defiantly struck up "Kingdom's Coming" and, after patriotic speeches were made on Main Street, the throng returned to camp where Captain Honeyman's artillery fired a 21-gun salute. According to the Gentiles, only one Mormon joined in this celebration.[43]

In an unexplained turnabout just eleven days later, Mormons joined enthusiastically in the festivities in Salt Lake City to celebrate Lincoln's second inauguration. Perhaps the leadership had been stung by previous criticism, or perhaps it was as Stenhouse claimed — when the Confederacy had prevailed, "the Spirit of the Lord was noisy; but when the Union cause was in the ascendency, the preaching in the Tabernacle became more conservative . . . and, on the reinauguration of President Lincoln, the Mormons were most loyal."[44]

A huge parade was held, with several companies of soldiers from Camp Douglas and an even larger number of the Nauvoo Legion. There were two brass bands, throngs of marchers, and sleighs and carriages to carry Grand Marshal Sharp Walker, General Connor and other dignitaries. Two of Ben Holladay's stagecoaches were decked in red, white and blue. Sleighs were draped with banners proclaiming such mottoes as "Uncle Sam's right hand pocket — Bingham Canyon — Gold, Silver and Copper united," and "Give us the Pacific Railroad and we will pay the National debt in ten years." Members of the Young Men's Literary Association were jammed into a large carriage that had portraits of Washington and Lincoln on either side and "between them, held aloft very appropriately by an exceedingly dusky American of African descent, was a beautiful lithograph copy of his immortal 'Proclamation of Emancipation.'" Seen also were a number of conveyances "overflowing with young humanity, who were themselves in similar condition of enthusiasm and made the welkin ring with their rejoicings."[45]

Young Gentile drifter James Miller, in observing the parade, commented on the presence of the 1,300 infantry and 200 cavalry of the Nauvoo Legion. He confided to his diary that the Mormons were uncouth, ragged and undisciplined, and were carrying every variety of weapon known to civilized nations — all rumored to be loaded. He was sure some secret motive had impelled these people, known to be hostile to the government, to turn out with so much display to celebrate Lincoln's inauguration.[46]

After the procession, speeches were given by Chief Justice Titus, representing the Gentiles, and William Hooper, the Mormons. General Connor and his staff were on the speakers' stand, along with Governor Doty, Mayor Smoot, and several prominent Mormons, but Brigham Young was conspicuously absent. Artillery salvos were fired to conclude the ceremonies, and then the Mormon cavalry under Colonel Burton, as a display of courtesy, escorted Connor's troops back to camp.

At four p.m. Mayor Smoot and the city council entertained Colonel George and staff officers at City Hall. Here, the officers were said to have responded heartily to Captain Hempstead's toast to the Mormon civic authorities and they, in turn, "joined noisily" in a tribute to Connor. It was said the general was absent because the affair was "somewhat impromptu" and he was called to camp before the committee could meet with him.[47]

Stenhouse claimed that Connor was greatly moved to see the mass of working people parading and cheering in the streets and by the patriotic sentiments expressed by speakers. The general, he said, approached him with "gentlemanly frankness" to express his pleasure and to let Stenhouse know that he wanted differences to be forgotten. Connor supposedly even proposed bringing an end to the journalistic conflict with the *Telegraph*, saying that "if the Mormon people were desirous of making 'a new departure,' the silence of the *Vedette* was the proper thing."[48]

Indeed, a March 8 editorial in Connor's newspaper, entitled "Let Us Understand Each Other," expressed a willingness to accept at face value the sudden outpouring of Mormon patriotism, But, while its tone would change for a short few months, the bitter tirades of the paper soon returned, inspired by the Reverend McLeod.

On the seventh of March, the evening before he departed Utah for Denver and his new command, General Connor was the honored guest of city authorities at an expensive banquet and ball at the Social Hall. Mormon ladies were supper partners for some twenty-three officers from Camp Douglas. The general drew as a partner Mrs. Smoot, one of the mayor's wives. In spite of rationalization to the contrary, this affair really served only to highlight the depth of division, since Brigham Young, his councillors and their women were conspicuously absent, as were most of the wives from Camp Douglas, who adamantly refused to meet the Mormon women.[49]

It seems likely that an accommodation might have been reached at this point, had Young deigned to show himself at either the parade or the banquet a few days later. A caustic letter the prophet wrote to Daniel Wells and Brigham Jr. on March 13, however, reveals how unchanged he remained in spite of others' attempts toward reconciliation. Noting that the few volunteers remaining in Utah possessed scarcely a single horse fit for use, Young exclaimed "What a change we here behold! . . . You know how lofty they held their heads and how much they hoped to accomplish when they came here," he said, "gaily and jauntily, with all the pomp and circumstance that would be likely to impress the citizens here with respect and fear . . . [and] with horses fat and fine."[50]

Organizing a Campaign 10

"Do tell me what is the popular opinion of this Indian war in the States, no news papers we get even speaks of us, they are all gloating over the close of the war in the south and don't seem to remember the soldiers out here fighting a race, whom it would be flattering to call men."[1]

— Private Hervey Johnson, June 15, 1865, writing from Platte Bridge Station, Dakota Territory to his sister Sybil

I

Not long after Patrick Connor assumed command of the new "District of the Plains" on March 30, 1865, General Dodge sent him clear orders to take control of the entire overland route, "push right on" and make "vigorous war on the Indians." With forces on hand and those being promised, Connor was instructed to keep the hostiles on the defensive and well away from the mail and telegraph lines. Dodge expressed confidence in Connor's ability to infuse new life and discipline in the forces on the plains, and proposed to give him great latitude in his actions in spite of their being strangers to one another. Both he and Connor had been given to understand by Pope that the tribes were to be punished at all costs.[2]

Plans already had been made for General Alfred Sully, commander of the District of Iowa, to leave Sioux City about the first of May with a column of 1,200 cavalry and proceed to the Powder River, some 175 miles north of Fort Laramie. Here he was to establish a large post from which he could operate against the Sioux.

Connor, likewise, was expected to make an immediate expedition northward, cooperating with Sully, but not bound by his movements.

General Connor had won for himself a task of enormous proportions. His command now included the former districts of Utah, Colorado and Nebraska. The telegraph route along the North Platte and Sweetwater Rivers also was still the main trail for westward emigration. This route, together with the Cherokee Trail used for overland mail, comprised over 2,200 miles of road for the new commander to protect, while at the same time trying to prepare for a campaign.

It didn't take the general long to realize he couldn't soon field an expedition. After making an inspection tour from his Denver headquarters eastward to Fort Kearny in early April, he began to see his problems. He initially had only four undermanned cavalry regiments at his disposal — the Eleventh Kansas, Eleventh Ohio, Seventh Iowa and First Nebraska — plus what he had in Utah, and the Colorado militiamen about to be mustered out. Except in his Utah companies, there existed a widespread lack of discipline brought on by a combination of bad leadership, the proximity of war's end and expectation of imminent discharge. Citizens of the region complained, in fact, that their property was in more danger from the volunteer soldiery than from the Indians.[3]

The Sixteenth Kansas Cavalry, intended as the principal unit with which Connor could make an early expedition, was to give him endless fits. The regiment, commanded by Lieutenant-Colonel Sam Walker, took two months to travel from Fort Leavenworth to Fort Kearny, causing General Pope to complain that they had had "time enough to walk to Kearny and return twice."[4] In an attempt to get some reliable cavalry, Captain Brown at Fort Bridger was sent a supply of grain and ordered to march California Companies L and M to Fort Laramie.

Another factor hindering the planned expedition was the almost total lack of logistic support. Wagons, teams, pack mules, camp equipage, commissary stores and ammunition all were in short supply. But lack of horses — and forage for those available — would prove the biggest obstacle, not only to starting an expedition, but simply to protecting the road. It had been a dry spring, the grass was poor and corn forage was consumed faster than it could be received. The trains of corn and other supplies that had started west from Fort Leavenworth in recent months invariably had been seized by army commanders who helped themselves to the contents. When short of transportation, these same officers had adopted the habit of "appropriating" wagons of passing civilians after throwing the owner's possessions onto the road.

Both Generals Connor and Dodge expected that they would be fully supported until the hostiles could be thoroughly subdued. They had, accordingly, made plans for the long term. From the outset, Connor was told to lay in at least a year's worth of supplies at his depots for 12,000 men on the plains and 2,500 in Utah. He also was told to plan on supplying Sully's expedition from stocks at Fort Laramie.

Although Dodge initially cautioned Connor against making purchases or contracts on his own authority, it seems he eventually gave him permission to buy some items on the open market until contracts could be let. Most of the contracts would be made by staff officers in Washington, and would not be completed until May 1. Much to everyone's later surprise, the contractors were given until December 1 to fulfill them. This flaw would prove devastating to the plans that had been laid.

Connor fell to with a will. He organized his command into four sub-districts, each with its respective headquarters at Fort Laramie, Denver, Fort Kearny and Camp Douglas. A staff was formed that included several of his trusted California and Nevada officers. Among other efforts to infuse discipline, he issued a strict set of standing orders to officers in the district, enjoining them to stop their slandering of other officers, to pay their debts on time, and to zealously guard their soldiers' rights — but to stop socializing with them, since the practice was subversive of good order and military discipline.

To protect the roads, Connor hoped to keep the Indians north of the Sweetwater and North Platte. The Third U.S. Volunteer Infantry arrived in early April — the first of several regiments Connor would receive comprised of paroled Confederate prisoners led by Union officers. Companies of these "whitewashed rebs," or "galvanized Yankees," were headquartered at Forts Kearny and Laramie and other smaller posts and then dispersed, twelve to fifteen men per telegraph and mail station. Some cavalry would remain scattered along threatened sections of the telegraph line to aid in repairing damage, but most mounted troops, after relief by infantry, were concentrated at the major posts for use in responding to emergencies.

II

The commander of Connor's North Sub-District at Fort Laramie was Thomas Moonlight, colonel of the Eleventh Kansas Cavalry. As noted earlier, he had for a time been commander of the District of Colorado after Chivington. Moonlight had distinguished himself earlier in the war, but his frustrated ambitions since being assigned to his present duty had made him a most discontented man. Judging from his actions, it appeared that he himself badly wanted to command the expedition planned for Connor. Unhappily, the majority of the forthcoming Indian problems would occur in Moonlight's area.

There had been sporadic attacks along the telegraph line west of Fort Laramie, near Rocky Ridge and Deer Creek. These, along with evidence from scouting forays he had made, convinced Moonlight that Cheyennes were responsible, and that they were operating from a large village somewhere on the Wind or Big Horn Rivers. On May 8, with Connor in St. Louis conferring with General Dodge, the colonel threw together a cavalry force of some 300 and left Platte Bridge, intending to strike the village "by rapid night marches."[5]

A two-day snowstorm, covering what little grass was available, ended Moonlight's ambitions. With James Bridger leading his scouts, a trail was discovered on a tributary of the Wind River that indicated the Indians had moved across to the Powder, but the condition of his horses caused Moonlight to return to Platte Bridge by May 17. In his report of this excursion, Moonlight's recommendations for attacking the Powder River villages sounded suspiciously like the sort of tactics he knew Connor favored and already was planning to use.[6]

Moonlight's frustration at failing to find some Indians to fight may help explain the next incident he was involved in. On May 18 some Indians were discovered to be camped ten miles east of Fort Laramie on the north side of the Platte. The Indian agent, Mr. Elson, took a party of Indian soldiers and, on the twentieth, captured a Sioux chief called Two Face and several of his band, who had in their possession a certain Mrs. Lucinda Eubanks and her one year old daughter.

The twenty-four year old Eubanks, her two small daughters, a six-year old nephew and a neighbor, Miss Laura Roper, had been captured on August 8, 1864 when Cheyennes attacked the Eubanks' home on the Little Blue River. Lucinda had been raped by an old chief and then kept as his wife for a time before being traded in the fall to Two Face, who in turn traded her to Black Foot, another Sioux. Black Foot treated her cruelly, and eventually traded her back to Two Face. She traveled all winter on the North Platte with the Sioux as they made frequent forays against the whites, bringing in scalps and stolen livestock. Her older daughter, age three, and the nephew had been taken away right after capture, and eventually were ransomed by Major Wyncoop, but both had died in Denver before Mrs. Eubanks herself was freed.

One source has said that Two Face was seeking peace and had brought in the white prisoners in response to negotiations for their ransom — that he wanted to trade Eubanks for large quantities of commissary stores.[7] If so, he had kept his merchandise in a wretched condition. Mrs. Eubanks was emaciated and almost naked when she was recovered. After she told Moonlight the location of Black Foot and his village, a party of Indian soldiers found it northeast of Laramie on the Snake Fork. Black Foot surrendered without a fight and was thrown into Moonlight's Fort Laramie guardhouse with Two Face and four others.

According to Moonlight, the chiefs boasted openly that they had killed white men and that they would do it again if let loose. This being the case, on May 26 the colonel "concluded to tie them up by the neck with a trace chain, suspended from a beam of wood, and leave them there without any foothold."[8] Two Face, Black Foot and one other Indian were hung. The three were still swinging in the wind two months later on the bluff northeast of the fort.

Connor's Judge Advocate, Captain Zabriskie, later took the statements of Mrs. Eubanks and of a Mrs. Martin who had been captured from a wagon train traveling at the same time and in the same area as the Eubanks attack. All eleven men in Mrs. Martin's train were killed and she and a nine year old boy were carried off by a party of over sixty-five warriors. During her travels she had seen

Mrs. Eubanks and Miss Roper in a Cheyenne village and, like Eubanks, she had been exposed to a gruesome variety of atrocities before being ransomed and brought to Deer Creek. The testimony of the two women undoubtedly provided General Connor with additional information regarding the warriors' summer plans to leave their families high up on the North Fork of the Powder while they attacked the road.[9]

Whether or not Moonlight's confinement and hanging of the chiefs had anything to do with it, within a few days of their capture, the country west of Fort Laramie came alive with Indians. Two hundred or more swooped down on Deer Creek Station and stole twenty-two horses before being repulsed by the soldier detachment. Five hundred attacked Three Crossings on the Sweetwater, cut large sections of the telegraph wire and burned the poles. Following this, the stage stations at Green River and Rocky Ridge, and the telegraph station at St. Mary's were burned to the ground.

Cavalry detachments sent in pursuit from Forts Laramie and Bridger proved luckless, either arriving too late or finding themselves unable to cross the Platte on their weakened horses. Moonlight distributed the Eleventh Kansas by companies from Platte Bridge to Laramie, and Connor decided he had better garrison every station all the way to Salt Lake City. He also issued instructions for soldiers to carry telegrams by hand to the next station whenever a break in the line should occur. Sub-district commanders were told to organize travelers into trains of at least 100 wagons at Fort Kearny and Junction. Travelers in that year's immense emigration were told to use only the mail road, so that Connor could provide better protection on a single route.

New troubles also broke out west of Fort Halleck. On June 2, after stages stopped running, Lieutenant James Brown of the Eleventh Ohio left the fort with thirty-one men to reopen the route between there and Fort Bridger. Brown and his detachment found Sage Creek Station deserted, and four miles farther on, two dead emigrants were discovered near the road. The next two stations, Pine Grove and Bridger's Pass, were also deserted. The missing stock tenders and drivers, and part of the livestock from the abandoned stations, were found to be congregated farther on at Sulphur Springs.

A tri-weekly service was resumed but, on June 8, a large band of Indians once again attacked Sage Creek, where Brown had left only five troopers. After an hour-long fight the soldiers and two civilians tried to escape and make their way westward to Pine Grove. Although well mounted, they were surrounded the moment they left. In a desperate eight-mile fight, only two of the cavalrymen survived. The soldiers at Pine Grove and at Bridger's Pass joined these two in fleeing even farther to Sulphur Springs.

Next morning, the troopers started back, their backbones stiffened by the arrival of Sergeant McFaddin of the Eleventh who was up the road on escort duty with ten men of Company K. The bodies of two privates were found lying in the road, horribly mutilated. One of the civilians was also found, but the remaining two victims were never discovered.[10]

III

A short distraction from his problems, but perhaps a welcome one to Connor, came in the form of Schuyler Colfax, the speaker of the House of Representatives, who was crossing the plains on his way to Utah and the Pacific coast. Traveling with the forty-two-year-old speaker were Lieutenant-Governor Bross of Illinois, Samuel Bowles, editor of the Springfield, Massachusetts, *Republican* and Albert Richardson of the New York *Tribune*. Colfax — who was destined to be elected U. S. Grant's vice-president in 1868 — had been the publisher of the leading Whig newspaper in northern Indiana before helping to organize the Republican Party in that state and being elected to Congress in 1855. He had served as speaker since 1863.

Colfax and party left Atchison, Kansas, on May 22. Not by chance, Connor and his aide, Captain Jewett, rode in the same coach, returning from the visit with General Dodge in St. Louis. Just a few days before, trouble had broken out on the eastern end of the road. On the Little Blue, some normally peaceful Pawnees had ambushed a detachment of about twenty soldiers — mostly converted Rebels of the Third U.S. Volunteers — who had been sent without arms in a wagon from Leavenworth to Fort Kearny. Seven of the men were killed and the rest wounded. Following this, the eastbound stage between Fort Kearny and Atchison and three stations in the vicinity had been attacked, although without hurt to anyone.[11]

Although exceedingly shorthanded, Generals Connor and Dodge had given much attention to ensure that the speaker went through unharmed. Thus, while Colfax saw a lot of houses and barns ruined in previous depredations, and must have gotten an earful of massacre stories and of Connor's current troubles west of Fort Halleck, his trip was without incident. In recounting it, editor Bowles noted the thorough precautions that had been taken all along the route, assuring his readers that "General Connor has taken command of our party."[12]

Prompted by what he had seen — and probably by what Connor told him — Colfax wired Secretary Stanton from Fort Kearny on the twenty-fourth that "Indians, broken up in small forces, intend attacking whole stage line from bridge, Missouri River."[13]

General Connor got off at Julesburg, where he had moved his headquarters in early May. Bowles described it as being just a village of tents, turf forts and barns, but he considered it well located for Connor's plans. Before the stage resumed its journey, Connor delighted the speaker and his friends with a parting "field" breakfast of canned chicken and oysters eaten from tin plates.

Many opinions had evidently been exchanged, and our P. Edward Connor had made a most favorable impression. Bowles noted that although their host had been in command only two months, "every body hereabouts notes with pride and confidence" the changes already introduced. Soldiers had ceased being thieves and bullies; a better "social tone" was visible in all the mining region; the laws were better respected; soldiers were guarding the whole central line of travel; and there was no longer any real danger — or would not be as soon as a few more troops arrived. All in all, Connor had shown himself to be "both a genuine gentleman and valuable commandant... most fit and efficient for restraining the Indians... [and] for settling the Mormon problem."[14]

The discussions that would have been most startling to overhear — had you and I been in that bouncing stagecoach with these nineteenth century leaders and molders of public opinion — were those concerning the future of the Indians. Of this subject Bowles said:

"Whether the Indians shall be wholly exterminated; or forced into submission and half civilization in limited territories. . . . The choice belongs to the Government. . . . But General Connor will certainly restrain them from violence, and punish them for their barbarities. He believes they may be made useful in building the Pacific Railroad and he has proposed to furnish two thousand of one or two tribes who have already submitted to his authority, and whom he is now supporting at an enormous expense far distant from his base of supplies, to the railroad company for an experiment."[15]

Schuyler Colfax went on to Denver, and thence to Salt Lake City to examine, at first hand, polygamy — one of those "twin relics of barbarism" spoken of at his political party's 1856 convention. The first, slavery, had been disposed of and now Colfax had in mind the elimination of the second. Nearly everyone agreed that the stop at Salt Lake served to make the speaker more determined than ever to act vigorously against it. Historian Tullidge later said that the visit marked the start of a new epoch in Utah — "the crusades" against Mormonism — because of the influence Colfax would come to have as Grant's vice-president.[16]

IV

Generals Dodge and Connor didn't let their preparations for Indian campaigns interfere with the more basic interest the two of them had in nation-building and commerce. Each had projects going which used up soldier manpower that might otherwise have been wielded in the ongoing struggle.

Routes for the Union Pacific Railroad were to be surveyed west of Omaha that summer of 1865. In April, Dodge, who had a vested interest, directed Connor to provide army supplies and assign an escort of fifty men from Fort Kearny to protect and "render all aid" to the railroad division engineer and his surveyors.[17] The general also took a great deal of time and trouble to obtain two army wooden pontoon bridges and have them emplaced across the Loup Fork near Columbus, Nebraska, and across the Platte at Fort Kearny, perhaps to help solve a future transportation problem for the railroad.

In Connor's case, he involved soldiers in a major project to build a new road from Salt Lake City to Denver via Springville, the Uintah

Valley, Hot Sulphur Springs, and Berthoud Pass. This route, combined with the new Smoky Hill Trail from Kansas City, would have allowed direct east-west service through Denver instead of requiring that the mile-high city be served by branch lines. The Colorado legislature had granted Ben Holladay and some associates the right to build a road over the route and, in April 1865, Holladay's agent, Bella M. Hughes, came to Denver to get started. Here he apparently convinced General Connor to provide the necessary manpower.

Connor directed his Utah commander to assist Hughes in doing the work. He explained that he had already decided to build a military road along this route and, when he found that the mail company had a charter from Colorado to build it, he had decided to help. Such a road would open new areas for settlement and save 200 miles, Connor claimed, and would pass through a fertile and well-timbered country where there would be little danger of Indian attack.

Lieutenant-Colonel William M. Johns, commander of the Third Infantry since Jeremiah Moore's resignation, left Camp Douglas with Companies A and B of the battalion on June 8 for what was to be a four-month job. When their task was completed and they arrived in Denver in late September, the Volunteers received a hero's reception. The *Rocky Mountain News* of the twenty-eighth declared that a great work had been done for the people of Colorado and the nation by "opening an infinitely more feasible route."

In spite of the hoopla, work on the road had not been fully completed nor, indeed, was it ever to be finished by the Holladay interests. The soldiers were paid $60 each for their work by Hughes, after which some were discharged and went to work for him, while the remainder returned to Camp Douglas.[18]

V

By the end of May, General Sully still had not gotten away on his Black Hills expedition, but it little mattered because now General Pope cancelled his participation in it. Fears of raids on border settlements by large bodies of Sioux had been expressed recently by General Henry H. Sibley at St. Paul and, at Sibley's urging, Pope ordered Sully to move to Fort Rice, far up the Missouri River. From there he was to operate against the Indians at Devil's Lake.

But Pope was still under political pressure for an expedition. A. W. Hubbard, a congressman from Iowa, had helped obtain an appropriation to survey and build a wagon road from the mouth of the Niobrara River in Nebraska to the Virginia City, Montana, gold fields. The scheme had been cooked up by Hubbard and others interested in building up the commerce of Sioux City. In order to appease competing interests, the act of March 3, 1865, which authorized the road, also provided funds for three others. James A. Sawyers had been named superintendent of the Niobrara project by the secretary of the interior and was at this moment moving with his eighty-five wagons and a military escort toward the Niobrara, from which point he would depart on June 13.

Pope told Dodge that now Connor must get after the Indians and build the Powder River post as soon as possible — by August for certain — so that the wagon road parties could do their work. Pope promised Dodge all the troops he might need for such service and told him, "I have assured Judge Hubbard that you will clear out those Indians. Do not therefore, fail to do it."[19] Dodge, in turn, told Connor — who had only heard of Sawyers' project on April 24 — that the two of them would now have to "take care of the Indians up there."[20] Connor was to establish the new post near the route of travel from Fort Laramie to Montana and strike as soon as possible, even if it meant making two campaigns.

Connor, of course, had been trying to get going ever since he had taken command. After the missing Sixteenth Kansas had been found, he had chosen not to leave because of the condition of his animals and the drain on manpower caused by increased Indian attacks along the line. Now he was waiting for his California cavalry with their good horses to arrive. With General Lee's surrender in April, and with the great national war machine about to be dismantled, the retention of the men Connor already had became questionable. When Dodge received an order to muster out some cavalry in Connor's district, he suspended the order and stated that none would be let go until replacements had arrived. General Grant sustained the suspension but, anticipating future losses, Dodge had begun attempts to procure more cavalry and infantry regiments with plenty of time remaining to serve.

Dodge also laid plans about this time to move a large column from Omaha, up the Loup Fork and along the east base of the Black

Hills. The Second Missouri Regiment of Light Artillery, commanded by Colonel Nelson Cole, was chosen as the main element of this "right" wing of the thrust against the hostiles. This column would be under Connor's control and would act in conjunction with his "left" column, which would be moving to Powder River along the west base of the Black Hills.

As Indian attacks intensified, so did the badgering from Pope. On June 7, he told Dodge, who was in Leavenworth trying to speed things up: "Be sure to attend to the Cheyennes in the Black Hills. I shall rely upon you for this."[21] Dodge, in turn, began harassing Connor, and made plans to travel west to see that Pope's orders were carried out as soon as he could get Connor's promised troops on the way.

Pope was a bitter opponent of soft policies toward Indians and of the treaty system, with its many abuses. When Governor Newton Edmunds of Dakota Territory suggested making peace with the Indians threatening the upper Missouri, Pope replied that no treaty could possibly be made until Sully and Connor had dealt with them.[22] John Pope, exceedingly proud of these Indian views of his, expounded upon them to everyone he could, including General Grant. In correspondence of May 18, the general-in-chief was told of Pope's 1864 letter on the subject to Secretary Stanton. Grant was assured that if Pope's policy was sustained by the government, it would bring "peace at a small cost of money or life."[23]

Orders came down from General Dodge, on June 8, to put a force of 800 to 1,000 cavalry in the field after the Cheyennes, under another officer if necessary, without waiting for more troops. To accomplish this, Connor was told to strip his line of cavalry and Dodge would replace it with more from Leavenworth. The replacements Dodge had in mind were five veteran regiments that had been with Sheridan when Lee surrendered and were supposedly well-mounted, equipped and up to complement. Three of these regiments, belonging to Brigadier General Peter Stagg's Michigan cavalry brigade, had hurriedly left Washington for the plains on the evening of the Grand Review of May 23.

By now, many of Connor's stores were on their way — over 2,000 wagons loaded with supplies for all points on the plains — and what troops were available had been distributed to protect the road. The condition of horses and lack of corn and grass were still matters of concern. The plains commander was just waiting for some corn to arrive before leaving with the Sixteenth Kansas and his two California cavalry companies, which had just arrived at Fort Laramie from Bridger. Unfortunately, the hapless Colonel Moonlight was to spoil these plans.

On June 11 Captain Fouts and about 140 men of the Seventh Iowa Cavalry left Fort Laramie, escorting to Julesburg the 1,500 supposedly friendly Sioux General Connor had thought might be useful in building the railroad. Connor had ordered them moved to Fort Kearny to remove them from the influence of hostile Cheyennes who had been operating from the north against the mail and telegraph lines for several months. Some of these Indians — Spotted Tail's band — had been subsisted at Laramie since the previous winter but others, some sixty lodges of Little Thunder's band, had just "surrendered" in mid-April. Charles Elson, the Indian agent at Laramie, was with Fouts' soldiers and in direct charge of the band. He had a company of civilians to assist him and had brought along some rations for the Indians.

Since they were outwardly friendly and seemed pleased with the move, Colonel Moonlight had not bothered to disarm or dismount the warriors. That Fouts was also confident of a trouble-free journey can be seen by the fact that his family and that of another officer were making the trip — as was the recently-rescued Mrs. Eubanks. After three days, uneventful save for some curious smoke signals to the north, the expedition camped on Horse Creek, sixty miles east of Laramie. That evening the Sioux had a "dog feast" and over 300 warriors sat in secret council.

Next morning at sunrise, Captain John Wilcox of Company B was sent two miles ahead with the advance guard to halt and wait for the wagons and Indians to close up before proceeding. Just as the wagons were arriving, he heard firing to the rear and, assuming trouble, corralled the train. A messenger arrived to report that Fouts had been killed by the Indians while trying to hurry them up, and that now they were arguing amongst themselves. Troops who had been with Fouts reported to Wilcox that they had been unable to stand and fight because their now-dead leader had not thought it necessary to issue them ammunition.

Wilcox went to the scene with an armed detachment to find that Fouts had been stripped and mutilated and the Indians had fled several miles away to the Platte. Wilcox tried to convince them to return but, instead, hundreds of the Indians charged the soldiers. Wilcox extricated his men in a fight in which some of them "acted badly" and, as the troopers retreated to the corral, they were able to recover the mutilated bodies of four more comrades who had been killed.[24]

Reinforcements Wilcox had requested arrived at nine a. m. from Camp Mitchell, but the captain decided against a further fight after he learned that the Sioux had been reinforced by warriors from the north side of the Platte, with whom they had been communicating for days. Colonel Moonlight told Wilcox to join him across the river the next day to chase the Sioux as they fled north, but Wilcox found it impossible to cross. The Indian ponies had made it, but Wilcox said his worn-out horses could not do so. The captain was ordered by Connor to bring his command immediately to Julesburg.

Moonlight's pursuit of the Sioux was to turn out no better than any other of his ventures. By the morning of June 18 he and the three companies of cavalry he had taken with him were well to the northeast of Fort Laramie on Dead Man's Fork. During a halt for breakfast and grazing, Indians surprised his camp and ran off 75 horses. Some of Moonlight's men were Californians of the Second Cavalry under Captain Albert Brown, and 27 of the stolen horses had been theirs.

Captain Brown went in pursuit with about 25 mounted men but, upon finding that the stolen horses were surrounded by over 400 Indians spoiling for a fight, he let discretion get the better of him and withdrew. Moonlight then ordered the tack and saddles of the missing horses destroyed, after which he and many of the men walked 120 miles back to Laramie.

Moonlight's time had run out. The California officers were quick to blame him for the indignity of the walk, and they told Connor so. According to them, Moonlight had disregarded their advice — and that of nearly every trooper — to picket the horses. He had, instead, put them out on herd. Moonlight, in turn, maintained that many of Brown's men didn't have picket ropes or pins. Needless to say, Connor believed the Californians, and his rage at losing so many good horses caused him to summarily relieve Moonlight of command and order him to be mustered out. Frustrated by renewed attacks on the Overland, loss of the horses and contractor delays, Connor told Dodge: "Everything appears to work unfavorably — I will overcome all obstacles, however, in a short time.[25]

VI

By mid-June, the plains around Julesburg were dotted with the tents of the Powder River expedition. Troops and supply trains were crossing the South Platte on a rickety ferry to proceed to the concentration point at Fort Laramie as fast as Connor could push them. The Sixteenth Kansas Cavalry had already gone forward. A few supplies had begun to arrive from the Missouri River, and the troops were said to be ready to march as soon as enough subsistence stores arrived.

Indian attacks were so intense by now that every mile of the two routes required protection. The telegraph line west of Fort Laramie was being cut almost daily and became next to impossible to keep in repair. The area between Sweetwater Station and Three Crossings was perhaps the hardest hit. On the twentieth, the operator at Sweetwater — a soldier of the Eleventh Ohio named Edgar Gwynn — was killed by Indians while out repairing the line with other soldiers. He was later found naked with nineteen arrows in his body, scalped, his hands cut off, the sinews taken out of his legs and arms, and his heart and liver removed.[26]

The mails west of Denver were still being frequently interrupted as well. For ten days in June they were stopped when all of the mail company's horses on the hundred-mile stretch between Fort Halleck and Duck Lake were driven off. Upon Connor's orders to see that the mails were delivered without fail, the guard was increased at each station from Big Laramie as far west as available troops would reach. Until the mail company regained its courage and replaced its livestock, cavalry horses were used to haul stages, and soldier drivers were put in the boxes. Writing for the benefit of the papers, Captain Price said of the orders: "There is the old Utah ring in that dispatch. General Connor does not intend that the 'noble red men of the forest' shall run the Overland Mail coaches."[27] When service was interrupted a second time in early July, General Connor went himself to Camp Collins and once again got things moving using wagons and large escorts.

During this latest outbreak there occurred the first of several mutinies that would come to plague Connor's efforts. Three companies of the Eleventh Kansas had just arrived from Laramie as reinforcements for the troubled area. When the commander at Camp Collins ordered one of them to go down the road and relieve the Ohio cavalry, the soldiers refused, claiming they were out of the service. Another company of the same regiment offered to support the mutiny, but finally other troops on duty at the post compelled the Kansans to go.[28]

The enlistments of the men of the Eleventh had in fact expired, and before his departure, Colonel Moonlight had told them they would be let go at Fort Laramie. Moonlight was himself rebelling at that moment at Fort Kearny. In his case, he refused to provide the proper data required to muster him out. Connor ordered it done without the data.

The frustrated General Connor had by now lost any compassion he might have had for his Indian tormentors. He told Dodge that none of them were to be trusted and they must be "hunted like wolves." Colonel Potter, the sub-district commander at Denver, was ordered to treat all Indians found near the mail route as hostile and henceforth to "show no quarter to male Indians over twelve years of age." In another instance, at Connor's direction, Captain Price instructed the commander at Fort Kearny to receive a small party of Sioux being brought there under escort, keep them disarmed, feed them and treat them kindly, but to "hang any who try to escape."[29] The men were to be made to work for their keep.

Colonel Nelson Cole's right column of Connor's expedition would be the first to get into motion. General Dodge had told staff officers at Leavenworth to furnish Cole's soldiers with ammunition, rations for sixty days, plenty of transport to carry everything, and then to ship the whole lot by steamer to Omaha. His men were expected to start marching the moment their feet touched the dock, but Cole delayed eleven days at Omaha procuring wagons, teamsters and mules and awaiting the arrival of the remainder of his equipment and commissary stores.

Connor had planned that Brevet Brigadier-General H. H. Heath should command Colonel Cole's forces but, unfortunately, once in Omaha, Cole embarrassed everyone by raising the question of rank. Heath, it seems, had never been assigned to duty in his brevet grade by the president, so he was relieved and instructed to pass the verbal orders Connor had given him on to Cole. These included instructions to buy side hobbles for the horses and to hire some good guides who knew the country.

The balance of Cole's commissary and quartermaster stores were expected by steamer in a few days but, on June 30, pushed by Dodge, Connor ordered Cole to purchase what he needed in Omaha and leave immediately. Cole bought about $15,000 worth of goods and tried to get moving, but was further delayed when two companies of his regiment refused to march. The men had not been paid for eight months and wanted to provide for their families before leaving civilization. General Dodge arranged for a paymaster to meet the column on its route and so, at last, the column started its trek on the first of July.

The command comprised eight companies of Cole's Second Missouri Light Artillery — equipped as cavalry — and eight companies of the Twelfth Missouri Cavalry, numbering in all some 1,100 to 1,400 men. The large and cumbersome train consisted of 140 mule-drawn wagons and a section of 3-inch rifled guns.

Cole's written instructions and a map marked with the routes of all the columns were to be hand carried from Connor by a courier who would meet Cole on the Loup Fork near Columbus. The instructions included a set of fire-signals for Connor's use in directing the column and orders that Cole was not to receive overtures of peace or submission from Indians, but instead would "attack and kill every male Indian over twelve years of age."[30] Once again, Cole was told to hire good guides from among the Pawnees at the Indian agency, to which he replied that his command had everything it needed.

Connor and his staff moved to Laramie on July 1, personally escorting some 600 horses he had finally received from the East. At this point, many items of the ration still were missing, as well as ammunition, horseshoes and a variety of other essentials. In reaction to the intense pressure from Dodge and Pope to get moving, Connor himself had ordered large quantities of corn. His contracts had been made with Edward Creighton of the Pacific Telegraph Company at Omaha and a certain Mr. Nolan. In doing this, Connor had bypassed completely the quartermaster in Denver, and that officer became so incensed that he asked to be relieved of duty.[31]

Connor was beginning to curse the "rascally" contractors for the delays. One, Henry S. Buckley, who arrived at Laramie on July 15, refused to transport his stores to Powder River, saying he had already furnished more than his contract called for. To get the job done, Connor took it upon himself to hire Nolan's sixty-four wagons and teams.[32] Frustrated by both the Indians, who were presently enjoying the "best of it," and his suppliers, Connor venomously remarked: "I wish they had Contractor Buckley under their scalping knives."[33]

But the delay could no longer be laid exclusively at the feet of contractors. Heavy rains were falling during most of July, overflowing streams and rivers throughout the entire country and making the road from Fort Leavenworth a morass in which the missing subsistence trains floundered. Some trains took forty days to travel 100 miles. General Dodge, like his subordinate, was totally frustrated, but he told General Pope that, in spite of the many obstacles, "we will overcome it all if it will only stop raining and let us have a few weeks solid road."[34]

Connor now knew where the Indians were and wanted to get at them badly. From some of the Sioux who had killed Captain Fouts, he learned that a large band was at Bear Butte intending to move to Powder River, and that other bands were there and on the Tongue River. Another report had a large band on the Heart River, and Connor was prepared to travel that far and to continue the campaign during the winter if necessary. Connor thought, however, he could finish the business long before that if given a free rein. Dodge assured him the government wouldn't interfere and make peace, and that the handling of it would be left to the army. In this regard, Dodge said, he had sent a dispatch of Connor's relating to the subject to General Grant.[35]

The forces that were to be available for the expeditions and plans for utilizing them had now been finalized. In addition to Cole's force, there would be a push up the center of the Black Hills by Lieutenant-Colonel Sam Walker and his 600 officers and men of the troublesome Sixteenth Kansas. He would leave from Fort Laramie, travel light and, like Cole, would be expected to meet Connor at a general rendezvous on the Rosebud River. Walker would receive the same instructions as Cole regarding killing of male Indians twelve years and older.

General Connor himself intended commanding the left column, leaving direct from Laramie to establish the military post on the headwaters of the Powder or Tongue. After this, he too would proceed to the general rendezvous. His 760-man force would consist of cavalry companies of the Second California, Seventh Iowa, Eleventh Ohio and Colonel J. H. Kidd's Sixth Michigan. There would also be about eighty-four Winnebago and Omaha scouts and a large contingent of Pawnees under Captain Frank North. Connor would take about 195 wagons as well as detachments of artillery and the signal and quartermaster corps. Except for the Michigan companies, all of Connor's men had a good deal of experience in Indian warfare.[36]

While Connor and Dodge had hoped to have a grand total of 12,000 men on the plains, including at least 1,500 cavalry in each of the three columns, less than 6,000 total would finally be obtained for the entire district and only about 2,500 mounted soldiers in the aggregate for the expeditions. The promised regiments had either failed to arrive or, upon arrival, proved to be small, poorly equipped and either dismounted or with large numbers of unserviceable horses.

In the final weeks before departure, more mutinies arose. In each case the men claimed that, since the war was over and they hadn't enlisted to fight Indians, they were entitled to discharge. On July 14 at Fort Leavenworth the Sixth West Virginia Volunteers rebelled when ordered to march to Fort Kearny. When part of the First Nebraska Cavalry at Fort Kearny mutinied a week later, Connor ordered the commander of the sub-district to suppress it with grape and canister and to bring the leaders to trial. Within hours the affair was settled. Dodge's policy remained unchanged. He insisted that no troops could yet be released. Connor was to tell them that they must cheerfully obey the orders, and when the troubles were settled their cases would be considered.[37]

General Connor prepared detailed instructions for his sub-district commanders regarding protection of the road during his absence. If any Indians got past Connor and attacked, they were to be pursued relentlessly, ignoring sub-district lines if necessary. Twenty days' rations were to be ready for instant use, and troopers were to carry salt so they could subsist on game if necessary while in pursuit. Anyone abandoning a trail without first punishing the

Indians would be recommended for dismissal from the service. While no "outrages" were to be committed on women and children, there would be no parlaying until first chastising the offenders.[38] Adjutant Price, who knew Connor's plans, and whom he most likely trusted more than any other subordinate, was left to handle district affairs. Connor planned to communicate frequently with Price by means of express and vedettes.

The worst attack on the line during General Connor's tenure on the plains came only a few days before he left on his expedition. On July 25 about one thousand Sioux, Cheyenne and Arapaho gathered north of the river across from Platte Bridge Station, near what is now Casper, Wyoming. They crossed and attempted to run off livestock from the post, but were repulsed after a skirmish in which both Indian and white losses occurred. The following day, Lieutenant Caspar W. Collins, who just happened to be at the post, was placed in charge of a detail of Eleventh Kansas cavalrymen to relieve a government train arriving from the west.

Collins' party was surrounded and attacked soon after leaving the post, and fought its way back only after another party was sent out to assist, eight soldiers being killed in the retreat. Collins was himself struck down while attempting to aid a wounded soldier. The train they had been trying to reach was surrounded, overwhelmed and all its members, save two, were killed. More than twenty-five whites were killed in the two days of fighting.

The attack disrupted Connor's plans somewhat. On the twenty-seventh, with the Indians destroying the telegraph line west of the bridge, he sent nine cavalry companies to the relief of the garrison and, for a short time, considered marching the entire left column to the bridge. The excitement quickly abated, however, and Connor left Fort Laramie with his staff on the twenty-ninth to join elements of his column forming upstream at La Bonte Station.

At last Connor was in the saddle, riding out to do what he knew best. After having waited five weeks for supplies, without appreciable result, he had obtained what he needed by special purchases, by diverting all subsistence trains bound for Denver and Julesburg to Laramie, and by stripping rations from Fort Kearny and Cottonwood. Now, knowing that a large contractor's train would be only a few days behind him, he could get going.

En route to La Bonte, on the last day of July, Connor received word from Captain Price that part of Walker's Sixteenth Kansas back at Fort Laramie had mutinied the previous night. The mutineers were refusing to go after Indians because their enlistments would expire before the expedition returned. When Walker asked for assistance, Price sent the two California companies and some Eleventh Ohio Cavalry with two howitzers, double-shotted, with orders for Walker to "do his talking with grape and cannister." Price reported that the mutineers had "weakened on the turn,"[39] completely cowed, and that before Walker and his troops left to become Connor's center column, enough men were standing by the colonel to maintain discipline. Price had seven of the ringleaders clapped into irons.

At attempt to suppress information on the movement north had not been successful. Small parties of warriors had already begun to retreat to their villages and the movement must have been completely known amongst the tribes. At Fort Bridger, Shoshoni braves came in from the Powder River region to report that hostile Indians were camped on that stream in large force — about 1,000 lodges in all. Washakie, the *Vedette* confidently reported, "who understands the plan of the campaign, and has perfect knowledge of the locality, declares that the Indians cannot escape."[40]

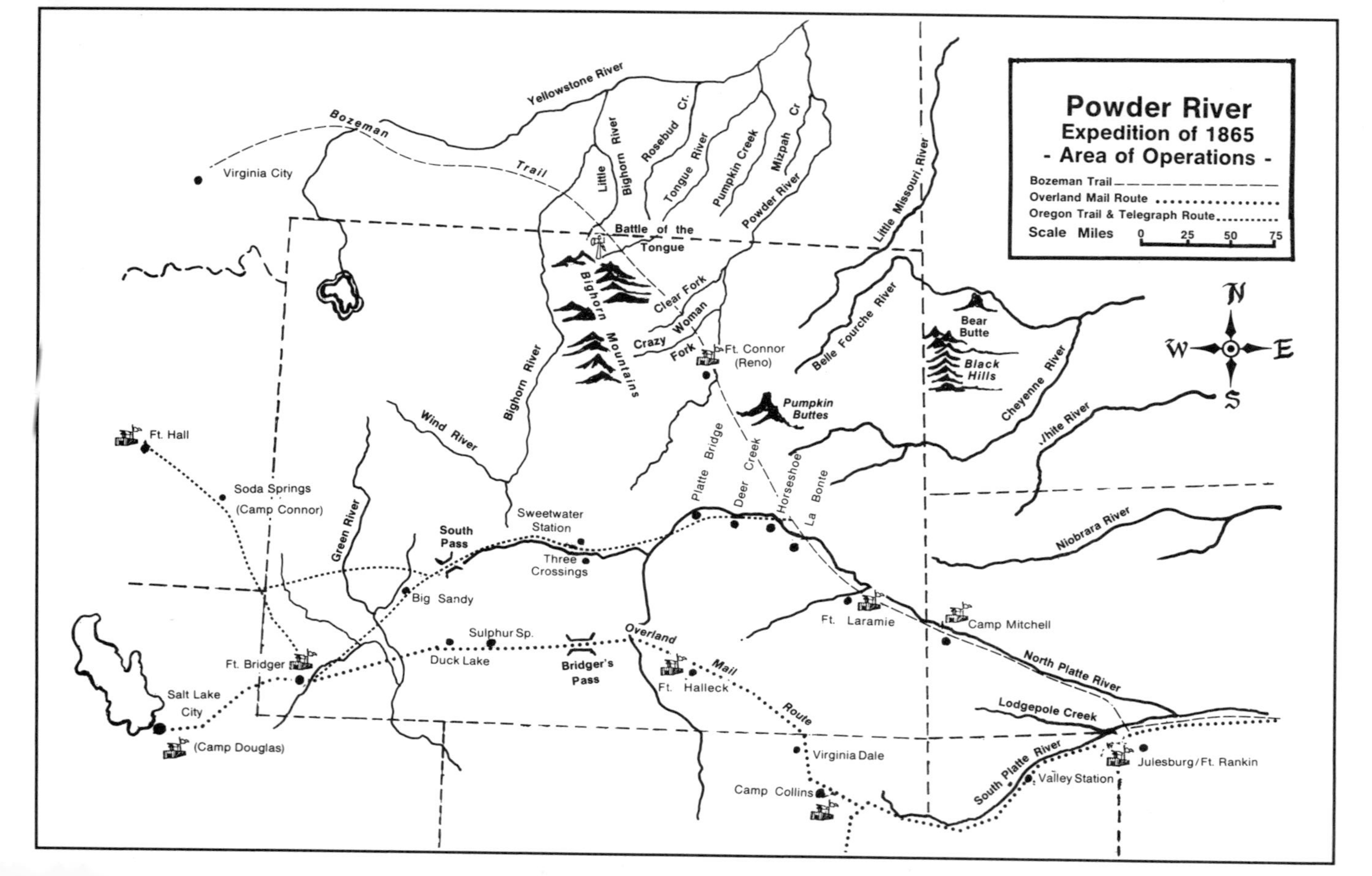
Powder River
Expedition of 1865
- Area of Operations -
Bozeman Trail
Overland Mail Route
Oregon Trail & Telegraph Route
Scale Miles
0
25
50
75
N
S
E
W
Virginia City
Bozeman
Trail
Yellowstone River
Little
Bighorn River
Rosebud Cr.
Tongue River
Pumpkin Creek
Mizpah Cr
Powder River
Little Missouri River
Battle of the
Tongue
Bighorn Mountains
Clear Fork
Woman
Crazy
Fork
Ft. Connor
(Reno)
Belle Fourche River
Bear
Butte
Black
Hills
Cheyenne River
Pumpkin
Buttes
Bighorn River
Wind River
Ft. Hall
Soda Springs
(Camp Connor)
Green River
South
Pass
Sweetwater
Station
Three
Crossings
Platte Bridge
Deer Creek
Horseshoe
La Bonte
Niobrara River
Big Sandy
Sulphur Sp.
Duck Lake
Bridger's
Pass
Overland
Mail
Route
Ft. Bridger
Salt Lake
City
(Camp Douglas)
Ft. Halleck
Ft. Laramie
Camp Mitchell
North Platte River
Lodgepole Creek
Virginia Dale
Camp Collins
South Platte River
Valley Station
Julesburg/Ft. Rankin

Powder River Expedition 11

"During this time there arose disaffection,
And when we required help from the nation,
They talked 'friendly Indian' instead of protection,
And answered our quest with 'investigation.'
Yet an Indian fighter they gave us at last,
To rule o'er our district and whip the red devils,
The 'Hero of Bear River' his lot with us cast,
And we seemed in a way to be rid of these evils;
Brave General Connor went gallantly forth,
Against our cowardly, merciless foe,
And won new laurels away in the north
To deck his honored and worthy brow."

— Denver, Colorado *Rocky Mountain News*, 1866[1]

I

Only a brief summary report, several pages in length, was ever submitted by General Connor after the Powder River expedition, but a number of colorful accounts were written by subordinates. From these and the dispatches surrounding individual events, the progress of the expedition can be traced with considerable accuracy.[2]

General Connor, his guides and the Pawnee scouts arrived at the La Bonte crossing of the North Platte on July 31. By the next day, the remainder of the command — the Californians, the four companies of the Sixth Michigan and the troops from the Seventh Iowa and Eleventh Ohio — all had assembled. With them was perhaps the most impressive array of guides ever seen on a western expedition. Led by the famous Major Jim Bridger, the group included the half-breed brothers Nick and Antoine Janise, Mich Boyer, Jim Daugherty, Antoine LaDeau, J. I. Brannon, mountaineer Jack Stead and Indian traders John Resha (or Richard) and James Bourdeaux.

After some difficulty in finding a ford across the rain-swollen river, the column, with its large train of wagons, traveled for several days up the north bank along the old Mormon Road. At Horse Shoe (near Douglas, Wyoming), on the morning of August 4, Captain Brown and his "west" column of Californians, a train of pack mules, and the seventy Omaha scouts under Captain Nash were detached to proceed upriver to Platte Bridge, thence northwest to reconnoitre the south slope of the Big Horn mountains and into the Wind River valley before rejoining in about three weeks near the Crazy Woman's fork of the Powder.

The headquarters column turned northward, leaving the Platte, to travel a route up Sage Creek valley to the Dry Cheyenne, Antelope Springs and then down the Dry Fork to the main Powder River itself. The terrain proved rough going for wagons but, nonetheless, the roadometer on the headquarters ambulance clicked off about thirteen miles each day. Stagnant pools were often the only source of water.

The general was careful to keep Pawnee scouts out at all times, both ahead and on the column's flanks. No Indians would be seen on this leg of the journey, but apprehension remained high because of the many trails that were crossed. A grass fire caused by the carelessness of some soldiers greatly alarmed Connor and his guides, and raised fears that Indians, seeing the smoke, might congregate and attack.

On the sixth, the command turned nearly north and, by that afternoon, could see the Pumpkin Buttes which rise above the prairie only thirty miles from Powder River. From this point onward, game was more prevalent. The Pawnees began killing buffalo for the camp, lessening the need to eat beef from the herd of some 200 cattle. The scarcity of water was still a problem however and, in his fashion, Connor took charge to see that it would not limit his expedition. On August 8, while stopping for a day to recuperate the mules, the general, his aide Lieutenant Jewett, Jim Bridger, J. I. Brannon and one of the Janise brothers departed on an early morning scout for the next water hole, intending to combine the search with a buffalo hunt.

Invited along was Captain B. F. Rockafellow of the Sixth Michigan Cavalry, one of the diarists whose vivid record of the expedition has survived. A veteran who bore wounds from the Wilderness battle, Rockafellow earlier had expressed resentment that Connor intended to retain personal command of the left column instead of giving it to Colonel Kidd of the Sixth. In Rockafellow's opinion, his regiment would likely see a great deal of hard work from its new Irish leader, for which it would receive but little credit. The captain's assessment of Connor would change after riding alongside him on this day's diversion.

Rockafellow's attempts to bring down several buffalo by firing at them with his revolver, Connor dismissed as being akin to "p— — —g against the wind." To show how it should be done, the general promptly killed a large bull and then finished off another that had already received three ineffective shots from Rockafellow. Later, while chasing a small buffalo herd near the edge of a high bluff, Rockafellow related that "Genl Connor went so much faster than we could that he flanked them and kept them there while we popped into them."

Late in the day, Rockafellow took a bad spill from his horse, putting an end to the hunt. An attentive Connor furnished the captain some whiskey from his flask to rub the hurt and also bade him to "take some inwardly." The men remained at a spring until moonrise, and then moved three miles to make a camp where the bruised captain might recuperate. The general awoke at four a. m., and after giving Rockafellow the last of his "stimulant," ordered the men "to horse" without breakfast. They were soon back with the column, where they learned that scouts had been sent out for them in the fear that they had perished. Of the overnight excursion, Connor was said to have stood it better and with less growling than the rest.[3]

The first distant glimpse of the snow-covered Big Horn Mountains came on August 9, seen eighty-five miles distant to the northwest. To the east of the Big Horns, Bear Butte was visible and a faint outline of the Black Hills could be discerned. On the eleventh, the column moved down the Dry Fork, traveling past a three-week old Indian camp site which had contained over 250 lodges. Also seen throughout the day were a lot of "good Indians" laced up in buffalo skins and hanging from nearby trees. Camp that evening was made on the banks of a rapid and muddy Powder River, the command having traveled, in all, eighty miles since leaving La Bonte.

After a search of the immediate area for a favorable site, construction of Fort Connor, as it was first known, was begun on the fourteenth. The new post was built in stockade fashion on the northeast portion of a large mesa that rose about 100 feet above the west bank of the Powder and extended back about five miles to some bluffs. Twelve foot timbers were cut from a plentiful supply of large trees near the river and the fort, complete with blockhouses, was finished in short order by a combined work force of cavalry soldiers and teamsters.[4]

Opinion was universal that an excellent location had been chosen, situated as it was just south of the new Bozeman Trail and astride the best route for immigration to Virginia City. The place was described as most attractive, with plenty of wood, grass, water and buffalo — its only disadvantage being a lack of nearby hay lands.

With the fort abuilding, the serious business of finding Indians began. On August 15 one of Captain North's Pawnee scouts discovered a war party of Cheyenne about fifteen miles north of the fort. Connor instructed North to get after them, and the Pawnees with several staff officers and others left the fort at three p. m., riding hard. North tried to halt his Indians after dark, but they insisted on continuing. After moving slowly downriver with scouts out, the hostile camp was located in some timber a full sixty miles from the new fort. North and the Pawnees surrounded and attacked the surprised war party, then engaged the enemy in a running fight.

Perhaps the most colorful record of the expedition is that of its egocentric staff quartermaster, Captain Henry E. Palmer of the Eleventh Kansas Cavalry. Of this chase and fight, he recalled that only a few staff officers "who were smart enough to get in front with the Pawnees" were able to keep up. The bloodthirsty Pawnees, Palmer said, rode "like mad devils, dropping their blankets behind them, and all useless paraphernalia," rushing into the fight "half naked, whooping and . . . howling."[5]

The twenty-four hostiles were greatly outnumbered and, in a short engagement, all were killed and scalped without loss to North's contingent. Included in the slaughter were one or two women and a man with a badly-wounded leg who "would in all probability have died" anyway.[6] One of the squaws killed was Yellow Woman, the Cheyenne mother of the Bent brothers. North's victims evidently had been returning from the mail road. They had in their possession eleven government and mail company horses, and a number of white scalps, including one from a blond, curly-haired girl. Their plunder also included government saddles, white women's and children's clothing, and two infantry coats that Colonel Moonlight had issued that spring to the Indians who subsequently killed Captain Fouts and his men of the Seventh Iowa.

Captain Palmer was astonished at the savage delight the aroused Pawnees took in the victory as they rode back to camp with the Cheyenne scalps tied to the end of sticks, "whooping and yelling like so many devils." And, in spite of having been up more than thirty hours, North's Indians danced in celebration that evening. To Palmer, it was the most hideous scene he had ever witnessed, the Pawnees brandishing hatchets and the bloody scalps of their hereditary foe, all the while howling "Hoo yah, hoo yah, hoo yah, hoo you"[7] in time with a drum. The dance continued until well after midnight when a disgusted General Connor ordered the officer-of-the-day to stop it. This victory celebration was renewed several nights running, but with an imposed ten p.m. curfew.

II

General Connor had been communicating frequently by means of express riders to Deer Creek, from which place mail or telegraphic messages could reach Captain Price and thence be sent to Generals Dodge and Pope. Both superiors had been informed of the expedition's progress thus far. After commencing the new post, Connor made known his requirements for an additional four companies of infantry as a permanent garrison, and he asked Captain

Price to ensure that the fort would have 400,000 rations and a million pounds of corn for the coming year. Dodge was informed that Connor's livestock was in fine condition and that the march would be resumed within a few days, after a supply train arrived from Laramie. At this time, Connor still intended to build a second fort on the Tongue River.[8]

The plains commander was stunned to receive by return mail, on August 20, two very sharp reprimands from General Pope. Nine days earlier Pope had received copies of Connor's orders to his commanders regarding the killing of all male Indians over twelve years of age. Pope labeled the orders "atrocious" and "disgraceful," and in direct violation of his own repeated instructions. Dodge was told to have them countermanded, Pope threatening to have Connor's commission, "if not worse,"[9] if they were carried out.

Of course Pope was himself no stranger to ruthlessness or of giving the appearance of it. When he had taken command in northern Virginia in 1862, he had issued a harsh decree calling for the execution of any civilians found aiding guerrillas or breaking the oath of allegiance he required them to take.

General Connor's second rebuke sprang from Pope's having heard "unpleasant news" about Connor ignoring the quartermasters and commissaries in making contracts himself. Dodge was instructed to "stop all this business at once, and order all officers to conform to law and regulations."[10]

Pope's ire in this case was caused by Connor having made the contracts for corn and the civilian transport he needed to carry stores to Powder River. A complaint also had been received from Commissary-General Haines that Connor had ordered the commissary officer at Camp Douglas to contract for fresh beef with Howard Livingston without first advertising for bids. The commissary, Captain E. J. Bennett, had refused to do so and, on Connor's orders, had been arrested for disobedience by the commanding officer at Douglas. Pope ordered Bennett released, and Haines ultimately contracted to have the fresh beef supplied from Kansas.[11] Livingston, the man whom Connor desired to have the contract, was one of the Gentiles who had helped supply Camp Douglas during the difficult winter of 1863-64, when scarcities and Mormon manipulation had caused high prices.

Dodge passed the reprimands along without comment to Connor, saying he had no knowledge of either transgression. A seemingly chastened and dutiful Connor said he would follow Pope's instructions implicitly and would make explanations when he returned. Pope later qualified his initial harsh words — at least with regard to the making of contracts. "I do not mean to say that these expenses were not necessary," he said, "but hereafter, I am sure that with proper management the necessity will not again arise."[12]

John Pope's irascibility toward Connor was, no doubt, due in part to the intense pressure and criticism he himself was experiencing. Even before the Powder River expeditions had left their respective jumping-off places, forces were in motion that would bring censure and embarrassment to Pope, Dodge and Connor and that would ensure failure of their plans, regardless of any success achieved in the field.

First of all, a whirlwind rush to reduce forces and spending had begun at war's end. On May first of that year over a million men had been in army ranks; by November 10, only 183,000 would remain. A second factor adverse to conducting punitive expeditions was the ground swell of Eastern public opinion that arose about this time protesting the inhumanity of national policy — if indeed there was one — toward the Indian peoples. Leading Eastern papers were lobbying vigorously against any further campaigns, urged on by religious societies, all the while waving the bloody shirt of Chivington's barbarity as their example.

Jesse Leavenworth of the Upper Arkansas Indian Agency, thinking peace was possible with the several tribes of his region, went to Washington in April and conferred with General Halleck and Wisconsin Senator James R. Doolittle of the Committee on Indian Affairs. The result was formation of several joint congressional subcommittees to investigate the condition of Indian tribes. Doolittle and one such subcommittee toured Kansas, New Mexico, Colorado and the Indian Territory in June, and intervened to stop an expedition planned by Dodge against hostiles south of the Arkansas River. Following this, on July 25, President Johnson approved the appointment of commissioners to meet with Indian tribes in "grand council" on September 1 at Fort Gibson, Indian Territory.

Such was the state of things when Quartermaster-General Meigs reported to Secretary of War Stanton that requisitions had been received from Grenville Dodge's department for an expedition whose expense was "beyond the capacity of existing appropriations." Transportation estimates alone, Meigs said, exceeded $2,000,000 per month. General Grant was away from Washington for an extended period but, on July 28, Stanton wired him that both Meigs and the commissary-general were in a "state of alarm," and Grant was asked to investigate the matter.[13]

Grant claimed he knew nothing of it, and immediately sent similar telegrams to Generals Sherman and Pope asking them to look into the matter, stop all unnecessary expeditions, and reduce necessary ones to the level actually required. Grant told Pope he thought the cavalry force in the Department of Missouri might be materially reduced.

Having been instructed to cut back, General Pope became a changed man. His first priority was now retrenchment, not punishing Indians. "You don't understand the pressure from Washington on this subject," he told Dodge, as he ordered him to reduce troops and supplies to the lowest possible level.[14] Just as Connor was about to cross the Platte and begin the expedition, he was questioned about his huge supply estimates and, in reply, told Dodge that those in Washington did not understand "the necessities of the service" on the plains; that he required supplies for a greater number of men than were actually assigned, since the troops had to be mobile in winter when supplies were difficult to move.[15]

But Dodge agreed with this, remembering, like Connor, the difficulties they both had experienced in mounting an expedition that spring and summer for want of supplies. Consequently, he urged Grant, through Pope, to maintain a level of supplies for 12,000 men in Connor's area and 7,000 in the southern part of his own department, and to provide more troops in Utah to prevent the Mormon troubles he expected to occur during the winter. But this was not to be.

On August 2, only days after Connor had departed, Pope ordered Dodge to revert to a simple protection of the overland routes as soon as the expedition returned, and to plan on only 4,500 infantry and 2,500 cavalry for that purpose. Utah forces, Pope determined, would be only one infantry and one cavalry regiment. All other troops were to be mustered out by October 15, regardless of how the expedition ended. Dodge was to hurry his expeditions since there existed "a determination" not to keep on the plains or elsewhere in his command during the coming winter any larger force.[16] While Pope had sent Dodge's objections to General Grant, he had no hope they would change the government's goal of reducing troops and supplies.

General Meigs was now at Fort Leavenworth conducting an investigation, and this was causing Pope to continue to fret and look for a place where he might lay the blame. He recently had been relegated downward to command Dodge's Department of the Missouri, and Dodge likewise had been given a lesser responsibility, south and west of the Missouri River, as the Commander, U. S. Forces, Kansas and the Territories. Pope complained that when he had arrived to assume command at Dodge's former headquarters he had found "more than twice as many clerks and five times as many orderlies as were in any manner needed,"[17] and that Dodge did not seem to appreciate the necessity for breaking up posts, mustering out troops, and cutting down on supplies.

Dodge refused to become a scapegoat. On the twelfth he sent Pope an angry response, reminding him that reduction of troops on the plains had come after supplies had been forwarded in accordance with plans presented to Pope and General Grant, which Grant had instructed Pope to carry out. Dodge also said that surely both Pope and General Meigs were aware he had issued instructions that no more supplies were be sent to the plains except by his order. He hoped that Pope would "inform Government of the true state of affairs," so as not to cause prejudice against him.[18]

General Dodge would much later get a peep at Navy Secretary Gideon Welles' diary for the ten days or so beginning August 8, which disclosed, in Dodge's opinion, the abysmal ignorance and incompetence at the presidential and cabinet levels regarding Indian affairs. As recorded by Welles on August 8, Secretary Stanton finally revealed to the cabinet, erroneously and somewhat reluctantly, that "three columns of twenty-two thousand troops were moving into Indian country, with a view to an Indian campaign."[19] Based on his investigation, General Meigs had by now told Stanton that the total expense involved was at least fifty million dollars.

Stanton queried Grant again on the twelfth, telling him of the president's concern and the secretary of the treasury's inability to meet such a large and unexpected expenditure "not sanctioned by the Government."[20] Grant replied he was not aware of the necessity of the expeditions, and they had been planned under Pope's direction. However he would go to St. Louis in a few days and look into the matter and, in the meantime, recommended that all extraordinary requisitions be disapproved.

By August 15, the embarrassed Stanton was telling his cabinet colleagues that the forces moving against the Indians would be reduced to about 6,000 by the first of October. A few days later, Senator Doolittle, freshly returned from his mission on the southern plains, sat in on a cabinet meeting. Secretary Welles thought the Senator's comments in relation to Indian affairs showed well the "folly and wickedness of the expedition which has been gotten up by somebody without authority or the knowledge of the Government." Welles was confident a check had just been put on "a very extraordinary and unaccountable proceeding."[21]

General Grant, still absent, hadn't been working overtime on the problem. In a dispatch to Sherman on August 21, he continued to deny any responsibility for these "expeditions fitting out for [an] Indian hunt."[22] Apparently uninformed as to what Pope had already done, he asked Sherman to consider whether or not the troops in each column might be reduced, or if perhaps the peace council soon to take place at Fort Gibson might render some of Pope's expeditions totally unnecessary.

But General Connor knew nothing yet of these dealings at higher echelons. He knew only that he had just been harshly chastened by the mercurial Pope, and that he must continue his work to a successful conclusion to justify his actions and prove his critics wrong.

III

More scouting parties were sent out from Fort Connor while awaiting the supply train. They reported seeing bands of up to one thousand Indian warriors on different occasions. One well-traveled trail six miles west of the fort, some smaller Indian parties were attacked, resulting in the killing of a few warriors and recovery of some government livestock. One of the dead braves had in his possession letters and a book belonging to soldiers of the Seventh Michigan cavalry.[23]

These sightings and encounters convinced General Connor that the Indians his men were seeing were coming directly from the mail and telegraph lines, abandoning them to reach their families to the north before the soldiers could do so. He believed them to be playing right into his hands.

The supply train arrived and was unloaded on the twenty-first. The following morning, Connor and a force of 250 cavalrymen and 150 Indian soldiers headed north for the general rendezvous at Panther Mountain. A part of the Sixth Michigan under Colonel Kidd was left behind to garrison the fort.

The expedition was now traveling somewhat lighter, but was still encumbered by a large train carrying 50,000 rations and other supplies to support all three columns when they joined. On the second afternoon, camp was made at a place on the Clear Fork of the Powder, with splendid grass and plenty of sparkling, cold water. The troopers had a delightful time bathing and fishing for trout with hooks made of willows. In the evening, an impromptu buffalo drive into a wagon corral near camp netted fifteen animals for the cooks. Captain Palmer recorded that, from this point on into Montana, the country was "perfectly charming" with good grass, rushing streams in every valley, wild cherry, and plentiful groves of cottonwood and quaking aspen.

At this camp, forty-three miles north of Fort Connor, Brown's "west" column rejoined after its excursion through the Big Horns. Brown had come via Fort Connor, and he brought the news that Colonel Sawyers' wagon road party would arrive at the fort that day after having been under attack by Indians.

Sawyers' large expedition had started as scheduled on June 13. His 147-man military escort, under command of Captain George W. Williford, comprised two companies of "galvanized yankees" from the Fifth U. S. Volunteer Infantry and a small detachment of the First Dakota Volunteer Cavalry. The wagon road party had traveled without incident until August 13, when it had been attacked for three days, and three of its members killed, by about 500 Indians. In corral on the fifteenth, Sawyers parleyed with half-breed Charlie Bent and, for a wagon load of goods, obtained a promise of safe passage. Bent and some of the other hostiles reportedly wore army uniforms and traded part of their plentiful supply of greenbacks with the whites for other goods. The Cheyennes present were said to be the same who had killed Lieutenant Collins and his men at Platte Bridge.[24]

Sawyers' scouts had found General Connor's trail down the Dry Fork of the Powder and his company was following it to reach the safety of Fort Connor. His infantry escort, however, was refusing to proceed any farther and had threatened to return to Fort Laramie. Sawyers' plea for help was conveyed by Captain Brown to Connor on the Clear Fork and resulted in Connor ordering Colonel Kidd to assign an escort from the Sixth Michigan.[25]

Thinking he had settled Sawyers' problem, Connor proceeded along the Bozeman Trail past large coal deposits and a flowing oil well. On the morning of the twenty-sixth, the ridge dividing the Powder and Tongue River valleys was reached. From here, through field glasses, could be seen the north end of the Big Horn range and, farther on, the outline of mountains that rose from across the Yellowstone. Directly ahead lay the valley of Peno Creek and, beyond that, the valleys of the Tongue and its tributaries.

On this clear, bright morning, sitting on his horse beside Jim Bridger, Captain Palmer thought this to be surely the grandest view he had ever seen. Palmer had been riding alongside the old scout, listening to tales of forty years on the plains. The two surveyed the scene before them — Palmer with a telescope and Bridger with only his eyes shaded by his hands. The captain later recalled the events which, he claimed, led to the discovery of an Indian village:

"As I lowered my glass the Major said: 'Do you see those 'ere columns of smoke over yonder?' I replied: 'Where, Major?' to which he answered: 'Over by that saddle,'. . . pointing at the same time to a point fully fifty miles away. I again raised my glass to my eyes and took a long, earnest look, and for the life of me could not see any columns of smoke even with a strong field glass. . . . Yet, knowing the peculiarities of my frontier friend, I agreed with him. . . ."

When Connor came up to join Palmer and Bridger, the general was told of the smoke. Even after several careful looks he, like Palmer, was unable to see it. At this, Bridger quietly mounted his horse and rode on. When Palmer caught up with him he found the scout muttering about the "damn paper collar soldiers,"[26] telling him there were no columns of smoke. Bridger seemed indignant that the officers should doubt his ability to outsee them, even aided by their field glasses. Palmer didn't believe the major had seen any columns of smoke either, although an Indian village would later prove to be near the point he had sighted. Bridger understood well enough that it was a favorite locality for Indians to camp, and that, at almost any time, a village could be found there.

On the twenty-seventh and eighth, Connor and his men traveled down Peno Creek and Tongue River. Just after sunset of the second day, as the various messes were fixing their suppers within the wagon corral, two of Captain Frank North's Pawnees came in with news that a large Indian village had been discovered about forty miles distant. Palmer wrote that General Connor — to satisfy Bridger — had sent North and seven Indians in the direction of the supposed smoke two days earlier to reconnoitre. According to Connor's report, however, it was only after arriving at the Tongue River, that very day, and discovering a fresh Indian trail, that scouts were sent out.

Regardless of how the discovery had come about, Bridger and Connor engaged in an animated consultation and plans were soon afoot for an attack. Palmer was called to Connor's tent and told to take charge of the train and livestock, keeping the wagons in corral until his return. The captain was crushed. He had "never been baptized with Indian blood, had never taken a scalp, and now to see the glorious opportunity pass was too much." With tears in his eyes he begged the general to allow Lieutenant Brewer of the Seventh Iowa, who was sick, to remain with the train in his stead so that he, Palmer, could join in "the glorious work of annihilating the savages." How could Connor refuse him?[27]

Supper was hurriedly eaten and, at eight p.m., leaving behind enough troops to guard the train, the remaining men were in the saddle, with Connor leading, riding through the darkness in an attempt to reach the Indian camp before daybreak. Orders were issued for the men not to speak above a whisper; if horses should attempt to whinny, they were to be jerked up with a tight rein. Captain North joined the force shortly after it got underway and he and Bridger guided it up the valley of the Tongue. Progress was difficult as the men wound their way through fallen timber, underbrush and rocky defiles, with only stars to illuminate a black but cloudless night.

By daylight of the twenty-ninth, the Indian camp had not yet been reached. General Connor pushed his men onward, keeping them hidden behind what little cover was available and sometimes having them ride at the water's edge under the river bank in single file to avoid detection. At last, about 7:30 a.m., on a bend of the Tongue, a bit over a mile south of what is today Ranchester, Wyoming, the soldiers found what they had been seeking.

There are as many versions of the discovery of the village and the initial charge into it as there were recorders of the event and, of course, nearly all the chroniclers would take credit for being in the forefront of the battle. Palmer says he had become reckless in his determination to reach the Indian village ahead of Frank North and had worked himself in the advance just as they crossed the Tongue. As he climbed up the bank of a deep ravine, and reached the top, he was startled to see before him an extensive mesa, on which was gathered a huge herd of Indian ponies. To his left about a half-mile was a large Arapaho village.

Palmer threw himself from the saddle and, while keeping his horse silent, retreated back down the bank to tell North and General Connor — who was close behind — that he had discovered the village. Orders were whispered down the line for the column to close up and follow, but not to fire a shot until Connor so indicated. Captain J. L. Humfreville of the Eleventh Ohio was told to take 200 cavalry across the deep ravine and draw up facing the village. Connor followed quickly with the remaining troops and Indian scouts whom he brought into line on the edge of the ravine at right angles and on the flank of Humfreville's troops, forming a large crescent.

The Arapaho — some 700 under chiefs Black Bear and David — may have previously detected Connor. Although one account has the village asleep when the battle began, another says the natives were then in the process of breaking camp. This latter version — Palmer's — says that tepees were down and packed, and that most of the warriors had gotten their horses from the herd of several thousand. In any case, once the troopers began forming to make their charge, the Indian ponies covering the mesa set up a tremendous whinnying and galloped toward the village.

When the last man emerged from the ravine and came into position, General Connor took the lead. The whole line then fired a volley from their carbines into the village, a bugle sounded the charge and the whites — already exhausted from their long midnight march — dashed pell-mell into battle. Outnumbered as they were, all knew their only salvation lay in a quick, unhesitating attack.

Finn Burnett, a freighter working for expedition sutler A. C. Leighton, had, like several other civilians, finagled permission to come along for the fight. His version tells of Leighton, himself, General Connor and the staff leading the charge. In the confusion, he said, they found themselves out in front, caught between fire from their own troops and the Indians. Connor ordered them to lie down on their horses and, just as they did, a ball struck Connor's bugler between the shoulders. The wounded bugler, Richard Yates of the Second California, continued carrying dispatches back and forth over the field the rest of the day.[28]

As for Captain Palmer, as his horse carried him forward almost against his will, he began having second thoughts about his decision to leave the wagon train the previous night. He reminded himself that he had "lost no Indians" and that scalping them "was unmanly, besides being brutal."

The soldiers and their Indian allies were quickly into the village, dealing death, each man acting more or less independently. In the close, sometimes hand-to-hand fighting against both the Arapaho warriors and their women, "unfortunately," Palmer says, the whites had no time to direct their aim. "Bullets from both sides and murderous arrows filled the air," and "squaws and children, as well as warriors, fell among the dead and wounded." Connor's Indian scouts were said to have been especially savage, deliberately killing men, women and children alike, and they themselves — being red men — became special targets for the Arapaho.

Standing near the Arapaho "sweat house," Palmer emptied his revolver into the bodies of three warriors, and then was implored by a fellow cavalryman to help remove an arrow that had passed through the man's open mouth and lodged in the root of his tongue. With only a hospital steward available, it was later decided that to get the arrow out the man's tongue must be — and was — cut out.

In a short time the defending warriors and most of the women and children succeeded in getting out of camp and across the river, in spite of an intense cannonade by the battery of mountain howitzers commanded by Major Nicholas O'Brien of the Seventh Iowa — he a vengeful survivor of the Julesburg raid the previous January. Their possessions abandoned, the Indians made their escape up Wolf Creek through the foothills toward the Big Horn Mountains about twelve miles distant.

General Connor remained in close pursuit for ten miles, leading a running fight. About eleven a.m., when his quarry entered a canyon that looked suspiciously unsafe, he finally halted and discovered that he was accompanied by only three officers and ten men, the horses of his other men having given out during the chase. The Indians, seeing this, turned in an attempt to surround the overextended soldiers and, from this point on, the pursuers became the pursued. Connor and his few men quickly fell back to the Indian camp, contesting every inch of the way, and being reinforced every few moments by stragglers who had been attempting to keep up.

The majority of the Pawnees and Omahas, instead of pursuing the Arapaho, had remained back at the village site to take plunder and capture horses. When Connor returned there, about half past twelve, he ordered the camp destroyed. There were at least 250 — some said as many as four hundred — lodges in the village. Huge fires were made of the scores of buffalo robes, blankets, furs, the dried buffalo meat and tepee covers — all heaped on top of lodge poles. Estimates of the number of horses and mules captured ran from 500, as given by Connor, all the way to the 1,100 claimed by Palmer.

As their camp was being burned, the Arapaho pressed hard on the whites and made several attempts to recover their livestock, but were driven back by supporting fire from the howitzers. Most of the cavalrymen turned their tired horses into the Indian herd and remounted themselves from it, having no little difficulty in lassoing and getting aboard the skittish and bucking Indian ponies.

In the late afternoon, Connor and his men took up the line of march back to the wagon train, some forty miles distant. Captain North and his Indians rode ahead, driving the captured horses that were trying desperately to return to their former owners. The cavalrymen trailed behind to fight off the Arapaho as they dashed in from every side, sometimes to within fifty feet of the rear guard. Before darkness arrived, ammunition became frighteningly scarce, and Black Bear's warriors kept pressing and charging, until finally giving up the chase about midnight. Sanctuary at the wagon train was soon reached in the early morning hours of August 30. By then, Connor and his men were more dead than alive, having ridden over 100 miles to and from the battle, and without rest for more than forty hours. All that most of them had eaten was what jerked buffalo they had stuffed into their pockets at the Indian camp.

The ferocity of the fight with "John Rappaho," and the ruthless killing that took place is evident from some of the anecdotes that have survived. Finn Burnett, for example, told of Major O'Brien's shame when his reflex actions caused him to shoot a squaw who had just thrown a hatchet at him. Palmer recalled that, during the chase up Wolf Creek with the general, one of North's Pawnees picked up a little Arapaho who had fallen by the trail, and the youngster was saved from certain death only by the intervention of a kind-hearted cavalryman.

Humfreville tells of another incident, this one occurring on the return down the canyon. French-Canadian guide Antoine Ladeau, noticing an Indian pretending to be dead under a heap of buffalo skins, rose in his stirrups and shot the hidden Indian with his carbine. The Arapaho "jumped two or three feet from the ground after being shot, and fell a corpse, one of the troopers facetiously remarking, 'Be quiet after this, please,'" which caused a grim smile.[29]

Of his forces, Connor reported only one Omaha scout killed that day, yet other chroniclers mention two whites and three or four of North's Indians being found among the dead. Palmer also mentioned placing "our dead" on the burning piles of plunder so that their bodies would not be later mutilated.[30]

Seven soldiers were wounded. These included General Connor's aide-de-camp, Lieutenant Oscar Jewett, three of the general's orderlies and a sergeant of the signal corps, all of whom Connor said were near him during the engagement. Jewett was shot both through the thigh and hand, yet managed to stay in the saddle for the forty-odd mile ride back to the wagon train. The signal corps sergeant, Charles M. Latham, was shot in the heel. He was a bemedaled veteran of the Army of the Potomac who had passed through the Eastern war unharmed, but who now would die within a few days of tetanus.

General Connor estimated that his men had killed sixty-three warriors, but others put the toll much higher and claimed that the son of Black Bear was one of these victims. Four women and seven children were taken prisoner and brought back to the wagon train. Connor told General Dodge in his reports that these prisoners thought Black Bear would now gladly make peace. Within a few days, Connor gave the captives ponies and sent them with a conciliatory message asking the Arapaho chief to meet him at Fort Laramie about the middle of October.

IV

Connor soon started his elated men northward again down the Tongue and toward the rendezvous. He was now exceedingly concerned about Cole and his right column, having heard nothing of their progress since they passed Columbus, Nebraska Territory on July 6. The general knew that Cole would by now be nearly out of supplies, and fully expected him to be waiting anxiously on the Yellowstone.

The dismal story of Colonel Cole's march is taken mostly from a report he sent to General Grant in 1867, some seventeen months after the event. Two earlier and shorter versions had been submitted, but it appears that Cole later wished to defend against attacks regarding his leadership, and thought an expanded version might "be some value to the Government."[31]

Cole apparently could have used a few of Connor's many good guides. Those employed he described as being "unfamiliar with the country," and the only map he admitted having was that of Lieutenant G. K. Warren, furnished by the chief engineer of the department. After leaving Omaha on July 1, Cole followed along the Platte to Columbus, buying "a sufficiency of forage" and fifty beef cattle from the many farms along the river. At Pawnee Mission, 110 miles from Omaha, civilization was left behind, and the column proceeded up the Loup Fork.

General Connor's orders and prescribed route were received by officer courier on July 12, near the mouth of the north branch of the Loup. After continuing up the Loup Valley, Cole moved generally westward and northwestward, across what is now northern Nebraska and western South Dakota, finally arriving at Bear Butte on August 14. He then took his column around the north base of the Black Hills and, as ordered, struck across country in a north-

rain and snow storms. On September 3, with it still storming, Cole turned back to find grass but, before traveling far, his stock began to die. On this and the following day, over 200 mules and horses would perish from exhaustion, starvation and the extreme cold which followed in the wake of such excessive heat. A number of wagons and a lot of stores, which were "no longer needed," now had to be destroyed.[34]

On the fourth, Cole relocated a few miles away in an area of better grass. A detachment of the Twelfth Missouri, which had been sent back to finish destroying the abandoned property, was set upon by about seventy-five of the "Idaho Militia," as the cavalrymen came to call their Indian enemies. This band was easily repulsed but, as the column was preparing to move the following morning, somewhat larger numbers of warriors were seen in the hills to the west, attempting to cut off Cole's herders. A three hour fight ensued. Early in the battle, only small parties of warriors were involved, rushing the camp to try to draw the soldiers off. But, before long, all of the surrounding hills were covered with Indians. One charge, which resulted in the killing of several soldiers, was made by an estimated one thousand braves. Cole's use of artillery finally drove most of the attackers out of sight, and he was able to move his column upriver twelve miles to better grass.

V

Nelson Cole wasn't the only one beset by red men that September fifth. James Sawyers' wagon road expedition was again under siege a number of miles upstream on the Tongue. Sawyers had left Fort Connor on August 26 and followed in Connor's path up the Bozeman Trail to the Tongue. Here, on the evening of the thirty-first, Captain O. F. Cole of the newly-assigned escort was brought down with four Indian arrows through his body while in advance of the train with another officer. The next morning, just a few miles from the Arapaho's recent defeat by Connor, Sawyers' entire party was set upon by those same angry Indians. Two civilians were killed in the onslaught, and their bodies buried with that of Captain Cole within the corral.

After several days, the Arapaho asked Sawyers to parley, and an arrangement was made whereby each side would send several messengers in company to General Connor — the Arapaho wanting their horses back and Sawyers wanting more protection. This being done, several warriors were held by Sawyers as hostages and the wait was begun for news from the general. On September 4, the three Arapaho who had started as messengers came back into Sawyers' camp to report that many white men were coming, causing all the Arapaho, including hostages, to hastily depart. The white men proved to be Captain James W. Kellogg and twenty-seven men of the Sixth Michigan. While returning from delivering mail to General Connor they also had been attacked by Indians and, after meeting Sawyers' messengers, had decided to make for the camp of the wagon road party. Kellogg sent word of Sawyers' predicament and, when Connor received it on September 5, he quickly dispatched Captain Brown and his company, along with Captain Nash and the Omaha scouts, to render assistance and serve as escort.

Sawyers broke corral on the thirteenth, and headed back for Fort Connor after nearly all of his men and some of the escort refused to go on without help. That evening, the familiar cry "Indians" was heard, but these red men turned out to be Captain Nash's Omaha scouts arriving just in advance of Brown, Jim Bridger and Company L. Sawyers and those who had stood beside him against the mutineers were overjoyed at the sight of the Californians, and nothing in the camp was too good for them. Brown was treated to a bottle of brandied peaches, and the whole company was "wined and dined after the most approved soldier style that circumstances would permit."[35]

The Michigan troops were sent back to Fort Connor, and Sawyers' train started out again toward its goal, now making good time over rolling country and across the Little Big Horn near the place where, eleven years later, Custer would fall. They were threatened once more by Arapaho, but the Indians backed off after seeing Brown's force. Soon after getting Sawyers' party across the Big Horn in wagon box rafts, Brown and most of his men returned to Fort Connor, with Sgt. James Yoacham and seven men detailed to accompany Sawyers' party to Virginia City and then proceed to Camp Douglas.

The sergeant did his duty well, getting Sawyers to Virginia City by October 12. In his report of the expedition, Sawyers expressed gratitude to Yoacham and to General Connor for furnishing reinforcements when he, himself, was surrounded by hostile Indians. The Iowan was most appreciative, however, of Captain Brown, of whom he said: "A better officer than himself, or better troops than those under his command are not to be found in the service."[36]

VI

The groping search by Cole, Walker and Connor to locate one another had become frantic by September 6. On that day, when the headquarters column was near what is now Garland, Montana, General Connor's scouts returned from the Rosebud and the mouth of the Tongue, having found no evidence of the missing columns. Connor theorized that perhaps Cole and Walker's men had deserted so fast that the colonels were compelled to turn back. By means of a large, well-armed express to the Platte, he asked Captain Price to return immediate word if such had been the case.[37] Then, reluctantly, the general began retracing his steps to better grass and Fort Connor. He sent out Captain North and twenty Pawnees toward the Powder River, and Captain Humfreville and part of his company for another look at the Rosebud. Other small scouting parties were sent in every direction in an all-out effort to locate Cole. Connor had seen no Indians since his battle.

Cole and Walker were continuing up the Powder, making eight to twelve miles each day. On the eighth, they were attacked again by a large war party, but managed to repulse them with the aid of artillery. That night, while the two commands were camped together, another hail and snow storm struck, accompanied by a bitter freeze. It continued the next day, forcing the soldiers to move a few miles away into timber for shelter. Huge fires were built and livestock was fed cottonwood boughs but, in spite all that could be done, animals again began dying in large numbers. Walker later would tell how his starving men pounced on the fallen horses to feast on their raw flesh.[38]

In all, 414 horses and mules belonging to Cole and over 100 of Walker's perished in the thirty-six hour storm. The trail was littered with dead animals and the many more wagons, harnesses, saddles and other equipment the two commanders were now forced to destroy. For years afterward, remains of saddles and cinch rings still could be seen at this site near Powderville, Montana.

Still dogged by Indians, Cole and Walker moved up the east bank of the Powder, using artillery to cover their frequent crossings of the quicksand and mud-bordered stream. The storm cleared, but at this point — en route for over seventy days, on one-quarter rations and eating mules and horses to survive — Cole despaired of the future. He thought his soldiers had a right to wonder "why old Indian fighters had not, with their knowledge, planned a more consistent campaign . . . not had a command starving here, unfit to cope with the Indians everywhere around them. . . ."[39]

Across on the Tongue, the storm had also killed several of Connor's animals and had caused the river to rise two feet. Crossing it was impossible for two days. On September 11, the latest scouting parties returned. While others had found nothing, on the Powder Captain North had come across the hundreds of dead cavalry animals and the burned equipment that marked the trail of the missing columns. Seeing signs of the thousands of Indians in the vicinity, and noting that most of the livestock had been shot at the picket line, North had concluded that Cole had been forced to shoot his animals because he had been unable to allow them to forage. More concerned than ever, Connor sent scouts back to the Powder that day with instructions, for both Cole and Walker, to follow them either back to his position or to Fort Connor.[40]

The men who first left with this dispatch were driven back by Indians, so Connor sent it once again on the morning of the fourteenth, adding instructions on the outside of the envelope for the two colonels to bring their columns over to the Tongue immediately. Entrusted with the message this time was Sergeant C. L. Thomas of the Eleventh Ohio, who volunteered, along with another soldier and two Pawnees. Thomas was instructed to travel only by night and to run the gauntlet at all hazards, so that those in the missing columns might not perish with an abundance of food and ammunition so close by.

The same evening that Thomas left, an apparently still concerned Connor sent another one hundred of his soldiers and Pawnees, under Captains North and Marshall, with instructions to fight their way through to Cole and Walker and not to return until they had found them. With Captain Brown away assisting the Sawyers party, the general had, by now, left himself with very few men to protect his train.

Sergeant Thomas reached Cole and Walker on the fifteenth. For his gallantry in leading the scouts in this exploit, he would later be awarded the Congressional Medal of Honor. Both of the colonels chose to ignore the order to join Connor and decided instead to follow the Powder upstream to Fort Connor, thinking it would be impossible to cross the rugged country to the Tongue without water or grass.

After having done all he could for his lost commanders, General Connor laid over for two days to recuperate his weakened mules, then continued up the Tongue. On the evening of the seventeenth, Thomas, the Pawnees and Lieutenant Jones of Cole's Second Missouri Artillery finally rode into camp with the first news of Cole's location. Connor kept moving toward the fort and, on September 22, just two days out, met a detachment sent with information that the destitute columns had reached that place on the twentieth, with half of Cole's men barefoot and one-fourth or more dismounted — in all, a completely disgusted and discouraged outfit.

The detachment carried another message equally as vital, but of more personal interest to Connor. It was a crushing letter from Major-General Pope, telling of the dissolution of the District of the Plains, and ordering its erstwhile commander to proceed at the "earliest practicable moment" to Utah where he was once again to command only that district.[41]

VII

Just a day after General Connor had marched his men northward from Fort Connor to fight the Arapaho, Pope had abolished the Plains district and created once again, in its stead, a number of smaller ones, all under the command of regular army officers. Major-General Frank Wheaton, assigned to the Nebraska district, was ordered to take command of Connor's posts without delay. He was told of the force reductions that were to take place, and the planned reversion to a simple defense of the overland routes. Pope also informed Wheaton of Connor's expedition moving against the hostiles in "five columns." Finally — as though Pope himself had not been involved — the new Nebraska commander was told to collect and store the surplus supplies sent to the plains by Dodge, his "predecessor in command of this department."[42]

Pope made his district changes while Dodge was away, making a long trip to "straighten matters" on the plains. Dodge traveled to Fort Kearny, Julesburg, Fort Laramie and thence to Fort Connor, where he arrived on September 8, 1865, with an escort of 100 Pennsylvania cavalrymen. It was during his two-day stay at the fort that Dodge left Pope's unpleasant orders for Connor, and he departed still unaware of the recent victory on the Tongue or of the fate of Cole and Walker. Dodge had made one last proposal to salvage something of the show. Writing to Pope on August 31, he said that, if he were allowed to keep Connor in the field with about 2,000 men, he would guarantee a satisfactory peace with the Indians by spring. All of the supplies, forage, etc. were already paid for and on hand or en route. If Connor were ordered back, Dodge said, the "tribes will be down on our lines, and we will have our hands full, and more too."[43]

Pope would reply only that the pressure on him about expenses on the plains was tremendous, that the commissioners would meet the Indians as planned, and that, "whether reasonable or not, the demands of the Government must be complied with."[44]

Trying to clarify his orders — or, more likely, having second thoughts — Pope telegraphed Dodge on September 5 that the new district arrangements were to affect Connor only *after* his operations were ended and he resolved to return himself.[45] But Pope's change of heart came too late. Dodge was in the boondocks, and likely didn't see Pope's message until his return to the telegraph line on September 15. There is no evidence that he ever acted on it.

Two days after reaching Fort Connor, the dejected General Connor left for Laramie, leaving Cole to command the combined columns as they returned by slow marches. Captain North and his Indians accompanied the general, driving what remained of the captured Indian horses — some 500 or 600 head. On the day he left, traveling in his ambulance, Connor passed part of Cole's men starting out on the road. Seeing that some of them were barefoot, he took the boots from his own feet and gave them to the men. He also directed a train of forty wagons to carry some of the more footsore.[46]

From Connor's arrival at Fort Laramie on the thirtieth, until he left four days later for Denver, dispatches went out to the press glorifying the campaign and lobbying for its continuance. Four pitched battles were said to have been fought with Cheyennes, Sioux and Arapaho, resulting in 400 to 500 Indians having been killed and an entire village destroyed. The Arapaho were represented as now being thoroughly cowed and supposedly en route to Laramie, suing for peace, but the Sioux and Cheyenne were "not yet half whipped." Not less than 1,500 men should be stationed at Fort Connor, and the campaign continued into the winter to keep these tribes from coming back down on the mail and telegraph lines.[47]

One can see Connor's broken plans and sense of rejection poking through his post expedition report and the other documents that have survived. He was eager to go on fighting, and would have continued the campaign for at least forty more days. He had planned to return to Fort Connor, reorganize, and then go after the large bodies of Sioux and Cheyenne that he believed were camped on the headwaters of the Little Missouri or on the small streams near where the Powder River empties into the Yellowstone. Captain Brown, knowledgeable of the plan, later said that this "was the destination long sought for by Connor, and an opportunity to settle by one quick, decisive blow the whole Indian troubles of the Plains."[48]

Another observer, Finn Burnett, said an angry Connor planned to disobey the order to cease hostilities and suffer the consequences, but that his officers pleaded with him not to do so because he would be cashiered and dishonored. If the order had been disobeyed, Burnett thought, "there would have been no Fetterman massacre, no Custer battle, no eleven years of Indian atrocities, thousands of lives would have been saved, and the settlement of the West could not have been retarded for years." Burnett implied that those opposing Connor had ruined the life of a "fine brave officer," had defeated the "finest organization of veteran Indian fighters that had ever been organized in the West." These persons had then destroyed Connor's records to cover their "nefarious" work.[49]

Grateful Coloradans gave General Connor a hero's welcome. On October 15, in Denver, he gave a revealing interview to Orvando J. Hollister of the Black Hawk, Colorado, *Daily Mining Journal.* The deposed commander spoke of the loosely-made contracts for supplies, over which the generals in the field had no control. He told of these supplies not arriving at Laramie until the expedition had returned, and of his stripping other posts and going to Denver to get what he needed to depart. He told Hollister that three-fourths of his troops had been with Cole and Walker, who had failed for some reason to rendezvous as directed on Rosebud Creek, from whence he intended to embark with pack animals on a sixty-day campaign, and follow that with a winter campaign, if necessary. Connor expressed his dismay at the abrupt termination of the campaign, believing that the troops were, in a sense, driven out of the country by the Indians.

Hollister, who would later come to Utah — perhaps at Connor's suggestion — and work for the intensely anti-Mormon *Salt Lake Tribune*, said the general did not "feel sore over the treatment accorded him personally." He described Connor as a "man of superior good sense, of uncommon sagacity and persistence, scrupulously honorable and more tender of the honor of the service, if possible, than his own; an upright, incorruptible, patriotic man."[50]

Cole and Walker were especial objects of Connor's contempt. In his report to Dodge, Connor bluntly accused his subordinates of disobeying orders. Cole, he said, had only sent out one small scouting party and thereafter had made no effort to reach the rendezvous. He thought that if Cole's scouts had reached the Tongue, as reported, it would have been impossible for them not to have discovered the trail of his column. From all the information Connor could obtain, he was sure Cole's men had gone only as far as Pumpkin Creek, a small stream between the Powder and Tongue Rivers. As for Walker, he had satisfied himself with the single scout made by Cole.[51] In another communication, General Connor called Cole and Walker's troops "mutinous and not well-commanded."[52] Perhaps it was these highly critical remarks that caused General Dodge not to forward Connor's report to higher authority, thus giving rise to rumors that it had been lost or purposely destroyed.

There seems to have been plenty of blame to share by all concerned with the expeditions. Dodge might be faulted for not paying greater attention to Cole's outfitting. He and Connor might also have provided Cole with a few reliable guides from the many who apparently were available to them. A rendezvous point might have been chosen which would not have necessitated marching Cole and Walker through the probable zone of operations. The extremely bad weather had certainly been a factor; poor morale another. Cole and his men were exhausted from the war. The previous year, the Twelfth Missouri had been in the Battle of Nashville and others, and had marched thousands of miles, many of them chasing Bedford Forrest through middle Tennessee.

All of these things could have been overcome, however, by greater determination on the part of Connor's two colonels. It is clear that neither made enough effort to locate the headquarters and supply column. With the men available to them, Cole and Walker might have sent out large, armed scouting parties and found Connor. Larger, well-armed parties might also have been able to stretch the ration by hunting farther afield in what was obviously a region alive with large bands of elk and other game. Cole, though the senior officer, made no attempt to assume command of the two forces after Walker inadvertently joined him. Instead, the two proximate columns merely acted more or less independently.

Connor's plan to carry the fight to the enemy by concentrating his columns in their country had been a good one. During his bold thrust northward, the Indians on the road had been forced to fall back quickly in defense of their villages, and the mail and telegraph lines both became relatively quiet. Captain Price, who did a commendable job of running the district while the expeditions were in the field, was able to report by August 25 that there wasn't a hostile within fifty miles of the road.[53]

In spite of the abortive ending to the campaign and Pope's imputations regarding Connor's honesty, Dodge, at least, was well pleased with the performance of his subordinate. He recommended that Connor be promoted for having organized the district, protected the routes under his charge, and for the "successful management of his expedition, all under the most embarrassing circumstances and overwhelming difficulties."[54] In other comments, Dodge pronounced the Powder River fight "the most brilliant in the history of Indian warfare" and stated that Connor had "thoroughly exploded the idea so commonly advanced . . . that the Plains Indians on the warpath cannot be overtaken and whipped in battle."[55]

New York City newspapers were not so complimentary of the former Plains commander. The *Times* called his battles "massacres" and the *Tribune*, telling its readers Connor was in command "somewhere in the Indian country," lumped him with Colonel Chivington and other sanguinary western soldiers for his barbarity toward Indians. The *Tribune* editor expressed regret that "some sensible plan," more worthy of a civilized America, couldn't be adopted toward "the poor Indian race," instead of the present one which seemed to be only to plunder, degrade and destroy.[56]

The decision to recall the expeditions before their work had been completed would be criticized for years to come, as would the basic structure of the government's Indian policy. Soon after Connor's withdrawal — thinking he had been defeated — the tribes descended on the roads again. Coloradans took the occasion to berate Doolittle's commission and "red-taped Major Generals"[57] for having given the Indians the prestige of victory and time to recuperate. They were in favor of abolishing the agency method of controlling the tribes and of giving total control over them to the War Department, as had been the case prior to 1849. In late January 1866, the territorial legislative assembly memorialized the president to this effect, asking specifically for Connor to be assigned to Colorado. The following year, the same assembly presented his name in Washington as a candidate for governor of the territory.[58]

The continuing depredations — including the Fetterman massacre — prompted Senator Wilson to follow up on the Colorado recommendation and introduce a bill in February 1867 to restore the War Department to jurisdiction over Indians. The proposed bill — which failed — would have named General Connor specifically to duty "in connection with Indian afairs."[59]

But, in spite of the protestations of Coloradans and other loyal supporters, General Connor's success, had he remained in the field that fall and winter of 1865, was far from assured. Many of his animals were dead and many more were played out. He still had all of his original command and morale problems to deal with, and his Indian enemies were congregating in increasingly large numbers. Charles Bent, at the parley with Sawyers, had expressed great fear of Connor but indicated that the tribes were concentrating everything they had to meet him. General Sully had also told Pope that the Sioux in his area were all working toward Connor. Under the best of circumstances, P. Edward would have had a tough fight.

Connor arrived back in Utah on October 1865 to a warm and supportive welcome from friends and confidants. At one mostly military, mostly Irish party, given in his honor, the toasts were frequent, expansive, and revealing of the sentiments of the moment. "Major" J. E. Barrow saluted his crony, the general, as "an experienced Indian fighter and a terror to the whole 'Lo Country.'" Captain Lewis, Connor's former adjutant, proposed a drink to "Bullets and Bayonets," the "surest guarantee of peace with the Indians," to which Major Hempstead responded "in his usual eloquent style." More cups were drunk to the "widows of Utah," the Fenian Brotherhood, the Republic of Ireland, *Union Vedette*, General Dodge, etc. — the festivities continuing on and on, one supposes, into the night.[60]

But despite all the jocularity of the mess table, it is apparent that Patrick Connor returned from Powder River a man broken in spirit. That reckless moment on the Tongue, charging hell-bent into the Arapaho camp, would prove to be the apogee of his particular, imperfect star.

Major-General Connor in later years. (Courtesy Utah State Historical Society.)

First Gentile of Utah 12

"The old Connor mansion in front of the court house square, hidden by the neglected trees, itself falling piece by piece away, is to us a melancholy reminder of days when so many now old were young, so many now dead were alive, so many now careworn were full of carelessness . . ."

— San Mateo *Times–Gazette*, December 16, 1891

I

By the end of July 1866, the Volunteer era in Utah had run its course. Connor's District of Utah had been disestablished, and his men mustered out after being relieved by a few companies of regular infantry at Camp Douglas and Fort Bridger.

One of Patrick Connor's last acts as a military commander, in his attempt to bring an end to "Brighamism," was to testify before Congressman James M. Ashley's Committee on Territories, which was then investigating polygamy and the Mormon question. At Connor's urging, Joseph Smith III of the Reorganized (Josephite) Church also appeared before the committee. While in Washington, Connor was breveted as a major-general of volunteers and then mustered out of the service. It was also during this trip that the old patronage professional managed to obtain for himself several choice plums, being named both as collector of customs for the District of Montana and Idaho, and as sutler at Camp Douglas.[1]

During these months of transition, a wave of terror swept Salt Lake City which would drive Connor and many other Gentiles completely out of Utah. With only a small military force in the territory, and with a sympathetic Andrew Johnson in the White

House, Brigham Young once again reasserted his full authority, preaching violence against Gentile claim jumpers of Mormon lands and beds.

It began in April when Squire N. Brassfield, a young freighter, was ruthlessly killed after having married the second wife of a man then on a mission in Europe. Next, on September 24, midnight attackers roughed up and threatened Captain Albert Brown and Surgeon Jonathan M. Williamson — both former Second California Cavalry officers — who had preempted quarter-sections of land on the west bank of the Jordan River. Shortly thereafter, *Vedette* editor Isaac M. Weston and two of his staff were whipped and threatened with pistols pressed to their heads until they promised to leave Utah.[2]

The most spine-chilling incident, however, was the October 20 killing of Dr. J. King Robinson, a discharged Second Cavalry surgeon. Robinson was thrice damned. He had married Miss Nellie Kay, apostate daughter of a respected pioneer Mormon; he had established a "bowling saloon" which catered to Gentile thirsts in defiance of Mormon liquor laws; and he was laying claim by preemption to the choice Salt Lake City Warm Springs property, upon which he intended to build a hospital.

One night early in October, Robinson's saloon was totally destroyed by armed ruffians with blackened faces, three of whom were recognized as police officers. A few days later, armed policemen peremptorily destroyed the doctor's buildings on the Warm Springs property and ejected him from the premises. Then, on Saturday night, October 20, Dr. Robinson was decoyed out of his house by an unknown caller to attend to the "broken leg" of an acquaintance. At the street corner nearest his house he was struck with two blows with a hatchet or bowie knife, then shot through the brain. Witnesses thought they recognized those fleeing the scene to be policemen.[3]

A final, sensational murder occurred on December 11, 1866, which, like the others, would go unsolved. Tom Colbourn, a well-known black attendant at the Salt Lake House, was found that evening lying at the head of Main Street with his head bashed in, castrated, two stab wounds in his body and with his throat cut. Attached to the corpse was a sheet of paper on which was inscribed: "Notice to All Niggers! Take Warning!! Leave White Women

Alone!!!"[4] The prevailing opinion amongst Gentiles was that Colbourn had been killed not for dalliance with white women but, rather, because he was about to give testimony in the Robinson affair.

After what seems to have been an appropriate waiting period, General Connor joined a host of terrorized Gentile merchants and former soldiers in the flight from Salt Lake City. On January 8, 1867, he took Johanna and his three children to Stockton, Utah, to live. He was an extremely disheartened man at this point in his life, with his honesty once again under attack and his business enterprises foundering.

Thus far, Connor had spent about $80,000 of his own money in mining, smelting and other pioneer ventures, with only a negligible return. And, as he now recognized, in spite of all his expansive claims designed to attract capital, the efforts to economically smelt Utah silver ores had failed miserably. In Rush Valley, experiment had followed experiment. By late 1866 four smelters were in operation at Stockton: a large reverberatory furnace belonging to Finnerty and Connor; another of the same type belonging to a Mr. Chase and former cavalry sergeant James W. Yoacham; a cupelling furnace, for separating lead from silver, belonging to Messrs. Mondheim and Johnson and, finally, the smelter and cupelling furnace of J. W. Gibson. Connor, Finnerty and others of the "Connor Smelting Company" had even employed various metallurgists and "practical smelters"[5] to design and run their works.

Connor and Grenville Dodge — by then chief engineer of the Union Pacific — corresponded frequently during the postwar period. For a time, in fact, Connor attempted to locate iron and coal claims in Utah for the railroad.[6] Writing now to Dodge, Connor confessed that he had exhausted his capital in the effort to find a method of treating the Rush Valley ores. He also complained of the abuse he was then receiving from Mormon press and pulpit, and claimed that he dared not go alone on Salt Lake City streets after dark since the Robinson killing. Connor said that, unless the government took action against the Mormons, or unless the Union Pacific were to commence building its road at Salt Lake soon, he intended to leave his $35,000 worth of property and move to California.[7]

The verbal abuse being suffered by Connor was largely the result of inspection visits to Utah the previous summer by two of General Grant's favorite officers, Generals Orville E. Babcock and Rufus Ingalls. Both of these men had taken the Mormon side of things and, further, had implied that General Connor had manipulated contracts for his own profit during the war — although neither man offered any proof to back the allegations. Nonetheless, rumors of these investigations, combined with reports of Connor's testimony before the House Committee on Territories, prompted vicious attacks, principally in Stenhouse's *Salt Lake Telegraph*.[8]

The question of Connor's guilt in the matters of which he was accused is a difficult one. All of the questionable dealings of his earlier days in California certainly suggest a lack of conscience where it came to making money. There are other suspicious, but tenuous, incidents, such as the disregard of commissaries and quartermasters that had aroused General Pope's ire. Also, while Connor was in command on the plains, Lieutenant Colonel George had reported to him large, unexplained deficiencies in the Camp Douglas quartermaster department, about which, strangely, nothing further was heard. In another instance, General Dodge felt it necessary to question Connor on a number of contracts at Camp Douglas and Fort Bridger which had seemed excessive both in quantity and price.[9]

One must also consider the turnabout in Connor's relations with Judge W. A. Carter, the sutler at Fort Bridger. Shortly after the Californians arrived in Utah, Connor accused the judge of inventing Indian troubles to get troops sent to Bridger, so that he might line his pockets. Before long, however, the two became fast friends and Carter was the recipient of most contracts to supply Fort Bridger's needs. Aside from Carter, the general is known to have evinced cronyism toward Edward Creighton, Howard Livingston and Major J. E. Barrow.

There is no doubt that Connor manipulated a number of contracts, but there is no available evidence showing that he ever purposely defrauded the government or tried to line his own pockets. His actions seem to have been motivated either by a desire to cut red tape, or to counter Brigham Young's attempts at economic strangulation, or as a means of repaying friends who had stood by him in that fight. All who knew Connor best during this period were uniformly consistent in commenting on his honesty and integrity.

A third senior army officer, in fact, thought the charges of corruption made against Connor had originated with Mormon leaders. Brevet Major-General W. B. Hazen, inspector-general for the Department of the Platte, had been in Salt Lake City during October, and had seen at first hand the circumstances surrounding the Robinson murder. The result was a strongly anti-Mormon letter in February addressed to Congressman John Bidwell of California. While Hazen thought Connor had been harsh, he credited him with being a strong and true representative of the government. Of Brassfield and Robinson murders, the inspector-general said that there was no doubt they had been inspired by church influence and teaching.[10]

A tormented Pat Connor finally packed up and returned to his old California home in early May 1867. Writing to Secretary of War Stanton to resign the sutlership at Camp Douglas, he spoke of his concern for his family's safety due to the "deadly hostility of Brigham Young and his fanatical followers."[11] Wounded, but not mortally, the Irishman gave notice that his commitment to the struggle in Utah would last a lifetime. As he told his old friend Dodge, he intended to go back again as soon as the railroad got within a few days' ride of Salt Lake and — if God spared him — he would "fight it out on that line with Brigham."[12]

II

True to his promise, Patrick Connor's sabbatical in California proved to be a short-lived one. While awaiting the coming of Dodge's railroad he busied himself raising the capital he would need to return to Utah. First, he incorporated and sold shares in his Stockton municipal water system and then, sometime in the fall of 1867, moved his family to San Francisco.[13] Here he became involved with *Alta California* publisher, Fred McCrellish, and others, in organizing the "San Francisco and Humboldt Bay Railroad Co." Plans were announced for a line from Sausalito to Humboldt Bay, via Marin, Sonoma, Mendicino and Humboldt counties. The group obtained the rights to build the road from the city of

Petaluma, for which they would receive a large subsidy. Before any serious work began, however, McCrellish convinced wealthy boy-wonder Asbury Harpending to buy in for better than ninety percent of the deal — including the entire interest of himself and Connor.[14]

With his pockets once more ajingle, Connor journeyed to Chicago in April 1868 to attend to business matters and to represent San Joaquin County at the Republican national convention. After helping to nominate Grant and Colfax, he returned briefly to California, then headed once again for Zion.[15]

By this time, construction crews of the Union Pacific and Central Pacific were fast closing the gap which separated them, and Connor fell to with a will to take advantage of the new prosperity that the roads were expected to bring. In December he launched a little side-wheel steamer — the *Kate Connor* — planning to use it first on the Salt Lake for towing telegraph poles and ties from the south shore to the Promontory area, and then to outfit it to carry passengers.[16]

Soon after the Union Pacific entered the Salt Lake Valley in March 1969, its division engineer laid out a new "Gentile" town on the west bank of the Bear River, near where it empties into the Great Salt Lake. This new "Burg on the Bear" was called Corinne. A flourishing, wild and bawdy town sprang up almost overnight and, within weeks, it boasted over 1500 people and some 300 buildings — including twenty-nine saloons and two dance halls. In its early days, the town was often referred to as "Connor City," since the general was closely involved in the development of the place as a center for transportation to Helena and the Montana mines. Large numbers of Salt Lake merchants moved their businesses to the new town and major freighting outfits soon began operating northward. Hoping to establish a regular water route to Corinne on the lake for ore and freight, Connor confidently built two more boats — the schooners *Pluribustah* and *Pioneer*.

With the coming of the railroad, there began a tremendous development of Utah mining which would lead to the territory becoming one of the richest silver-producing regions of the West. Within a year, General Connor's old West Mountain Mining District near Stockton came alive again with the discovery of rich and more easily smelted "horn", or chloride, silver ores in East Canyon. Mining camps called Ophir City, Silveropolis and Mercur — the "Johannesburg of America" — sprang up in the district. Connor's smelters and his "Silver King" and "Bolivia" mines were reopened. During these years of boom, Patrick Connor was constantly shuttling between Utah, Nevada, California, Chicago and the nation's capital, involved in starting new projects, attracting investors, and then selling out to begin still different ventures.

Although the two schooners and little *Kate Connor* proved to be unreliable for use on the lake, a larger steamer — the *City of Corinne* — was built and launched by Connor and other faithful supporters of the water route on May 23, 1871. This same year, the Alger Reduction Works were built in Corinne to handle ores from the Rush Valley mines.

City of Corinne operated intermittently until 1875, carrying ore and bullion from Stockton, as well as a few passengers and freight — but the water route was never a great success. Other means of transport were more efficient and, by 1872, with the mysteries of smelting largely solved, there were twenty-one reduction works with a huge capacity operating in the territory.[17]

The busy Irishman was also heavily involved in Nevada during these years. In Pioche — situated in Nevada's Meadow Mountain district — Connor's agent, Phil Shoaff, completed a system in 1872 to bring water to that booming but parched new town from Highland Springs six miles away. To supply much-needed lumber to the town, Connor and Henry W. Lawrence operated a steam sawmill near Beaver, Utah, some sixty miles away.[18]

Apparently Connor saw a decline coming in the fortunes of the Meadow Valley area since, by end of 1872, he had disposed of his water works, and he and some of his former soldiers had sold out their interests in the "Mammoth," "Panaca" and the other ledges they had claimed there in 1864. He next was reported to have purchased the financially-troubled Oreana Smelting Works near Unionville and some mining properties near it in the "Arabia" district. Right after this, he joined W. W. Raymond, John Ely, General Page, Hill Beachy and several other men of "abundant means" in organizing a corporation to build the "Eureka and Palisade" narrow-gauge railroad, which by 1875 would tie Eureka to the Central Pacific main line and make it a major shipping center.[19]

When the general joined in the Nevada railroad enterprise he had already recently started two others in Utah. In June 1872 elaborate ground breaking ceremonies were held at Corinne for his "Utah, Idaho and Montana Railroad," which Congress had recently chartered. That same year Connor and General E. M. Barnum organized a company to build another narrow-gauge road — the "Salt Lake, Pioche and Sevier Valley" — intended to connect Salt Lake City with Pioche some 300 miles distant, serving the mines and smelters along a route through Stockton, Tintic, Sevier Valley and Beaver River.[20]

Judging from his failure in railroad schemes, one must assume that Connor was hurt badly in the panic of 1873. By 1874 he was no longer involved with the Eureka and Palisade, although that road would prove successful. After grading his Utah, Idaho and Montana line for only ten miles, it was abandoned and, within a few years, the Mormons would build the Utah Northern to Silver Bow, Montana, up the same route Connor had planned to use. As to the Salt Lake, Pioche and Sevier Valley, only the first twenty miles had been graded and a small amount of track laid by August, 1874 when the road was bought out completely by Mormons and renamed the Utah Western. The new company, with Brigham Young's son John as president, assumed Barnum and Connor's debts and gave them stock in the new company in exchange for their equity in equipment and bridges. This road would eventually be purchased by the Union Pacific system.[21]

In 1877, when applying for membership in the Territorial Pioneers of California, Connor referred to himself as a "dealer in mines." In his Stockton, Utah, enterprises, he was at various times identified as the "manager" or "managing director" of the General Connor Tunnel and Mining Company, the Rush Valley Mining and Smelting Company, and the Great Basin Mining and Smelting Company. Historian H. H. Bancroft credits him with owning the most complete concentrating works of the Pacific region, illuminated for night operations by the first electric lights introduced into Utah. In Nevada's Eureka district, the general was president and superintendent of the Eureka Tunnel and Mining Company and was connected with the Silver Peak mine. By 1880 Connor was said to have been managing more mines and mining property than any other man in Utah.[22]

"Kate Connor" locomotive of the Salt Lake, Pioche and Sevier Valley Railroad. (Courtesy Utah State Historical Society)

III

As best is known, after returning to Utah, Patrick Connor never again lived continuously with his family. Kate would later explain the unusual arrangements by saying that Utah's climate disagreed with her mother.[23] Realistically, Johanna probably had no desire to contend once again with the ostracism to be found amongst the Mormons. She was also probably tired of trying to keep pace with her ambitious husband, while at the same time bearing and rearing his children.

Another son, Eugene Titus, had been born in San Francisco in 1869. Sometime that year, Johanna took her brood to live at a hotel in Belmont, after which, in October 1870, Connor purchased the Redwood City home of real estate developer and politician Ben Lathrop. Here Johanna could finally put down roots.

The new house was large and many-gabled. It was once described as Redwood City's "most imposing residence... with all that wealth could provide," its doors open to all with a genuine welcome, and presided over by the "gracious and cultured" Johanna. Here were said to have often gathered "the men who were notable in the affairs of San Francisco, for General Connor was an entertainer who was not to be outdone by the men of his day."[24]

In 1873 another son, Hilary Grant, was born in the Redwood City house. Kate, much beloved by her father, visited him for two memorable vacations in Utah, when she was eight (1872) and again when she was sixteen. During one visit, she spent a week on the Salt Lake with both of her parents. She later wrote of taking a swim each morning before breakfast and of using her father's private railroad car for an excursion with her friends to the lake.[25]

As an Indian fighter, the general's reputation apparently lived on. The fifty-six-year-old was interviewed at Salt Lake after the Custer massacre and, in the best pot-calling-kettle fashion, he faulted Custer's "anxiety for personal glory," at the same time conceding that his death had silenced criticism. Custer and other army officers, Connor explained, were more accustomed to southern Indians and tended to underrate the well-armed Sioux who, because of their horsemanship and fighting qualities, were "equal, man to man, with the whites." Calling for retaliation, the old war horse said he could quickly raise 4,000 volunteers in Utah and neighboring territories, and that "the boys" were "fairly itching"[26] to revenge poor Custer.

Connor's reactions when Brigham Young died in August 1877 were not recorded. He must have taken satisfaction, however, in knowing that prophesy is not always fulfilled, for he believed that Brigham had once predicted that he would live to bury the Irishman "head downward, and in his body plant a peachstone, which would sprout, grow up, and bear fruit that would gratify the Prophet's taste!"[27]

IV

General Connor continued to involve himself in territorial politics after his return to Utah. During the new wave of anti-Mormonism which began with Grant's inauguration as president, he was briefly appointed major general of Utah's militia when Grant's new governor put an end to the Nauvoo Legion.[28] Connor also served as midwife to the birth of the Liberal Political Party of Utah in July 1870. This party of anti-Mormonism began its life as a coalition of Gentiles and a group of disenchanted Mormons known as "Godbeites." The Godbeites counted amongst their numbers some of Utah's most progressive men, several of whom had recently been excommunicated from the church for speaking up against the total power of Brigham Young in business and political matters.[29] These dissidents had founded their own "Church of Zion," and were publishing the *Mormon Weekly Tribune*, which would later — under Gentile control — become a strident voice for change in Utah.

Both the Liberal Party and its rival Mormon "People's Party" battled one another at the polls for many years, but not even modest success would be achieved by the Liberals in gaining a share of political control until the 1880s. By then, some 32,000 of the 144,000 inhabitants of the territory were non-Mormon, and the mining economy that dominated the region was largely controlled by them. That decade would also see the relentless running to ground and prosecution of large numbers of polygamous men and the dissolution, by the Edmunds-Tucker Act, of the corporation holding title to most church-owned businesses and property. With Connor providing inspiration, a final push took place at the polls in 1889 which resulted in Liberals gaining control of the city governments of both Salt Lake and Ogden.

Although it had been evident for years, the Mormon leadership finally realized that it must temporarily abandon polygamy or risk losing further civil rights — that statehood and its attendant self-government wouldn't come until the practice was given up. On September 24, 1890, the current prophet, Wilford Woodruff, published his "Manifesto," which advised the Mormon people to refrain from entering into any more polygamous marriages, and which stated the intention of his church to submit to the laws of the United States. Mormon-Gentile animosities began to slowly abate, and, in 1896, Utah was at last admitted as a state.

On his seventieth birthday — St. Patrick's day, 1890 — Connor was feted by the Irish-American Association of Utah for having been the "Gladstone of Utah."[30] This honor must have cheered P. Edward quite a bit in what were otherwise lonely and difficult times. As his good friend C. C. Goodwin explained, Connor was not well educated and, in business, "he could never keep his details up with his enthusiasm," often erring in his judgements. Having fallen into straightened financial circumstances in these last years, the general had been unsuccessfully seeking appointment as United States marshal for Utah and also was soliciting Nevada's Senator William Stewart to obtain a pension for his Civil War service. While he was in Washington in 1889 lobbying for these causes, his faithful Johanna died — as she had mostly lived — without him nearby.[31]

The old general himself met his maker the evening of December 17, 1891, at the age of seventy-one. He was accorded a grand funeral by the army at what had by then become Fort Douglas. The Irish-Americans and various marching companies of the Liberal Party, called out to honor the man who "was to Utah what General Grant was to the nation," formed a huge cortege which made its way through a heavy snowstorm from the city up to the fort, along the same route traveled by the Volunteers in 1862. Here Connor was buried in the cemetery near the same spot where he had first camped with his Californians.[32]

V

Historian Edward Tullidge assessed General Connor as the "First Gentile of Utah in historical importance," giving him great credit, not only as the principal pioneer of the Utah mines, but also as the man who "substantially ended the constantly recurring Indian difficulties" for the Mormon people.

Tullidge recognized, however, that Connor and the Volunteers were an army of vigilance sent to Utah on a mission to purposely watch the Mormons, and that the general thus held Utah's fate in his hands at the most critical time in its history. No matter how inharmonious the relations which existed at first between the camp and city, Tullidge said, "General Connor had a part to perform... of an extraordinary nature... that required at once the honorable soldier and the magnanimous and humane man." Connor understood his part well, Tullidge admitted, and the historian credited the general's restraint and "preserving spirit" toward the people of the territory for preventing another "Utah War."[33]

Although Connor was intensely disliked by some who weren't close to him, he commanded the almost universal respect and admiration of the officers and men with whom he was directly associated. Most of his civilian contemporaries judged him in a similarly favorable light. Wilhelm Wyl said that to "name the old soldier is to name honesty and kindness, as everybody knows."[34] Goodwin credited him with being a patriot of the first order, and thought he had erred by not remaining in the army in 1866. "Born in a foreign land," he said, "not much accomplished in schools, coming to this country a poor emigrant, at the first call he offered his life, and that offer remained open until he died." When it came to his country Connor had been "true as steel" and his judgement as "clear as a diamond." And, behind it all was "a courage that was magnificent and a tenacity of purpose which lasted to the very end."[35]

The tenacity — which some might call stubbornness — was touched upon by the Salt Lake *Times*, along with some of his other characteristics:

"He never swerved from a principle. Never hasty in forming an opinion, yet when his mind was made up, he could no more be move than one of the peaks of the Wasatch. General Connor was a soldier, yet in his nature there was a limitless love for family and friends and that broad love for humanity that always marks true greatness. It is not believed that there was a man in the world who hated him. Those who were his friends loved him. His enemies admired him because he always fought in the open field."[36]

It would have been this willingness to do battle openly that prompted the only remotely good thing ever reputed to have been said by Brigham Young about the vexatious Irishman: "Men have been here before him; to our faces they were our friends; but when they went away they traduced, vilified and abused us. Not so with Connor. We always knew where to find him. That's why I like him."[37]

It is possible, but not likely, that Connor may also have had a similar, antagonistic respect for Young. A certain Mormon elder named Musser, traveling as a passenger in the same stagecoach with Connor in December 1871, reported that the general expressed himself strongly against the forthcoming prosecution of Brigham on cohabitation charges. Allegedly, Connor offered to sign bonds to the extent of $100,000, if the prophet could be admitted to bail. A few months before this, when the Desert Telegraph Company line was completed to Pioche, Connor was also said to have sent, along with others, a congratulatory telegram to the Mormon leader, thanking him for putting the mining community in touch with the outside world.[38] Both stories are out of character with all of Connor's other actions and stated opinions.

In spite of the glowing words of his eulogies and obituaries, Patrick Connor has remained a relatively obscure figure in Western history. While nearly everyone has heard of Brigham Young, practically no one is aware that there even were soldiers in Utah during the Civil War. Connor, of course, didn't begin to match the outward accomplishments of the Mormon "American Moses" as a builder and colonizer. In thirty years of work and with a powerful religious motive to drive his people, Young laid strong foundations for the future of his church.

Connor had little of Young's organizational ability or native canniness, and he was driven excessively by his desire for wealth and a need for personal accomplishment. What he did have, however, was that which Young had lost in earlier religious strife — a strong belief in his country and in the guarantees of intellectual and civil freedom that it offers. Joseph Smith III, whose Reorganized Church received so much assistance, was only one of several who remembered him with respect and gratitude for having had such strong beliefs, in spite of being a faithful Roman Catholic.[39]

The unlettered and impoverished thousands of Mormon converts from England, Denmark and other European countries brought to this country by Brigham Young were undoubtedly better off economically than they could ever have hoped to have been in their homelands. But they were likewise stifled and cut off from all meaningful association with their new country. They had heard nothing but abuse of the nation and its leaders from the priesthood. Connor, for all his many faults, performed a noteworthy service for the people of Utah. During the brief but critical period of the Civil War and until the coming of the railroad could ensure it, he not only helped keep them peacefully in the fold, but also did his best to protect for all people who came within his aegis — be they Josephite, Jew or Protestant — the right to function, free of religious dictate and dogma. He gave all who wished it the opportunity to enter the mainstream of American society.

VI

For those who, like myself, are curious about what became of the various people and places which played a part in the story of General Connor and his Volunteers, I have included here few of those histories which could be traced, and which seemed most interesting.

... Fort Douglas, has had a long and useful life as a western army garrison, and still is home to a limited number of military-related support activities. Fort Connor (Reno) in Wyoming and Ruby in Nevada were abandoned after only a few years of service.

... Edward McGarry, the ruthless and seemingly fearless cavalry commander, was made a brevet brigadier general of Volunteers for his gallant and meritorious service. In July 1866 he was appointed a lieutenant colonel of the 32nd Regiment of Infantry, regular army. About a year later, a fort was established in Nevada's western Humboldt County on the Applegate cutoff to Oregon, and named in his honor.

McGarry had been, for some time, an alcoholic. Complaint had been made against him in October 1864, in fact, by about twenty troopers of his regiment because of it.[40] This alcohol problem led to a death for the forty-five-year-old colonel which was as grisly and violent as had been those of the many Indians he had killed. After several weeks of heavier than usual drinking, he was found in his room in San Francisco's Occidental Hotel on New Year's morning, 1868, with his throat cut open, weltering in his own blood. Lying on the floor beside him was the pen knife with which he had presumably killed himself.[41]

... A number of the Volunteers who had served at Fort Ruby chose to return to the harsh northeastern Nevada region surrounding it. Major J. B. Moore settled in Ruby Valley to farm and raise livestock. He later served as a state senator and as deputy warden at the state prison. After failing in his smelting and sawmill endeavors at Stockton, Lieutenant James Finnerty moved to Halleck Station, twelve miles north of Camp Halleck, and died there of pneumonia in January 1875. Connor's artillery officer, Lieutenant Francis Honeyman, returned to Ruby Valley immediately upon his discharge and settled on a ranch. His wife Julia McDavid Honeyman died and was buried there in November 1867, leaving him with four children to rear.[42]

. . . Captain George F. Price was accepted in the regular army and served honorably with the Fifth Cavalry during the Reconstruction in the Carolinas and thence throughout the Indian campaigns of the 1870's against both the Apache and the tribes on the plains. Although recommended several times to brevet rank for gallantry, Price never held a rank above captain, either as a volunteer or a regular.

. . . Another of the volunteer officers who took commissions in the regular army was Colonel Robert Pollock, the former commander at Camp Douglas. He first served in the 32nd Infantry then later, as a captain of the 21st Infantry, served under General O. O. Howard in the Nez Perce War. He is said to have shown great personal bravery while commanding his company in the two-day Battle of Clearwater against the warriors of Chief Joseph. He also served during the entire campaigns against the Bannocks and Piutes, and all through the Modoc War. Pollock died in 1901 at Cornelius, Oregon, at age eighty-two.[43]

. . . The pitiless Captain Sam Smith went on to command Company H of the Eighth Regiment, U.S. Cavalry. Together with another former officer of the Second, Lieutenant Augustus Starr, he founded Fort Halleck, Nevada, on July 26, 1867. Smith was discharged November 1870 and ran a business for a time in Elko, Nevada. He died in Hamilton, Kansas, in 1911.

. . . After *Bulletin* correspondent and Chaplain John A. Anderson left the Third Infantry he served in various capacities for the U.S. Sanitary Commission. In 1868 Anderson accepted a ministerial call from the First Presbyterian Church at Junction City, Kansas, but found himself still unable to keep out of public affairs. He held the presidency of the Kansas State Agricultural College from 1873 to 1878. Elected to Congress in 1878, he served six terms and was responsible for making the agriculture department a full cabinet position. In 1891 Anderson became consul general at Cairo, Egypt. He died, after a very busy life, in 1892.

. . . Major Charles Hempstead continued to live and practice law in Salt Lake. The former provost marshal and *Vedette* editor became a frequent attorney for Brigham Young, helping to defend him both in his cohabitation and murder cases and in his well known divorce with Ann Eliza Young in 1873. Hempstead died in 1879, at age 47, of a stroke.

. . . Patrick A. Gallagher, who had so distinguished himself at Bear River by riding everywhere at the behest of General Connor, left Stockton, Utah, about the same time as his general. He joined the rush in 1867 to South Pass, Wyoming, and there, about fifteen miles north of Pacific Springs, he claimed a ledge. Calling himself an attorney, he helped draft a code of laws for South Pass City, and was elected judge of "Carter" county. When this played out two years later, Gallagher followed the rush to the new Caribou gold mines some fifty-five miles north of Soda Springs. By 1895 he was employed as secretary-treasurer in H. O. Harkness' large mercantile business at Pocatello, Idaho. After that his trail grows cold.[44]

. . . The dreaded Chief Pocatello killed no more whites after his last encounter with General Connor. The chief was baptized a Mormon on May 4, 1875. He died sometime during the period 1881 to 1884 and was buried in a deep spring near American Falls, Idaho.

. . . "Mich" Boyer, one of Connor's interpreter guides on the Powder River Expedition, died with Custer at the Little Big Horn. His bones have recently been positively identified by a team of archeologists and pathologists.

. . . Stockton, Utah, experienced a new prosperity during the initial mining boom of the 1870s but, like Corinne, it is now a tiny, extremely quiet and down-at-the heels village.

. . . Camp Connor, at Soda Springs, Idaho, was abandoned in June 1865. Several of the men who had helped establish it became prominent in the Blackfoot River valley of Idaho. Lieutenant Shoemaker married a Morrisite girl and spent the rest of his life there.

As soon as the soldiers left, Soda Springs began to shrink. The loss of government support and the cold weather combined to defeat most of the Morrisites. The town's renewal began in 1870 when Brigham Young and William H. Hooper bought land contiguous to Morristown on the northeast, and sent Mormon settlers to populate the area. What remained of the original Morrisite settlement eventually became known as "Lower Town," and soon disappeared after everyone moved away or to the new Mormon "Upper Town."

Today, Soda Springs is a tidy village with the broad streets and manicured churches typical of Mormon communities. The principal business of the area is the digging and processing of phosphates. That part of the old Morristown site not covered by the waters of Alexander Reservoir is now a horse pasture, owned by Clyde Anderson, the oldest survivor of that family. Neils Anderson's homestead and the old Morrisite schoolhouse cluster near the Bear River mud flats. Other than this, only occasional piles of rubble and the remains of stone foundations can be seen in years when the reservoir is low. The home of a prosperous Mormon family sits over the former outline of Camp Connor.

From a nearby hillside, the city cemetery overlooks the old town site. In the older part of the cemetery a few Morrisite graves can be found, huddled together as though seeking protection from oppressors that surround them even in death. Here is a large bronze tablet and a commodious bench from which to study it. It marks the resting place of Neils and Mary Christopherson Anderson. The Andersons never joined another church after the Morrisite affair, but the activities of Neils would eventually earn him the sobriquet "father" of the anti-Mormon party in Idaho. The singular headstone beneath which they are buried bears the names of their children and is inscribed with no less than 650 bitter words detailing the tragic drama of their Mormon and Morrisite experiences.

Notes to the Chapters

Notes to Chapter One

1. Frederick Lawrence Knowles, ed., *Poems of American Patriotism* (Freeport, N.Y.: Books for Libraries Press, 1970), 122-23.
2. Stockton, California *San Joaquin Republican*, August 24, 1861.
3. Hubert H. Bancroft, "Biographical Sketch of General P. Edward Connor" (Bancroft Library, Berkeley, ca. 1887), 1 (hereafter cited as "Biog. Sketch"). Also see Fred B. Rodgers, *Soldiers of the Overland* (San Francisco: The Grabhorn Press, 1939), 1-2.
4. San Mateo, California *Gazette*, June 7, 1873.
5. *General Taylor and His Staff: Comprising Memoirs of Generals Taylor, Worth, Wool, and Butler* (Philadelphia: Grigg, Elliot and Co., 1848), 159.
6. James H. Carleton, *Battle of Buena Vista* (New York, 1848), 104.
7. San Francisco *Daily Alta California*, April 7, 1854.
8. *General Taylor and His Staff*, 160.
9. Salt Lake City *Daily Tribune*, December 18, 1891;
10. "Biog. Sketch," 1. Connor evidently came through Mexico, then traveled by steamer to San Francisco (Territorial Pioneers of California, Roll of Members, California Historical Society Library, San Francisco, 2: 53).
11. Covert R. Martin, R. Coke Wood, and Leon Bush, *Stockton Album Through the Years* (Stockton Cal.: Simard Printing Co., 1959), 191. Also see Redwood City, California *Standard*, January 5, 1928.
12. Sacramento *Transcript*, April 20, 1850; also *Alta* of April 17.
13. "Biog. Sketch," 5-7; Hubert Howe Bancroft, *History of California* (San Francisco: The History Co., 1884-1890), 7: 501-504.
14. For the Murieta story see *Alta*, May 12, 13, and 16, 1853. Also *San Joaquin Republican*, June 21, August 6 and 11, 1853 and Joseph Henry Jackson, *Anybody's Gold, The Story of California's Mining Towns* (New York: D. Appleton-Century Co., 1941), 110-120.
15. San Mateo, California *Times-Gazette*, July 13, 1889; Biography of P. E. Connor, Richard Schellens Papers, Public Library, Redwood City, California.

16. Jill L. Cossley-Batt, *The Last of the California Rangers* (New York: Funk and Wagnall, 1928), 195-96.
17. Michael David Goodman, *A Western Panorama, 1849-1875: The travels, writing, influence of J. Ross Browne* (Glendale, Cal.: Arthur Clark Co., 1966), 289, quoting from Browne's *Crusoe's Island.*
18. George H. Tinkham, *History of Stockton* (San Francisco: W. M. Hinton and Company, 1880), 205.
19. Redwood City, California *Standard,* January 5, 1928. Octagonal houses were a fad in the decade following publication of an 1847 book by Orson Squire Fowler entitled "A Home For All or the Gravel Wall and Octagonal Mode of Building, New, Cheap, Convenient, Superior, and Adapted to Rich and Poor."
20. Clipping from the *Bee,* Miner F. Butler Papers, MS. 276, pt. 2, 16, California Historical Society Library, San Francisco. Also see *San Joaquin Republican,* March 2, 1859.
21. C. C. Goodwin, *As I Remember Them* (Salt Lake City: Salt Lake Commercial Club, 1913), 266; Salt Lake City *Daily Tribune* December 18, 1891.
22. Brig. Gen. Richard H. Orton, ed., *Records of California Men in the War of the Rebillion, 1861 to 1867* (Sacramento: California State Printing Office, 1890), 6.
23. *Republican,* August 3, 1861; also see Tinkham, 254.
24. Tinkham, 255.
25. San Francisco *Bulletin,* January 7, 1862; *Republican,* October 17, 1861.
26. *The War of the Rebellion, Official Records of the Union and Confederate Armies* (Washington, D.C.: Government Printing Office, 1880-1900), Series 1, vol. 50, pt. 1: 754 (hereafter cited as "O. R." Series 1 intended unless otherwise indicated).
27. *Bulletin* March 13, 1862. Also see editions of January 11 and 17.
28. Stockton, California *Daily Independent,* May 27, 1862.
29. Martin, Wood and Bush, 192-193.
30. *Bulletin,* June 22 and 23, 1862.
31. O. R., vol. 50, pt. 2: 6; Orton, 506.

Notes to Chapter Two

1. Charles Neider, ed., *The Selected Letters of Mark Twain* (New York: Harper and Row, Publishers, 1917), 30.
2. Salt Lake City *Deseret News,* May 28, June 10, 18 and 25, 1862.
3. Orson F. Whitney, *History of Utah,* (Salt Lake City: George Q. Cannon and Sons Co., 1893), 2: 31.
4. Brigham Young, et al., *Journal of Discourses Delivered by President Brigham Young, His Two Counsellors, the Twelve Apostles, and Others,* 1964 ed. (Liverpool: George Q. Cannon), 6: 342; also 7: 142 (hereafter cited as *Journal of Discourses*).

5. W. W. Drummond to Jeremiah Black, Attorney-General of the U.S., March 30, 1857, 35th Cong., 1st Sess., H. Exec. Doc. 71, 212.
6. *Deseret News*, May 20, 1857, published a letter from Drummond's wife revealing the Judge's indiscretion. Hubert Howe Bancroft, *History of Utah, 1540-1887* (San Francisco: The History Co., 1889), p. 490 states that Drummond introduced the prostitute as his wife and she sat beside him on the judicial bench.
7. Joseph Smith Jr. et al., *The Doctrine and Covenants of the Church of Jesus Christ of Latter-day Saints. The Pearl of Great Price* (Salt Lake City: Church of Jesus Christ of Latter-day Saints, 1982) Sec. 87 of D. and C., 164.
8. *Deseret News*, May 29, 1861.
9. Charles Lowell Walker, *Diary of Charles Lowell Walker*, ed. A. Karl Larson and Katherine Miles Larson (Logan: Utah State University Press, 1980), 1: 154-55, entry for December 30, 1860.
10. *Journal of Discourses*, 10: 250.
11. Walker, 1: 212, entry for January 3, 1862.
12. *Deseret News*, January 1, 1862. Detroit *Tribune*, January 24, 1862, as quoted by *Deseret News*, February 12, 1862.
13. Bancroft, *Utah*, 605.
14. Salt Lake City *Daily Union Vedette*, January 14, 1864.
15. Edward W. Tullidge, *History of Salt Lake City, and its Founders* (Salt Lake City: Star Printing Company, 1886), 252.
16. *Ibid.*, 253-54.
17. O. R., vol. 50, pt. 1: 1023-24. Also see Tullidge, *Salt Lake City*, 253 and O. R., Series 3, vol. 2: 29.
18. The most complete and balanced Morrisite history is contained in C. LeRoy Anderson, *For Christ Will Come Tomorrow: The Saga of the Morrisites* (Logan: Utah State University Press, 1981).
19. Salt Lake City *Daily Tribune*, March 9, 1879.
20. Wilford Woodruff, *Journal of Wilford Woodruff, 1833-1898*, ed. Scott G. Kenny (Midvale, Utah: Signature Books, 1984) 6: 58, entry for June 18, 1862.
21. J. F. Gibbs, *Lights and Shadows of Mormonism* (Salt Lake City: Salt Lake Tribune Publishing Co., 1909), 245.
22. Bancroft, *Utah*, 618. Joseph Morris' brother George said that the bodies were buried secretly.
23. Walker, 1: 232.
24. San Francisco *Bulletin*, July 15, 1862.
25. Richard Condy, Journal of the March from Camp Halleck, California to Fort Ruby, Nevada, July 12 to September 1, 1862, Haggin Museum and Galleries, Stockton California, 2. Also see *Bulletin*, July 19, 1862.
26. Condy, 2.
27. *Ibid.*, 5.
28. *Ibid.*, 6.

29. O. R., vol. 50, pt. 2: 48-49.
30. *Bulletin*, August 12, 1862.
31. Harlan D. Fowler, *Three Caravans to Yuma, The Untold Story of Bactrian Camels in Western America* (Glendale, California: Arthur H. Clark Co., 1980), 91-94.
32. O. R., vol. 50, pt. 2: 60-61.
33. *Bulletin*, August 29, 1862.
34. Condy, 7.
35. *Ibid.*, 8.
36. *Bulletin*, August 29, 1862.
37. Diary of Private Van B. DeLashmutt as quoted by Rodgers, 259.

Notes to Chapter Three

1. *Journal of Discourses*, 9: 157.
2. *Deseret News*, September 10, 1862.
3. Orton, 508 quoting Col. Connor's report to Gen. Wright of September 14, 1862.
4. *Deseret News*, July 16, 1862. Drake was from Pontiac, Michigan and was at this date sixty years old, of a thin, wiry frame and vigorous mind and a blameless life (Bancroft, *Utah*, 621).
5. Whitney, 2: 71-73.
6. Bancroft, *Utah*, 609.
7. Harding to Seward, August 30, 1862, Utah Territorial Papers, Record Group 59, National Archives.
8. *Deseret News*, August 6, 1862.
9. *Ibid.*
10. James D. Doty Report, H. Exec. Doc. 1, 37th Cong., 3rd sess., II as quoted by Virginia Cole Trenholm and Maurine Carley, *The Shoshonis: Sentinels of the Rockies* (Norman: University of Oklahoma Press, 1964), 193.
11. *Deseret News*, August 13, 1862. Attacks in early August are described in the *Deseret News* of August 27, 1862 and November 26, 1862.
12. Hamilton Scott, Diary, typescript extracts, Idaho State Historical Society, 8. Other details of the attack are found in the *Bulletin* of September 27 and October 8, 1862, and in the Jane A. Gould, Diary, typescript, Oregon State Historical Society, MSS 2680, Gould family papers, 27-99.
13. This skirmish took place just south of what is now Indian Springs Natatorium, near American Falls, Idaho.
14. Jane Gould diary, 28.
15. *Deseret News*, September 17, 1862; *Bulletin*, October 8, 1862.
16. *Bulletin*, October 8, 1862.
17. *Deseret News*, September 25, 1862. Also see edition of September 24, 1862.
18. *Bulletin*, September 16, 1862; O. R., vol. 50, pt. 2: 123-125. Only twelve

people, if any, may have been massacred at Gravelly Ford. Another ten might have been killed about the same time near the mouth of the south fork of the Humboldt River. (Carson City *Silver Age*, October 2, 1862, and Edna B. Patterson, Louise Ulph and Victor Goodwin, *Nevada's Northeast Frontier* (Sparks, Nevada: Western Printing and Publishing Co., 1969), 103. White Knives were a Shoshoni band whose range was from Goose Creek to the Humboldt.

19. O. R., vol. 50, pt. 2: 148-49.
20. *Bulletin*, October 4, 1862.
21. *Ibid.*, October 8, 1862.
22. *Bulletin* article dated September 24, 1862, as quoted by *Deseret News*, October 15, 1862.
23. O. R., vol. 50, pt. 2: 133.
24. *Bulletin* article as quoted by *Deseret News*, October 15, 1862.
25. Thomas B. Stenhouse, *The Rocky Mountain Saints* (London: Ward, Lock and Tyler, 1874), 608.
26. All the narrative above is from the *Bulletin*, October 30, 1862.
27. O. R., vol. 50, pt. 2: 180.
28. *Bulletin*, October 30, 1862. Stenhouse, 602 says that parties who would have benefited financially by the Volunteers occupying Camp Floyd tried to induce Connor to remain there and, failing that, they sought to intimidate him by saying that the Mormons intended to dispute the passage of the Californians over the Jordan River.
29. *Ibid.*
30. *Ibid.*
31. Hiram S. Tuttle, "Account of Service in Utah," photocopy Fort Douglas Military Museum, Salt Lake City., 5.

Notes to Chapter Four

1. Mark Twain, *Roughing It* (New York: Harper and Brothers Publishers, 1906), 1: 112.
2. *Deseret News*, October 29, 1862.
3. *Ibid.*, January 7, 1863; Also see edition of January 14.
4. Bernard DeVoto, *The Year of Decision, 1846* (Boston: Little, Brown and Co., 1943) 85.
5. *New York Times*, June 23, 1857. Also see *Deseret News*, September 2, 1857.
6. Tullidge, *Salt Lake City*, 143. The prophecy is said to have been made May 18, 1843, in these words: "Judge, you will aspire to the presidency of the United States; and if you ever turn your hand against me or the Latter-day Saints, you will feel the weight of the hand of the Almighty God upon you; and you will live to see and know that I have testified the truth to you, for the conversation of this day will stick to you through life." (*Deseret News*, September 24, 1856).

7. *San Francisco Bulletin,* November 17, 1862.
8. *Ibid.*
9. *Deseret News,* January 28, 1863.
10. O. R., vol. 50, pt. 2: 144.
11. McGarry's report is found in Orton, 172.
12. *Deseret News,* November 19, 1862.
13. *San Francisco Bulletin,* November 21, 1862. King was a noted California Unitarian clergyman who had first arrived there in 1860 from Boston. He was nationally prominent for his literary and patriotic interests. Chaplain Anderson had worked with him toward the reform of charitable institutions in California.
14. *Vedette,* January 30, 1864.
15. Joseph Smith Jr., *The Book of Mormon,* 1920 ed. (Salt Lake City: Church of Jesus Christ of Latter-day Saints), 102 (2 Nephi 30:6). In 1981, the *Book of Mormon* text was altered to read "pure and delightsome."
16. Brigham Young, "Message to the Legislative Assembly of the Territory of Utah," Fillmore City, Utah Terr., December 11, 1855, Utah State Historical Society, photocopy.
17. *Deseret News,* April 3, 1861.
18. Juanita Brooks, ed., *Journal of the Southern Indian Mission, Diary of Thomas D. Brown* (Logan: Utah State University Press, 1972), 25, entry for May 14, 1854. Brown said, in part: "Ephraim is the battle ax of the Lord. May we not have been sent to learn how to use this ax, with skill? . . ."
19. Orton, 172.
20. Church of Jesus Christ of Latter-day Saints, *Journal History of the Church,* Church Historian's Office, Salt Lake City (hereafter cited as *Journal History*), October 26, 1862.
21. Stockton, California *Stockton Daily Independent,* June 12, 1867. Also see *Bulletin,* November 17, 1862.
22. Mowry letter of September 17, 1854 as quoted in William Mulder and A. Russell Mortensen, eds., *Among the Mormons, Historic Accounts by Contemporary Observers* (Lincoln: University of Nebraska, Bison Books, 1973), 274.
23. O. R., vol. 50, pt. 2: 245.
24. *Ibid.,* 256-57.
25. *Ibid.,* 275.
26. Tullidge, *Salt Lake City,* 271-272.
27. Stephen S. Harding, *Message to the Territorial Legislature of Utah, Dec. 8, 1862.* 37th Cong., 2d sess., 1862. S. Misc. Doc. 37, 1-5. Also see *New York Tribune,* January 7, 1863. Parts of the address are also contained in Tullidge, *Salt Lake City,* 297-299.
28. Stenhouse, 603.
29. Harding letter of December 23, 1873, as quoted in Bill Hickman, *Brigham's Destroying Angel* (Salt Lake City: Shepard Publishing Co., 1904), 213.

30. *Deseret News*, December 31, 1862.

Notes to Chapter Five

1. *Vedette*, February 1, 1864.
2. Several companies of Dragoons, a total of 90 men, were stationed near Fort Hall the summer of 1860. They returned to Camp Floyd in late September, bringing with them 20 emigrant survivors of another major attack in the City of Rocks area.
3. Accounts of the Otter-Van Orman saga can be found in the *Deseret News*, October 31, 1860; Oregon City *Argus*, November 24, 1860, and in John D. Unruh Jr., *The Plains Across, The Overland Emigrants and the Trans-Mississippi West, 1840-1860* (Urbana: University of Illinois Press, 1979), 190-2.
4. Seymour Dunbar, ed., *The Journals and Letters of Major John Owen, Pioneer of the Northwest, 1850-1871*. (New York: Edward Eberstadt, 1927), 2: 242-48.
5. O. R., vol. 50, pt. 2: 61-62. I have used the spelling of Van Orman as contained in O. R. Another variant of the name is "Van Ornum."
6. *Deseret News*, November 26, 1862.
7. Orton, 509. In late September, Shoshoni or Bannocks had stolen forty horses in the Logan area. Mormon militia were unable to recover them in spite of a brief fight (*Deseret News*, October 8, 1862).
8. San Francisco *Evening Bulletin*, June 27, 1863.
9. Orton, 173.
10. *Deseret News*, December 3, 1862.
11. Newell Hart, *The Bear River Massacre* (Preston, Idaho: Cache Valley Newsletter Publishing Co., 1982), 84, quoting Henry C. Haskin in unspecified issue of the *Napa County Reporter*. Also see *Deseret News*, November 26, 1862.
12. Col. J. H. Martineau, "Military History of Cache Valley," *Tullidge's Quarterly Magazine* 1883), 2-1 (April 1882): 125.
13. Near present-day Colliston, Utah.
14. The Bannock Indian boy sent with the note was shot and killed a few weeks later by a man who had hired him to go after livestock the Indians had stolen (*Deseret News*, December 31, 1862).
15. *Deseret News*, December 17, 1862.
16. *Ibid.*
17. *Ibid.*, December 31, 1862.
18. *Deseret News*, January 14, 1863. Also see February 4, 1863, edition for events leading up to the battle.
19. O. R., vol. 50, pt. 1: 185.
20. Oration by Captain Charles H. Hempstead as quoted in *Vedette* January 30, 1864.
21. Rodgers, 70-71.

22. Lee's oral history, recorded by his daughter and as quoted in Hart, 130.
23. *Deseret News*, February 11, 1863.
24. Undated article in *Alta California*, as quoted in Orton, 176-177.
25. Franklin County Historical Society and Monument Committee, *The Passing of the Redman* (Preston, Idaho, 1917), 14.
26. Sacramento *Daily Union*, February 17, 1863.
27. *Army and Navy Journal*, December 15, 1866, as quoted by Rodgers, 74; Blackfoot, Idaho *Daily Bulletin*, June 11, 1929.
28. Tullidge, *Salt Lake City*, 289.
29. Daughters of the Utah Pioneers, *The Trail Blazer: History of the Development of Southeastern Idaho* (Preston Idaho: Cache Valley Newsletter Publishing Co., 1976), 13.
30. Mae T. Parry, "Massacre at Bia Ogai," in *The Trail Blazer*, 128.
31. *Passing of the Redman*, 14
32. Sacramento *Daily Union*, February 13, 1863.
33. Tuttle, 7.
34. *Daily Union*, February 13, 1863.
35. *Ibid.*
36. O. R., vol. 50, pt. 1: 187.
37. Tullidge, *Salt Lake City*, 288.
38. *Ibid.*
39. Hart, 129.
40. *Rocky Mountain News* of February 26, 1863, as quoted in LeRoy R. Hafen, *The Overland Mail* (Cleveland: Arthur H. Clark Co., 1926), 249.

Notes to Chapter Six

1. *Deseret News*, October 14, 1868.
2. C. B. Waite letter to Hon. Edward Bates, January 28, 1863, as quoted in Robert Joseph Dwyer, *The Gentile Comes To Utah* (Washington, D.C.: Catholic University Press, 1941), 10.
3. Bancroft, *Utah*, 610.
4. Harding to Seward February 3, 1863, as quoted in Dwyer, 11-12.
5. Stenhouse, 604.
6. Dwyer, 11-12.
7. Letter of February 16, in O. R., vol. 50, pt. 2: 314-315.
8. Letter of February 19, in O. R., vol. 50, pt. 2: 318-320.
9. Whitney, 2: 90; *Deseret News*, March 4, 1863.
10. O. R., vol. 50, pt. 2: 370-374.
11. Undated Young letter to Secretary Frank Fuller, Brigham Young Letter Books, Historian's Office, Church of Jesus Christ of Latter-day Saints, Salt Lake City. This letter was probably written near the end of March, and it en-

closed a copy of the speech. Another version can be found in the *Deseret News* of March 4, 1863.

12. Whitney, 2: 95-96.
13. O. R., vol. 50, pt. 2: 373.
14. *Deseret News,* March 4, 1863.
15. *Journal of Discourses*, 10: 107. The speeches as reported by Connor can be found in O. R., vol. 50, pt. 2: 370-371.
16. Stenhouse, 606.
17. O. R., vol. 50, pt. 2: 342.
18. William Ajax, Diary, University of Utah Library, Salt Lake City, 187.
19. O. R., vol. 50, pt. 2: 342.
20. Stenhouse, 604. Also see *Deseret News,* March 11, 1863.
21. Stenhouse, 605; Bancroft, *Utah*, 615.
22. O. R., vol. 50, pt. 2: 347. Also see vol. 48, pt. 2: 344-45.
23. O. R., vol. 50, pt. 2: 370-374.
24. Church of Jesus Christ of Latter-day Saints, *The Latter-day Saints Millennial Star* (London: Latter-day Saints Book Depot, 1840-1970), 24: 301-02 (hereafter cited as *Millennial Star*).
25. O. R., vol. 50, pt. 2: 359.
26. Hafen, *The Overland Mail*, 295-296; Dwyer, 7.
27. O. R., vol. 50, pt. 2: 357-358.
28. *Ibid.*, 369-70.
29. Stenhouse, 607.
30. *Deseret News,* April 1, 1863.
31. Harding letter of December 23, 1873, as quoted in Hickman, 218.
32. Howard Egan, *Pioneering the West, 1846 to 1878* (Richmond, Utah: Howard R. Egan Estate, 1917), 261.
33. O. R., vol. 50, pt. 2: 379. Also see Patterson, Ulph and Goodwin, pp. 4, 207 and 427.
34. This skirmish is reported in O. R., vol. 50, pt. 1: 201-03.
35. O. R., vol. 50, pt. 1: 200-01.
36. *Ibid.*, 205-08.
37. Peter Gottfredson, ed., *History of Indian Depredations in Utah* (Salt Lake City: Shelton Publishing Co., 1919), 118.
38. O. R., vol. 50, pt. 1: 205-08.
39. *Ibid.*, pt. 2: 415.
40. *Ibid.*, pp. 410-11 and 427.
41. Stenhouse, 608.
42. Tullidge, *Salt Lake City*, 322.
43. *Ibid.*, 323.
44. Stenhouse, 605.

45. *Ibid.*, 608-609.
46. Richard D. Poll, "The Mormon Question, 1850-1865: A Study in Politics and Public Opinion" (Ph. D. diss., University of California, Berkeley, 1948) as quoted by Leonard J. Arrington, *Brigham Young, American Moses* (New York: Alfred A. Knopf, 1985), 295.
47. Bancroft, *Utah*, 621.
48. *Ibid*; Stenhouse, 609.
49. Young letter of June 25, 1863 as quoted in Tullidge, *Salt Lake City*, 325.

Notes to Chapter Seven

1. Kate B. Carter, ed., *Heart Throbs of the West* (Salt Lake City: Daughters of the Utah Pioneers, 1939-41), 5:522.
2. Connor to Grenville Dodge, in O. R., vol. 50, pt. 2: 1185-86.
3. O. R., vol. 50, pt. 2: 411. Shoshoni and Bannocks spent summers in the area. They called the area "Tosoiba," or "land of sparkling waters" (Lula Barnard, Faunda Bybee and Lola Walker, *Tosoiba, Sparkling Waters* [Soda Springs, Idaho: Daughters of the Utah Pioneers, 1958], 1).
4. C. LeRoy Anderson, 160.
5. Hickman, 164.
6. The building of the ferry was apparently a joint venture of Hickman and Harry Rickards. It was known first as "Hickman's Ferry" and later as "Eagle Rock Ferry." (Barzilla W. Clark, *Bonneville County in the Making* [Idaho Falls, Idaho: 1941], 14).
7. *Vedette*, December 11, 1863.
8. *The Expedition of Captain James L. Fisk To the Rocky Mountains*, 38th Cong., 1st sess., H. Ex. Doc. 45, 30-31. The express Fisk used was probably that of Oliver and Connover, who put on a mail and express service by pack train early in the spring, and which was changed to light wagons carrying passengers in June. They had no mail contract (Barnard, Bybee and Walker, 138).
9. O. R., vol. 50, pt. 2: 453.
10. Statement by Abraham Anderson in Rodgers, 105.
11. O. R., vol. 50, pt. 1: 226-29. Also see *Deseret News*, June 3, 1863 and San Francisco *Evening Bulletin* of May 15, May 21, June 4, and June 27, 1863, for other accounts of the expedition.
12. Anderson statement in Rodgers, 105; Peter Anderson, 46.
13. *Vedette*, March 8, 1864.
14. The adobe building also served as the first courthouse for Oneida County when it was created. Ever the businessman, Connor set up a store in Soda Springs with civilian Fred T. Kiesel in charge. It may have been the store in this building. Kiesel, an agent for Gilbert and Sons, also had the contract to furnish supplies for Camp Connor. (Blackfoot, Idaho Daily *Bulletin*, June 11, 1929).

15. Patterson, Ulph and Goodwin, 104; O. R., vol. 50, pt. 2: 420.
16. O. R., vol. 50, pt. 2: 420; Orton, 182.
17. These events are described in Egan, 200 and the San Francisco *Bulletin*, May 22; June 4 and July 10, 1863.
18. *Vedette*, January 14, 1864; Orton, 182; O. R., vol. 50, pt. 1: 229.
19. O. R., vol. 50, pt. 2: 500.
20. *Ibid.*, 481; also vol. 50, pt. 1: 229.
21. O. R., vol. 50, pt. 1: 230.
22. Egan, 263-64. Orton, 567-69 gives the date of this ambush as July 6. The soldiers killed, all of Company E, were Privates Grimshaw, MacNamara, Myers and Pratt.
23. San Francisco *Bulletin*, August 1, and November 12, 1863.
24. *Bulletin*, August 7, 1863. Patterson, Ulph and Goodwin, 104.
25. O. R., vol. 50, pt. 2: 428-29, 479.
26. O. R., vol. 50, pt. 2: 474 and 479; Rodgers, 94; O. R., vol. 50, pt. 1: 229. Fifty of San Pitch's band were captured and brought to Fort Bridger.
27. Virginia Cole Trenholm and Maurine Carley, *The Shoshonis: Sentinels of the Rockies* (Norman: University of Oklahoma Press, 1964), 201.
28. O. R., vol. 50, pt. 2: 527; *Bulletin*, July 10, 1863.
29. *Bulletin* August 1, 1863.
30. O. R., vol. 50, pt. 2: 528-30.
31. *Ibid.*, 546.
32. *Ibid.*, 583-84.
33. *Ibid.*, 581, 582 and 585.
34. *Ibid.*, 547. Also see Trenholm and Carley, 204.
35. O. R., vol. 50, pt. 2: 588 and 631.
36. *Bulletin*, October 14, 1863. Also see issue of August 20, and O. R., vol. 50, pt. 2: 484, 496 and 501.
37. William Ajax diary, 269, entry for September, 27, 1863.
38. *Bulletin*, October 14, 1863. Also see O. R., vol. 50, pt. 2: 620.
39. Trenholm and Carley, 205; Rodgers, 97.
40. *Bulletin*, November 5 and 6, 1863.
41. Brigham D. Madsen, *The Bannock of Idaho* (Caldwell, Idaho: Caxton Printers, 1958), 146-47. In 1858 Le Grand Coquin had led the Bannocks that forced abandonment of the Mormon mission on the Lemhi River.
42. O. R., vol. 50, pt. 2: 659; 38th Cong., 2nd sess., H. Ex. Doc. 1, vol. II, 318-20 as quoted by Rodgers, 98.
43. Trenholm and Carley, 209.
44. *Bulletin*, December 2, 1862.
45. Accounts of the initial discovery are contained in Tullidge, *Salt Lake City*, 697-98, Rodgers, 110-11 and *Vedette*, November 27, 1863. Bishop Gardner was a Mormon pioneer of 1847 who was known as Utah's greatest mill builder.

46. O. R., vol. 50, pt. 2: 656-57.
47. *Vedette*, December 4, 1863.
48. *Vedette*, November 17; *Bulletin*, November 12, 1863.
49. O. R., vol. 50, pt. 2: 638-39.
50. Patterson, Ulph and Goodwin, 107.
51. *Journal of Discourses*, 10: 255.
52. *Vedette*, January 3, 1865.
53. *Ibid.*, November 20, 1863.
54. Tullidge, *Salt Lake City*, Appendix, p. 9; Rodgers, 133.
55. *Bulletin*, December 16, 1863.
56. Woodruff letter to George Q. Cannon of Dec. 25, 1863, as quoted in *Millennial Star*, 26: 140.
57. Brigham Young letter to George Q. Cannon, February, 1864. Brigham Young Letter Books.
58. *Expedition of Captain Fisk*, 31-32.
59. Letter of January 29, 1864 in *Millennial Star*, 26: 189.

Notes to Chapter Eight

1. *Vedette*, February 15, 1865.
2. "Medical History of Fort Douglas," prepared by Edward P. Vollum, Post Surgeon, 1870-76, in Rodgers, 118.
3. San Francisco *Bulletin*, November 30, 1863. Also see issue of February 15, 1864.
4. *Vedette*, February 1, 1864.
5. *Ibid.*, December 24, 1863. Also see *Bulletin*, October 14, 1863.
6. *Bulletin*, November 30, 1863; also *Vedette* December 11, 1863, February 8, 1864, and December 8, 1864.
7. *Ibid.*, January 1 and November 8, 1864; March 9, 1865.
8. *Vedette*, April 22 and June 6, 1864.
9. *Ibid.*, February 5, 1864; January 13, 1867, and March 3, 1865.
10. *Ibid.*, April 23, 1864.
11. *Ibid.*, March 10, 1864.
12. "Among the Mormons," *Atlantic Monthly*, April 1864 in Mulder and Mortensen, 351. Also see Wayne Sutton, ed., *Utah, A Centennial History* (New York: Lewis Historical Publishing Co., 1949), 2: 1006-09; Samuel Bowles, *Across the Continent* (1866; reprint, Ann Arbor: University Microfilms, 1966), 103-04.
13. *Bulletin*, February 8, and April 11, 1864; Sutton, 1006-09.
14. *Ibid.*, February 8, 1864.
15. Julia Dean had become a success at 15, after appearing in "The Lady of the Lake." After a decline in her popularity she went for a time to San Francisco

then, in 1865, toured the Rocky Mountain area, ending up in Salt Lake in late July.

16. *Vedette*, August 16, 1865.
17. *Ibid.*, December 3, 1864, and June 8, 1865; O. J. Hollister, "History of Independence Hall," typescript, Public Library, Salt Lake City, Utah.
18. *Vedette*, January 23 and February 4, 1865; March 2, 1867; Rodgers, 123. Also see James Knox Polk Miller, *The Road to Virginia City, The Diary of James Knox Polk Miller*, ed. Andrew F. Rolle (Norman: University of Oklahoma Press, 1960), 45.
19. *Vedette*, February 8 and 24, 1865; November 29, 1865; March 2, 1867.
20. *Ibid.*, October 1, 1864; Dwyer, 34.
21. Kate Connor Oliver, "Diary to Her Children," December, 1931, Mrs. George Goodlett, San Francisco, typescript, 1; "Biog. Sketch," 34.
22. Salt Lake *Telegraph*, July 4, 1864.
23. Bowles, 116. Also see Schuyler Colfax, "Hon. Schuyler Colfax's Journey From the Missouri River to California in 1865 (From His Journal)," *Tullidge's Monthly Magazine, Western Galaxy*, April 1888, 244.
24. *Vedette*, April 23, 1864.
25. Richard Williams lecture "The Great Basin," given before the Historical Society of Buffalo, N. Y., in *Vedette*, February 23, 1867.
26. O. R., vol. 50, pt. 2: 715-17.
27. *Ibid.*, 748.
28. *Vedette*, March 3, 1864.
29. O. R., vol. 50, pt.2 : 795; Rodgers, 115 and *Vedette*, April 12 and 22, 1864. Camp Conness was on the western side of the valley about 10 miles from Stockton, Utah.
30. O. R., vol. 50, pt. 2: 834 and 845-46.
31. *Ibid.*, 845; *Vedette*, April 30 and June 6, 1864.
32. O. R., vol. 50, pt. 2: 802-803, 1185 and pt. 1: 355-60; *Vedette*, June 25, 1864; *Alta California*, February 3, 1865; Arrington, *Brigham Young*, 357.
33. *Vedette*, June 22, 1864.
34. *Ibid.*, April 23, 1864. Also see June 25 edition.
35. *Ibid.*, Mining stock was usually sold in "feet" or shares. When capital was needed for development, owners were assessed in proportion to the number of feet owned.
36. Walker, 1: 125, entry for May 3, 1860. Also see Edmund C. Briggs journal, entries for August 11 and September 18, 1863, and Briggs in *Vedette* of March 29, 1864.
37. Briggs Journal, February 25, 1864.
38. *Vedette*, July 6, 1865. Josephites believe that polygamy was introduced into the Mormon Church by Brigham Young.
39. Joseph Smith III, "Memoirs," *The Saints Herald*, March 24, 1936, 369; San Francisco *Bulletin*, October 14, 1863; *Vedette*, April 28, May 1 and 3 and July 11, 1864.

40. Bancroft, *Utah*, 645 and John H. Beadle, *Life in Utah, or the Mysteries and Crimes of Mormonism* (Philadelphia: National Publishing Co., 1870), 429.
41. O. R., vol. 50, pt. 2: 887.
42. For both sides of this crisis see O. R., vol. 50, pt. 2: 887-94; *Vedette*, July 11, 1864; B. Young letter of July 16 to Daniel Wells in Cecil J. Alter, *Utah, The Storied Domain* (Chicago: American Historical Society, 1932), 1: 361-62.
43. Tuttle, 16-18.
44. Orton, 517.
45. O. R., vol. 50, pt. 2: 913-14.
46. Tullidge, *Salt Lake City*, 328-330.
47. O. R., vol. 50, pt. 2: 909-10.
48. *Ibid.*, 916-17.
49. *Ibid.*, 923.
50. *Ibid.*, 948.
51. *Vedette*, August 10, 11, 12 and 18, and September 22, 1864.

Notes to Chapter Nine

1. Goodwin, 265.
2. *Vedette*, July 13, 1864. Also issue of June 21.
3. *Ibid.*, August 18, 1864. Also see "Biog. Sketch," 30.
4. Sacramento *Daily Union*, September 29, 1864.
5. O. R., vol. 50, pt. 2: 1000 and 1112.
6. Salt Lake City *Telegraph*, October 28, 1864.
7. O. R., vol. 50, pt. 2: 1111.
8. *Ibid.*, vol. 41, pt. 2: 644.
9. *Ibid.*, pt. 3: 903.
10. *Vedette*, October 27, 1864. The report of Pocatello's activities can be found in the statement of Paul Coburn to Captain Hempstead, Salt Lake City, in Jeffery S. King, "'Do Not Execute Chief Pocatello:' President Lincoln Acts to Save the Shoshoni Chief," *Utah Historical Quarterly*, 53: 244.
11. *Vedette*, October 27, 1864.
12. Trenholm and Carley, 212. Also see William H. Dole to O. H. Irish, Salt Lake City, November 26, 1864, Office of Indian Affairs, Record Group 75, Letters sent, Roll 75, p. 471, National Archives.
13. O. R., vol. 50, pt. 2: 1014-15.
14. *Ibid.*, 1011.
15. *Vedette*, October 22, 1864.
16. *Ibid.*, October 27, 1864.
17. Tullidge, *Salt Lake City*, 700.
18. O. R., vol. 41, pt. 4: 259

19. *Ibid.*, vol. 50, pt. 2: 1036.
20. *Ibid.*
21. *Vedette*, December 6, 1864.
22. Stan Hoig, *The Sand Creek Massacre* (Norman: University of Oklahoma Press, 1961), 135; *Vedette*, December 6, 1864.
23. Denver *Republican*, May 28, 1890, as quoted by Hoig, 135-36.
24. O. R., vol. 41, pt. 1: 908-910.
25. *Vedette*, January 5, 1865.
26. O. R., vol. 50, pt. 2: 1101.
27. *Rocky Mountain News*, January 16, 1865, as quoted by Hafen, *The Overland Mail*, 263. Fort Rankin, later called Fort Sedgewick, had been established the previous May 17 on the South Platte, one mile east of the mouth of Lodgepole Creek.
28. Evidence of Connor's lobbying efforts can be found in O. R., vol. 48, pt. 1: 486-87, 498-99 and 522 and *Vedette*, January 10 and 11, 1865.
29. O. R., vol. 48, pt. 1: 598.
30. *Vedette*, October 5, 1865.
31. O. R., vol. 48, pt. 1: 714.
32. *Ibid.*, vol. 50, pt. 2: 1136.
33. William E. Unrau, ed., *Tending the Talking Wire, A Buck Soldier's View of Indian Country, 1863-1866* (Salt Lake City: University of Utah Press, 1979), 214.
34. O. R., vol. 48, pt. 1: 760.
35. *Ibid.*, 778.
36. *Millennial Star*, 27: 206.
37. Hickman, 167.
38. *Vedette*, January 24, 1865.
39. Hickman, 170.
40. *Ibid.*, 167.
41. Wilhelm Wyl (Wymetal), *Mormon Portraits; Joseph Smith the Prophet, His Family and His Friends* (Salt Lake City: Tribune Printing and Publishing Co., 1886), 255.
42. Hickman, 166.
43. *Vedette*, February 23, 1865.
44. Stenhouse, 610-11.
45. *Vedette*, March 6, 1865. Also see issue of February 28.
46. James K. P. Miller, 50, entry for March 4, 1865.
47. *Vedette*, March 6, 1865.
48. Stenhouse, 611-12.
49. *Journal History*, March 7 and 13, 1865; Stenhouse, 612.
50. *Journal History*, March 13, 1865.

Notes to Chapter Ten

1. Unrau, *Tending the Talking Wire,* 261.
2. O. R., vol. 48, pt. 1: 1295-96.
3. *Ibid.,* pt. 2: 274-76; Letter of Captain Albert Brown in Stockton *Daily Independent,* June 12, 1867.
4. O. R., vol. 48, pt. 2: 42.
5. O. R., vol. 48, pt. 2: 374. On March 7, 1865, Moonlight had telegraphed Dodge saying: "No word from Genl. Connor. Can I not have command of expedition against Indians? I can easily be spared for a month" (Grenville Dodge, Papers, Iowa State Historical Department, Des Moines, vol. 9. Hereafter cited as Dodge papers).
6. O. R., vol. 48, pt. 1: 255-56.
7. Richard N. Ellis, *General Pope and Indian Policy* (Albuquerque: University of New Mexico Press, 1970), 75. For other accounts of the Eubanks story see Hoig, 96, *Vedette,* August 19, 1865, and Diary of Captain B. F. Rockafellow in Leroy R. and Ann W. Hafen, eds., *Powder River Campaigns and Sawyer's* [sic] *Expedition of 1865* (Glendale: Arthur H. Clark Co., 1961), 167.
8. O. R., vol. 48, pt. 1: 277. Also see C. G. Coutant, *History of Wyoming* (1899; reprint, New York: Published for University Microfilms by Argonaut Press, 1966), 2: 443.
9. *Vedette,* August 19, 1865; Coutant, 2: 436.
10. These troubles west of Fort Halleck are described in O. R., vol. 48, pt. 1: 295-96 and *Vedette,* June 12, 1865.
11. O. R., vol. 48, pt. 2: 514.
12. Bowles, 9. Also see O. R., vol. 48, pt. 2: 555 and vol. 48, pt. 1: 280-82. Colfax's Journal of the trip was published in *Tullidge's Monthly Magazine, The Western Galaxy,* March and April, 1888.
13. O. R., vol. 48, pt. 2: 589.
14. Bowles, 26.
15. *Ibid.,* 27.
16. Tullidge, *Salt Lake City,* 358.
17. O. R., vol. 48, pt. 2: 227.
18. *Ibid.,* 238-39; *Vedette* June 8, October 4 and 5, 1865.
19. O. R., vol. 48, pt. 2: 756.
20. *Ibid.,* 708-09.
21. *Ibid.,* 807.
22. *Ibid.,* 392.
23. *Ibid.,* 493.
24. Most details of the Fouts incident can be found in O. R., vol. 48, pt. 2: 895 and vol. 48, pt. 1: 322-24.
25. O. R., vol. 48, pt. 2: 895. Also see vol. 48, pt. 1: 325-28; *Vedette,* August 4, 1865, and Coutant, 2: 459.

26. Unrau, *Tending the Talking Wire,* 262-64, entries for June 21 and 24, 1865; *Vedette,* July 21, 1865; O. R., vol. 48, pt. 2: 998.
27. Sacramento *Daily Union,* June 15, 1865, in *Vedette,* July 15, 1865.
28. O. R., vol. 48, pt. 2: 1060.
29. *Ibid.,* 1044, 1045 and 976 respectively.
30. *Ibid.,* 1049.
31. Captain Turnley to Col. Potter, July 28, 1865, Dodge papers, vol. 10.
32. *Ibid.* Also Connor to Dodge, June 30 and July 16 in vol. 10.
33. O. R., vol. 48, pt. 2: 1084.
34. *Ibid.,* 1132.
35. *Ibid.,* 1059, 1086 and 1112.
36. Finalized plans for the columns are contained in O. R., vol. 48, pt. 2: 1129-31 and in letter of Captain Albert Brown in Stockton *Daily Independent,* June 12, 1867.
37. O. R.., vol. 48, pt. 2: 1112, 1124-25.
38. *Vedette,* September 5, 1865.
39. O. R., vol. 48, pt. 2: 1145.
40. *Vedette,* August 19, 1865.

Notes to Chapter Eleven

1. As quoted by *Vedette,* January 16, 1866.
2. A transciption of Connor's end of campaign report, previously said to have been burned or lost in Utah, is contained in Grenville Dodge, "Personal Biography, 1831-71." Iowa State Historical Department, Des Moines, 2: 421-424 (hereafter cited as Dodge biography). Captain S. M. Robbins, Connor's Chief Engineer, submitted a separate report with topographical maps.
3. Hafen and Hafen, *Powder River Campaigns,* 176-78. Rockafellow's original diary is in the library of the State Historical Society of Colorado. Also see *Vedette,* September 11, 1865.
4. In November 1865, the name was changed to Fort Reno, in honor of Major Jesse L. Reno who was killed in the battle of South Mountain, Maryland. The fort was originally named after Connor by his officers, and was later changed to Fort Reno by a spiteful General Pope, according to Captain Brown, writing in the Stockton, California *Daily Independent,* June 12, 1867. In his post-campaign report, Connor says Colonel Kidd originally named the fort.
5. H. E. Palmer, "History of the Powder River Indian Expedition of 1865," *Transactions and Reports of the Nebraska State Historical Society, 1887*), 2: 208 (hereafter cited as Palmer account).
6. F. G. Burnett, "History of The Western Division of the Powder River Expedition," *Annals of Wyoming,* 8 (January, 1932): 573 (Hereafter cited as Burnett account). Also see Dee Brown, *Bury My Heart at Wounded Knee* (New York: Holt, Rinehart and Winston, 1970), 108.

7. Palmer account, 209.
8. O. R., vol. 48, pt. 2: 1051; *Vedette*, September 11, 1865; Connor to Captain Price, August 13, 1865, Dodge papers, vol. 10.
9. O. R., vol. 48, pt. 1: 356-57; Coutant, 2: 487.
10. Pope to Dodge, August 11, 1865, Dodge papers, vol. 10; O. R., vol. 48, pt. 1: 352.
11. Bennett to Haines, July 25; Captain Turnley to Col. Potter, July 28; Pope to Dodge, August 12. All in Dodge papers, vol. 10.
12. O. R., vol. 48, pt. 2: 1209.
13. O. R., vol. 48, pt. 2: 1127.
14. *Ibid.*, pt. 1: 350.
15. *Ibid.*, 352.
16. *Ibid.*
17. *Ibid.*, pt. 2: 1155; also pt. 1: 353.
18. *Ibid.*, pt. 1: 353-54.
19. Grenville M. Dodge, *Battle of Atlanta and Other Campaigns, Addresses, Etc.* (Council Bluffs, Iowa: Monarch Printing Co., 1910), 105. The figures in Meigs' second report (O. R., vol. 48, pt. 2: 1167) to Stanton agree closely with those in the diary.
20. O. R., vol. 48, pt. 2: 1178.
21. Dodge, *Battle of Atlanta*, 106.
22. O. R., vol. 48, pt. 2: 1199.
23. Rockafellow diary, entry for August 20, as contained in Hafen and Hafen, 183.
24. Williford to Lt. Colburn, Oct. 9, 1865, Dodge papers, vol. 11.
25. Connor to Captain Price, Aug. 24, 1865, Dodge papers, vol. 10.
26. Palmer account, 212-213.
27. *Ibid.*, 214.
28. Burnett account, 575. For another version of the fight see A. J. Shotwell account in Freeport, Ohio *Press*, May 3, 1916, as quoted by Rodgers, 203-204.
29. Lee J. Humfreville, *Twenty Years Among Our Hostile Indians* (New York: Hunter and Co., 1899), 355-56.
30. Connor's report to Dodge is dated August 30, 1885, from Camp 19 on Tongue River, Grenville M. Dodge, Record Books, Iowa State Historical Department, Des Moines, 5: 1026 (hereafter cited as Dodge record books). Also see Palmer account, 217.
31. O. R., vol. 48, pt. 1: 366-380. The original, shorter version of Cole's report dated September 25, 1865, can be found in O. R., vol. 48, pt. 1: 380-83. He also submitted a self-serving report directly to Dodge on September 21 from Fort Connor (Dodge papers, vol. 11)
32. O. R., vol. 48, pt. 2: 1048-49.
33. *Ibid.*, pt. 1: 370
34. *Ibid.*, 373.

35. N. Levering, "Locating the Government Wagon-Road From Niobrara, Nebraska, to Virginia City, Montana," *Iowa Historical Record*, January 1887, 424.
36. Sawyers' report, addressed to Secretary of Interior James Harlan, 39th Cong., 1st sess., H. Ex. Doc. 58, in Hafen and Hafen, 266. Also see Captain Williford's report of October 9, 1865, and Connor to Price, September 6, 1865, both in Dodge papers, vol. 11.
37. Connor to Price, September 6, 1865, Dodge papers, vol. 11.
38. Dodge biography, 2: 429. Walker's report can also be found in Misc. file 224, Ord, AGO, U. S. Army Records, Record group 165, National Archives.
39. O. R., vol. 48, pt. 1: 376.
40. *Ibid.*, pt. 2: 1224.
41. *Ibid.*, 1209. Letter is dated August 24.
42. *Ibid.*, 1206.
43. *Ibid.* Letter is dated Aug. 31, from Fort Laramie.
44. *Ibid.*, pt. 1: 355-56. Pope's message is dated Sept. 2, 1865, from St. Louis.
45. Dodge papers, vol. 11.
46. Charles H. Springer, *Soldiering in Sioux Country: 1865*, ed. Benjamin Franklin Cooling III (San Diego: Frontier Heritage Press, 1971), 63.
47. *Vedette*, October 2 and 4, 1865.
48. Captain Albert Brown Letter in *Stockton Daily Independent*, June 12, 1867.
49. Burnett account, 577.
50. *Daily Mining Journal* of Black Hawk, Colorado as quoted in *Vedette*, October 20, 1865.
51. Connor report in Dodge biography, 1: 422.
52. Undated telegram to Dodge, probably sent about Sept. 28 when Connor first reached a telegraph, Dodge record books, 5: 1144.
53. O. R., vol. 48, pt. 2: 1212.
54. *Ibid.*, pt. 1: 348.
55. Dodge letter to A. D. Richardson, of New York *Times*, dated September 26, as quoted in *Vedette*, September 30, 1865.
56. *Vedette*, November 29 and December 5, 1865, respectively, quoting the newspapers indicated.
57. Letter to the St. Louis *Republican*, as quoted by *Vedette*, November 29, 1865.
58. *Vedette*, January 31, 1866; *Rocky Mountain News*, October 12 as quoted in *Vedette*, October 14, 1867.
59. *Alta California*, February 11, 1867.
60. *Vedette*, October 28, 1855.

Notes to Chapter Twelve

1. *Vedette*, May 15 and August 18, 1866. Reorganized Church of Jesus Christ of Latter-day Saints, "Miscellaneous," *The Saints Herald*, April 1, 1866, 110;

Letter from Ashley to Smith in Joseph Smith III, Papers, P15 f 3, History Commission, Reorganized Church of Jesus Christ of Latter-day Saints, Independence, Missouri. Also see Connor to Smith, April 10, 1866, Artificial Collection, History Commission, RLDS Church, P. 31., f 1.

2. *Vedette,* April 4, 5, 7, 12, September 25, October 2 and 3, 1866, January 5, 1867; Virginia City *Territorial Enterprise,* April 24, 1866; Stenhouse, 615; *Millenial Star,* 364.
3. Juanita Brooks, ed., *On the Mormon Frontier, The Diary of Hosea Stout, 1844-1861* (Salt Lake: University of Utah Press, 1964), 2: 728; *Vedette,* March 26, October 13, 15, 29, November 12, 1866, January 13, 1867. Kate B. Carter, *Our Pioneer Heritage* (Salt Lake City: Daughters of the Utah Pioneers, 1958-76), 20: 409; *Millennial Star,* 34: 174-75; *Journal of Discourses,* 11: 281.
4. Beadle, *Life in Utah,* 211,12; Bancroft, *Utah,* 629; Achilles [pseud.], *Destroying Angels of Mormondom; or a Sketch of the Life of Orrin Porter Rockwell, the Late Danite Chief* (San Francisco: Bancroft Library, 1878), 34; *Vedette,* December 15, 1866; Charles Kelly and Hoffman Birney, *Holy Murder, The Story of Porter Rockwell* (New York: Minton, Balch and Co., 1934), 230-31.
5. The progress of smelting in Rush Valley can be traced in the *Vedette,* December 5, 1865; September 6, October 16, December 5, 1866, and February 14 and 21, 1867. Also see Edward W. Tullidge, "Patrick E. Connor," *Tullidge's Quarterly Magazine,* January, 1881, 179.
6. Dodge papers, vol. 12; Dodge record books, 6: 157 and 178.
7. Dodge record books, 6: 829. Letter is dated January 16.
8. *Telegraph,* January 6, February 14 and July 3 1867; *Deseret News,* April 24, 1867.
9. O. R., vol. 48, pts. 2: 501; Dodge record books, 5: 1203.
10. 39th Cong. 2nd Sess., H. Misc. Doc. 75, p. 4 as quoted by Dwyer, 50. Extracts of Hazen's letter can also be found in *Deseret News,* April 10, 1867.
11. Connor to Stanton, April 19, 1867, photocopy, Utah State Historical Society Library, Salt Lake City.
12. Dodge record books, 6: 605.
13. Stockton, California *Daily Independent,* February 13, 1866, August 2 and 6, 1867, March 11, 1868; *Vedette,* August 20, 1867; Kate Connor Oliver, Diary, 40.
14. *Daily Independent,* March 5, 1868, Gilbert H. Kneiss, *Redwood Railways* (Berkeley, California: Howell-North, 1956), 8-19.
15. *Daily Independent,* April 1, 7, June 10 and 12, 1868.
16. *Daily Independent,* November 14, 1868; Salt Lake *Daily Reporter,* December 11, 1868, as found in John Beadle, Scrapbook, 1868-69, A-12 Microfilm, Utah Historical Society, Salt Lake. The steamer was built by Gammon Hayward, a well-known Mormon boat builder.
17. The history of Corinne and the attempt to establish a water route on the lake can be found in the Corinne/Utah *Reporter,* issues of March 8, April 21, May

17 and 21, 1870, and May 27 and June 17, 1871; Corinne *Daily Journal*, May 23, 1871; Corinne *Daily Mail*, April 24, 1875; Alter, 408-410; Carter, *Heart Throbs* 4: 165-66; Tullidge, *Salt Lake City*, 701-02; Dwyer, 59-60; San Mateo *Gazette*, November 5 and December 17, 1869.

18. Pioche *Daily Record*, September 28, October 1 and 17, 1872.
19. *Ibid.*, November 1, 15, 21, 30, 1872; also see Corinne *Reporter* of November 30, 1872, and Virginia City *Daily Territorial Enterprise*, February 10, 1870.
20. Salt Lake City, *Utah Mining Journal*, September 20, 1872; also see issue of August 21 and *Deseret News* of June 22, 1872.
21. Alter, 499; Pioche *Daily Record*, March 29 and August 28, 1874.
22. Roll of Members, Territorial Pioneers of California, 1: 207 and 2: 53, California State Historical Society Library, San Francisco; Bancroft, "Biog. Sketch," 31-33; *Deseret News*, September 17, 1883.
23. Kate Connor Oliver, Diary, 1.
24. Redwood City, California *Standard*, January 5, 1928. Also *Redwood City's Lathrop House, 1863-1869* (San Mateo, Cal.: San Mateo Historical Association, 1969).
25. Kate Connor Oliver, Diary, 1, 13, 142; San Mateo *City Times and Gazette*, January 19, 1884.
26. *Alta*, July 11, 1876.
27. Stenhouse, 608. Kate Connor said the story came from one of Brigham Young's coarse sermons (Diary, 142).
28. Tullidge, 494-98; *Journal History*, November 1, 1870; *Elko Independent*, October 25, 1870.
29. Arrington, 356-61; also see *Deseret News*, October 26, 1869.
30. Salt Lake City *Daily Tribune*, March 16, 1890.
31. *Ibid.*, December 18, 1891; Also Stewart to Connor March 5, 1889, Wm. M. Stewart Collection, Letters, Nevada Historical Society, Reno; San Mateo *Times-Gazette*, July 13, 1889.
32. *Daily Tribune*, December 18, 21, 1891.
33. Edward W. Tullidge, "Patrick E. Connor," in *Tullidge's Quarterly Magazine*, January 1881, 345.
34. Wyl, 255.
35. Quotes are from Goodwin, 269 and Salt Lake City *Daily Tribune*, December 18, 1891, respectively.
36. Issue of December 18, 1891.
37. *Ibid.*
38. *Journal History*, December 21, 1871, and Tullidge, *Salt Lake City*, 559.
39. Joseph Smith III, "Memoirs," in *The Saints Herald*, March 24, 1936, 369.
40. Works Project Administration, "National Guard of California: California Volunteers and the Civil War," 1940. Typescript, California State Library, Sacramento, 3.
41. San Francisco *Examiner*, January 1, 1868, as quoted by Stockton *Daily Inde-*

pendent, January 3, 1868.

42. Myron Angel, *History of Nevada* (Oakland, California: Thompson and West, 1881), 390.

43. Rev. H. K. Hines, *History of the State of Oregon* (Chicago: Lewis Publishing Co., 1893), 291.

44. James Chisholm, *South Pass, 1868: James Chisholm's Journal of the Wyoming Gold Rush.* Ed. Lola M. Homsher (Lincoln: University of Nebraska Press, Bison Books, 1960), entry for Sept. 18, 1868; *Vedette,* October 31 and November 26, 1867; Stockton *Daily Independent,* June 18, 1868; Barnard, Bybee and Walker, 113-15.

Bibliography

Bibliography

Unpublished Material

Ajax, William. Diary. University of Utah Library, Salt Lake City.

Bancroft, H. H. "Biographical Sketch of General P. Edward Connor." Bancroft Library, University of California, Berkeley, ca. 1887.

Banks, John. "A Document History of the Morrisites in Utah." Thesis, University of Utah, 1909.

Banks, Karl. "A Brief History of John Banks and the Morrisite Movement." University of Utah Library, Salt Lake. Typescript.

Beadle, John H. Scrapbook, 1868-69. Utah Historical Society Library, Salt Lake City. Microfilm, roll A-12.

Briggs, Edmund C. Journal. History Commission, Reorganized Church of Jesus Christ of Latter-day Saints, Independence, Missouri.

Butler, Miner F. Papers. California Historical Society Library, San Francisco.

Church of Jesus Christ of Latter-day Saints. Journal History of the Church. Church Historian's Office, Salt Lake City.

Condy, Richard. Journal of the March from Camp Halleck, California to Fort Ruby, Nevada, July 12 to September 1, 1862. Haggin Museum and Galleries, Stockton, California.

Connor, P. E. Letter to Secretary of War Stanton, April 19, 1867. Utah Historical Society Library, Salt Lake City. Photocopy, Ms. A 1897.

________. Letter to Major John M. O'Neil, February 10, 1865. Fort Douglas Military Museum, Salt Lake City. Photocopy.

Dodge, Grenville M. Papers; Record Books, 7 vols.; "Personal Biography, 1831-71," 4 vols. Iowa State Historical Department, Des Moines.

Forscutt, Mark H. "Sketch of Joseph Morris." University of Utah Library, Salt Lake City. Photocopy.

Gould, Jane. Diary, Gould family papers, Mss 2680. Oregon Historical Society, Portland. Typescript.

Hollister, O. J. "History of Independence Hall." Public Library, Salt Lake City, Utah. Typescript.

Morris, George. "Reminiscences." Historian's Office, Church of Jesus Christ of Latter-day Saints, Salt Lake City. Microfilm, MSD 5566.

Oliver, Kate Connor. "Diary to Her Children," December 1931. Copy in possession of Mrs. George Goodlett, granddaughter of Mrs. Oliver. Typescript.

Rodgers, Fred B. "Notes on a interview with Adam Aulbach at Murray, Idaho in 1931." Utah Historical Society Library, Salt Lake City. Typescript.

Schellens, Richard. Papers. Public Library, Redwood City, California.

Scott, Hamilton. Diary extracts. Idaho State Historical Society, Boise, Idaho. Typescript.

Smith, Joseph III. Papers and Artificial Collection. History Commission, Reorganized Church of Jesus Christ of Latter-day Saints, Independence, Missouri.

Stewart, William. M. Letters. Nevada Historical Society, Reno.

Territorial Pioneers of California. Roll of Members, 2 vols. California Historical Soceity Library, San Francisco.

Tuttle, Hiram S. "Account of Service in Utah." Fort Douglas Military Museum, Salt Lake City. Photocopy.

Works Project Administration. "National Guard of California: California Volunteers and the Civil War," 1940. California State Library, Sacramento. Typescript.

Young, Brigham. Letter Books. Historian's Office, Church of Jesus Christ of Latter-day Saints, Salt Lake City.

________ . "Message to the Legislative Assembly of the Territory of Utah, Fillmore City, Utah Territory, December 11, 1855." Utah Historical Society Library, Salt Lake City. Photocopy.

Books, Monographs, Pamphlets and Articles

Achilles [pseud.]. *Destroying Angels of Mormondom; or a Sketch of the Life of Orrin Porter Rockwell, the late Danite Chief.* San Francisco: Bancroft Library, 1878.

Alter, J. Cecil. *Utah, The Storied Domain.* 3 vols. Chicago: American Historical Society, 1932.

Anderson, C. LeRoy. *For Christ Will Come Tomorrow: The Saga of the Morrisites.* Logan, Utah: Utah State University Press, 1981.

Anderson, Peter. "The Wound That Never Healed." *Frontier Times,* June-July 1965, 28.

Angel, Myron. *History of Nevada.* Oakland, Cal.: Thompson and West, 1881.

Arrington, Leonard J. *Brigham Young: American Moses.* New York: Alfred A. Knopf, 1985.

Bancroft, Hubert Howe. *History of California,* 7 vols. San Francisco: The History Co., 1884-1890.

________ . *History of Utah, 1540-1887.* San Francisco: The History Co., 1889.

Barnard, Lula; Bybee, Faunda; and Walker, Lola. *Tosoiba, "Sparkling Waters."* Soda Springs, Idaho: Daughters of the Utah Pioneers, 1958.

Baskin, R. N. *Reminiscences of Early Utah.* Salt Lake City: R. N. Baskin, 1914.

Bauer, K. Jack. *The Mexican War, 1846-1848.* New York: MacMillan Publishing Co., 1974.

Beadle, John H. *Life in Utah, or The Mysteries and Crimes of Mormonism.* Philadelphia: National Publishing Co., 1870.

Bowles, Samuel. *Across the Continent.* 1866. Reprint. Ann Arbor: University Microfilms, 1966.

Brodie, Fawn M. *No Man Knows My History, The Life of Joseph Smith.* 2d ed. New York: Alfred A. Knopf, 1985.

Brooks, Juanita. *John Doyle Lee: Zealot — Pioneer — Builder — Scapegoat.* Glendale: Arthur H. Clark Co., 1972.

________ . *The Mountain Meadows Massacre.* 2d ed. Norman: University of Oklahoma Press, 1962.

Brooks, Juanita, ed. *On the Mormon Frontier, The Diary of Hosea Stout, 1844-1861.* 2 vols. Salt Lake: Univ. of Utah Press and Utah State Historical Society, 1964.

________ . *Journal of the Southern Indian Mission, Diary of Thomas D. Brown*. Logan: Utah State University Press, 1972.

Brown, Dee. *Bury My Heart at Wounded Knee*. New York: Holt, Rinehart and Winston, 1970.

Burnett, F. G. "History of the Western Division of the Powder River Expedition." *Annals of Wyoming* 8 (January 1932): 571-79.

Carleton, James H. *Battle of Buena Vista*. New York, 1848.

Carter, Kate B., ed. *Our Pioneer Heritage*. 20 vols. Salt Lake City: Daughters of the Utah Pioneers, 1958-1976.

________ . *Heart Throbs of the West*. 12 vols. Salt Lake City: Daughters of the Utah Pioneers, 1939-51.

Chisholm, James. *South Pass, 1868: James Chisholm's Journal of the Wyoming Gold Rush*. Edited by Lola M. Homsher. vol. 2 of Pioneer Heritage Series. Lincoln: University of Nebraska Press, Bison Books, 1960.

Church of Jesus Christ of Latter-day Saints. *The Latter Day Saints Millennial Star*, London: Latter-day Saints Book Depot; 132 Volumes, 1840-1970.

Clark, Barzilla W. *Bonneville County in the Making*. Idaho Falls, Idaho, 1941.

Colfax, Schuyler. "Hon. Schuyler Colfax's Journey From the Missouri River to California in 1865 (From His Journal)." *Tullidge's Monthly Magazine, Western Galaxy*, March 1888, 32-39; April, 1888, 243-47.

Colton, Ray C. *The Civil War in the Western Territories, Arizona, Colorado, New Mexico, and Utah*. Norman: University of Oklahoma Press, 1959.

Coutant, C. G.: *History of Wyoming*. 2 vols. 1899. Reprint. New York: Published for University Microfilms by Argonaut Press, 1966.

Daughters of the Utah Pioneers. *The Trail Blazer, History of the Development of Southeastern Idaho*. Cache Valley Newsletter Publishing Co., 1976.

Dictionary of American Biography. 20 vols. and 6 supplements. New York: Charles Scribner's Sons, 1928-80.

Dillon, Richard. *Humbugs and Heroes, A Gallery of California Pioneers*. New York: Doubleday and Co., 1970.

Dodge, Grenville M. *How We Built the Union Pacific Railway*. 1910. Reprint. Ann Arbor, Michigan: University Microfilms. 1966.

———. *Battle of Atlanta and Other Campaigns, Addresses, Etc.* Council Bluffs, Iowa: The Monarch Printing Co., 1910.

Dove, George S., ed. *The Spirit Prevails: Containing the Revelations, Articles, and Letters Written by Joseph Morris.* San Francisco: George S. Dove and Co., 1886.

Dunbar, Seymour, ed. *The Journals and Letters of Major John Owen, Pioneer of the Northwest, 1850-1871.* 2 vols. New York: Edward Eberstadt, 1927.

Dwyer, Robert Joseph. *The Gentile Comes to Utah.* Washington, D. C.: Catholic University of America Press, 1941.

Egan, Howard R. *Pioneering the West, 1846 to 1878.* Richmond, Utah: Howard R. Egan Estate, 1917.

Ellis Richard N. *Gen. Pope and U. S. Indian Policy.* Albuquerque: University of New Mexico Press, 1970.

Faunce, Ruby C. "Biography of Mark Hill Forscutt." *The Saints' Herald,* January 30, 1934, 143-44.

Forscutt, Mark H. Letters to the Editor. *The Saint's Herald,* October 15, 1866, 142 and November 6, 1866, 175.

Fowler, Harlan D. *Three Caravans to Yuma, The Untold Story of Bactrian Camels in Western America.* Glendale, Cal.: Arthur H. Clark Co., 1980.

Franklin County Historical Society and Monument Committee. *The Passing of the Redman.* Preston, Idaho, 1917.

Fries, Rev. Louis J. "One Hundred and Fifty Years of Catholicity in Utah." *The Intermountain Catholic.* Salt Lake City, September 1926.

General Taylor and His Staff: Comprising Memoirs of Generals Taylor, Worth, Wool, and Butler. Philadelphia: Grigg, Elliot and Co., 1848.

Gibbs, J. F. *Lights and Shadows of Mormonism.* Salt Lake City: Salt Lake Tribune Publishing Co., 1909.

Goodman, Michael David. *A Western Panorama, 1849-1875: The travels, writing, influence of J. Ross Browne on the Pacific Coast, and in Texas, Nevada, Arizona and Baja California, as the first Mining Commissioner, and Minister to China.* Glendale, Cal.: Arthur Clark Co., 1966.

Goodwin, C.G. *As I Remember Them.* Salt Lake City: Salt Lake Commercial Club, 1913.

Gottfredson, Peter, ed. *History of Indian Depredations in Utah.* Salt Lake City: Shelton Publishing Co., 1919.

Greeley, Horace. *An Overland Journey from New York to San*

Francisco in the Summer of 1859. 1860. Reprint. New York: Alfred A. Knopf, 1964.

Grinell, George Bird. *The Fighting Cheyennes*. 1915. Reprint. Norman: University of Oklahoma Press, 1956.

Hafen, LeRoy R. *The Overland Mail*. Cleveland: Arthur H. Clark Co., 1926.

Hafen, LeRoy R. and Ann W., eds. *Powder River Campaigns and Sawyer's [sic] Expedition of 1865*. Glendale, Cal.: Arthur Clark Co., 1961.

Hart, Newell. *The Bear River Massacre*. Preston, Idaho: Cache Valley Newsletter Publishing Co., 1982.

Heitman, Francis B. *Historical Register and Dictionary of the U.S. Army, from its Organization, September 29, 1789, to March 2, 1903*. 2 vols. Washington: Government Printing Office, 1903.

Hickman, Bill. *Brigham's Destroying Angel*. Salt Lake City: Shepard Publishing Co., 1904.

Hines, Rev. H. K. *An Illustrated History of the State of Oregon*. Chicago: Lewis Publishing Co., 1893.

Hirshson, Stanley P. *The Lion of the Lord*. New York: Alfred A. Knopf, 1969.

Hoig, Stan. *The Sand Creek Massacre*. Norman: University of Oklahoma Press, 1961.

Humfreville, J. Lee. *Twenty Years Among Our Hostile Indians*. New York: Hunter and Co., 1899.

Jackson, Joseph Henry. *Anybody's Gold, The Story of California's Mining Towns*. New York: D. Appleton-Century Co., 1941.

Kelly, Charles, and Birney, Hoffman. *Holy Murder, The Story of Porter Rockwell*. New York: Minton, Balch and Co., 1934.

King, Jeffery S. "'Do Not Execute Chief Pocatello:' President Lincoln Acts to Save the Shoshoni Chief." *Utah Historical Quarterly* 53: 237-247.

Kneiss, Gilbert H. *Redwood Railways*. Berkeley: Howell-North, 1956.

Levering, N. "Locating the Government Wagon-Road From Niobrara, Nebraska to Virginia City, Montana." *Iowa Historical Record*, January 1887, 370, 422-28.

Long, E. B. *The Saints and the Union*. Urbana: University of Illinois Press, 1981.

Mack, Effie M. *Nevada*. Glendale, Cal.: Arthur H. Clark Co.; 1936.

Madsen, Brigham D. *The Bannock of Idaho.* Caldwell, Idaho: Caxton Printers, 1958.

________ . "Shoshone-Bannock Marauders on the Oregon Trail 1859-1863." Utah Historical Quarterly 35 (Winter 1967): 3-30.

Mansfield, Edward D. *The Mexican War, a History of Its Origin.* New York: A. S. Barnes and Co., 1848.

Martin, Covert; Wood, R. Coke; and Bush, Leon. *Stockton Album Through the Years.* Stockton, Cal.: Simard Printing Co., 1959.

Martineau, J. H. "The Military History of Cache Valley." *Tullidge's Quarterly Magazine* 2-1 (April 1882): 122-34.

Miller, James Knox Polk. *The Road to Virginia City, The Diary of James Knox Polk Miller.* Edited by Andrew F. Rolle. Norman: University of Oklahoma Press, 1960.

Morris, Nephi Lowell. *Prophecies of Joseph Smith and Their Fulfillment.* Salt Lake City: Deseret Book Co., 1920.

Mulder, William, and Mortensen, A. Russell, eds. *Among the Mormons; Historic Accounts by Contemporary Observers.* Lincoln: University of Nebraska, Bison Books, 1973.

Neider, Charles, ed. *The Selected Letters of Mark Twain.* New York: Harper and Row, Publishers, 1917.

Newell, Linda King, and Avery, Valeen Tippetts. *Mormon Enigma: Emma Hale Smith.* New York: Doubleday and Co., 1984.

Orton, Brig. Gen. Richard H., ed. *Records of California Men in the War of the Rebellion, 1861 to 1867.* Sacramento: California State Printing Office, 1890.

Palmer, H. E. "History of the Powder River Indian Expedition of 1865." *Transactions and Reports of the Nebraska State Historical Society, 1887* 2: 197-229.

Parry, Mae T. "Massacre at Bia Ogai." In Daughters of the Utah Pioneers, *The Trail Blazer, History of the Development of Southeastern Idaho.* Preston, Idaho: Cache Valley Newsletter Publishing Co., 1976.

Patterson, Edna B.; Ulph, Louise A.; and Goodwin, Victor. *Nevada's Northeast Frontier.* Sparks, Nevada: Western Printing and Publishing Co., 1969.

Reid, Agnes Just. *Letters of Long Ago.* Salt Lake City: Tanner Trust Fund, University of Utah Library, 1973.

Reorganized Church of Jesus Christ of Latter-day Saints, *The Saints Herald,* April 1, 1866, 110.

Ricks, Joel Edward. *The Beginnings of Settlement in Cache Valley*. Logan: The Faculty Association, Utah State Agricultural College, 1953.

Ridge, John R. *The Life and Adventures of Joaquin Murieta*. Norman: University of Oklahoma Press, 1955.

Roberts, Brigham H. *A Comprehensive History of the Church of Jesus Christ of Latter-day Saints, Century I*. 6 vols. Salt Lake City: Church Deseret News Press, 1930.

Rochlin, Harriet and Fred. *Pioneer Jews, A New Life in the Far West*. Boston: Houghton Mifflin Co., 1984.

Rodgers, Fred B. *Soldiers of the Overland*. San Francisco: Grabhorn Press, 1939.

San Mateo Historical Association: *Redwood City's Lathrop House, 1863-1869*. San Mateo, Cal., 1969.

Schindler, Harold. *Orin Porter Rockwell, Man of God, Son of Thunder*. Salt Lake City: University of Utah Press, 1966.

Smith, Joseph Jr. *The Book of Mormon*. 1830. Salt Lake City: Church of Jesus Christ of Later-day Saints, 1920 ed.

________. et al. *The Doctrine and Covenants of the Church of Jesus Christ of Latter-day Saints. The Pearl of Great Price*. Salt Lake City: Church of Jesus Christ of Latter-day Saints; 1982 ed.

Smith, Joseph III. "Memoirs." *The Saints' Herald*, March 24, 1936, 369.

Springer, Charles H. *Soldiering in Sioux Country: 1865*. Edited by Benjamin Franklin Cooling III. San Diego: Frontier Heritage Press, 1971.

Stenhouse, Thomas B. *The Rocky Mountain Saints*. London: Ward, Lock and Tyler, 1874.

Sutton, Wayne, ed. *Utah, A Centennial History*. 3 vols. New York: Lewis Historical Publishing Co., 1949.

Taylor, Samuel W. *The Kingdom or Nothing, The Life of John Taylor, Militant Mormon*. New York: MacMillan Publishing Co., 1976.

Tinkham, George H. *History of Stockton*. San Francisco: W. M. Hinton and Co., 1880.

Trenholm, Virginia Cole, and Carley, Maurine. *The Shoshonis: Sentinels of the Rockies*. Norman: University of Oklahoma Press, 1964.

Tullidge, Edward W. *History of Salt Lake City, and its Founders*. Salt Lake City: Star Printing Co., 1886.

________. "Patrick E. Connor." *Tullidge's Quarterly Magazine*, January, 1881, 179.

Twain, Mark. *Roughing It*. 2 vols. New York: Harper and Brothers Publishers, 1906.

Unrau, John D. Jr. *The Plains Across, The Overland Emigrants and the Trans-Mississippi West, 1840-1860*. Urbana: University of Illinois Press, 1979.

Unrau, William E., ed. *Tending the Talking Wire, A Buck Soldier's View of Indian Country, 1863-1866*. Salt Lake City: University of Utah Press, 1979.

U. S. Army. Misc. File 224, Ord. AGO, Record Group 165. National Archives.

U. S. Attorney General. John F. Kinney letter to Attorney General Black, Washington D. C., March 20, 1857. Attorney General Manuscripts, Utah File. National Archives.

U. S. Congress. House. *Letter of W. W. Drummond to Attorney-General Jeremiah Black*. 35th Cong., 1st sess., 1857. H. Ex. Doc. No. 71.

________. *The Expedition of Captain James L. Fisk to the Rocky Mountains*. 38th Cong., 1st sess., H. Ex. Doc. No. 45.

U. S. Congress. Senate. *Stephen S. Harding Message to the Territorial Legislature of Utah, Dec. 8, 1862*. 37th Cong., 2nd sess., 1862. S. Misc. Doc. 37.

U. S. Department of State. Letter of Governor Harding to Secretary Seward, August 30, 1862. Record Group 59, Utah Territorial Papers. National Archives.

U. S. Office of Indian Affairs. William H. Dole to O.H. Irish, Salt Lake City, November 26, 1864. Record group 75. Letters sent, Roll 75, p. 471. National Archives.

Waite, Catherine V. *The Mormon Prophet and His Harem*. Cambridge, Mass.: Riverside Press, 1866.

Walker, Charles Lowell. *Diary of Charles Lowell Walker*. A. Karl and Katherine M. Larson, eds. 2 vols. Logan: Utah State University Press, 1980.

Walker, Franklin. *San Francisco's Literary Frontier*. New York: Alfred A. Knopf, 1939.

The War of the Rebellion: A Compilation of the Official Records of the Union and Confederate Armies. Washington, D. C.: Government Printing Office, 1880-1900.

Whitney, Orson F. *History of Utah*. 4 vols. Salt Lake City:

George Q. Cannon and Sons Co., 1893.

Woodruff, Wilford. *Journal of Wilford Woodruff, 1833-1898.* 9 vols. Edited by Scott G. Kenny. Midvale, Utah: Signature Books, 1984.

Wyl [Wymetal], Wilhelm. *Mormon Portraits; Joseph Smith the Prophet, His Family and His Friends.* Salt Lake City: Tribune Printing and Publishing Co., 1886.

Young, Brigham, et al. *Journal of Discourses Delivered by President Brigham Young, His Two Counsellors, the Twelve Apostles and Others,* reported by G. D. Watt and J. V. Long. 26 vols. Liverpool: George Q. Cannon, 1854-1866. 1964 ed.

Young, Otis E., Jr. *Western Mining.* Norman: University of Oklahoma Press, 1970.

Young, Richard W. "The Morrisite War." *The Contributor Magazine* 11 (June, 1890): 281-84.

Newspapers

Blackfoot, Idaho, *Daily Bulletin,* 1929.

Carson City, Nevada *Silver Age,* 1862.

Corinne, Utah, *Corinne Daily Journal,* 1871.

Corinne, Utah, *Daily Mail,* 1875.

Corinne, Utah, *Utah Reporter/Semi-Weekly Reporter/Tri-Weekly Reporter/Weekly Reporter,* 1869-74.

Denver, Colorado, *Rocky Mountain News,* 1865.

Elko, Nevada *Elko Independent,* 1870.

Eureka, Nevada *Daily Sentinel,* 1874.

Gold Hill, Nevada, *News,* 1867.

New York *Times,* 1857.

New York *Tribune,* 1863.

Oregon City, Oregon *Argus,* 1860.

Pioche, Nevada *Daily Record,* 1872-75.

Redwood City, California *Standard,* January 5, 1928.

Sacramento, California *Transcript,* April 20, 1850.

Sacramento, California *Daily Union,* 1863.

Salt Lake City *Daily Tribune,* 1870-91.

Salt Lake City *Deseret News,* 1854-79.

Salt Lake City *Telegraph,* 1864-66.

Salt Lake City *Times,* December, 1891.

Salt Lake City *Union Vedette* and *Daily Union Vedette,* 1863-67.

Salt Lake City *Utah Mining Journal,* 1872.

San Francisco *Alta California*, 1849-68.
San Francisco *Bulletin*, 1860-64.
San Francisco *Chronicle*, April, 1889.
San Francisco *Herald*, 1869.
San Francisco *Morning Call*, June 1888 and November 1893.
San Mateo, California *Gazette/Times-Gazette*, 1870-91.
Santa Cruz, California *Sentinel*, July 1868.
Stockton, California *San Joaquin Republican*, 1853-1861.
Stockton, California *Stockton Daily Independent*, 1861-68.
Stockton, California *Stockton Journal*, 1853.
Virginia City, Nevada *Daily Territorial Enterprise*, 1862-63, 1866.

Index